MW00453571

PROGRESSI

Complete
Learn To Play
ROCK GUITAR
Manual

by
Peter Gelling

Visit our Website
www.learntoplaymusic.com

The Progressive Series of Music Instruction Books, CDs, and DVDs

2

CONTENTS

CONTENTS CONTINUED

4

CONTENTS CONTINUED

CONTENTS CONTINUED

For information about other books in this series, contact:

LTP Publishing Pty Ltd.
Email: info@learntoplaymusic.com
or visit our web page at:
www.learntoplaymusic.com

For more books and recordings by
Peter Gelling, visit:
www.bentnotes.com

COPYRIGHT CONDITIONS
No part of this book can be reproduced in any form without written consent of the publisher.
© 2003 L.T.P. Publishing Pty Ltd

INTRODUCTION

Progressive COMPLETE LEARN TO PLAY ROCK GUITAR MANUAL is the ultimate Rock guitar manual. It assumes you have no prior knowledge of music or playing the Guitar, and will take you **from beginner to professional level**. In the course of the book you will learn **all the essential techniques of Rock Guitar** along with how to read traditional music notation, guitar TAB, and rhythm notation. By the end of the book you will be ready to play both Rhythm and Lead guitar in a Rock band and be able to write your own songs and guitar parts.

The book is divided into sections, the first covering the basics of left and right hand technique, basic rhythms and chords, picking and music reading, along with **how to use an amplifier and guitar effects**. The later sections deal with using the whole fretboard, more advanced rhythms, scales and chords, and also techniques such as harmonics and right hand tapping. The examples and solos demonstrate a variety of Rock styles including Hard Rock, Southern Rock, Classic Blues Rock, Metal and Funk. The accompanying CDs contain all the examples in the book so you can play along with them. At the end of the book, there are also several **Jam–Along tracks** on the CD for you to practice your lead guitar playing with.

There is also a special section on how to play with a bass player and a drummer. Through the book you will have learned about many chord types and musical styles, so you may wish to learn more about some of them.

- To learn more about chords and their uses, see
  Complete Learn to Play Guitar Chords Manual.
- To learn more about lead guitar and improvising, see
  Complete Learn to Play Lead Guitar Manual.
- To learn more about Rhythm guitar and its related styles, see
  Complete Learn to Play Rhythm Guitar Manual.
- To learn more about Blues guitar and its related styles, see
  Complete Learn to Play Blues Guitar Manual.
- To learn more about fingerpicking with the right hand, see
  Complete Learn to Play Fingerpicking Guitar Manual.
- To learn more about Classical guitar, see
  Complete Learn to Play Classical Guitar Manual.
- To learn more about Jazz guitar, see
  Complete Learn to Play Jazz Guitar Manual.

All guitarists should know all of the information contained in this book.
The best and fastest way to learn is to use this book in conjunction with:
1. Buying sheet music and song books of your favourite recording artists and learning to play their songs.
2. Practicing and playing with other musicians. You will be surprised how good a basic drums/bass/guitar combination can sound even when playing easy music.
3. Learning by listening to your favourite CDs.

Also in the early stages it is helpful to have the guidance of an experienced teacher. This will also help you keep to a schedule and obtain weekly goals.

USING THE COMPACT DISCS

This book comes with **two compact discs** which demonstrate almost all the examples in the book. The book shows you where to put your fingers and what technique to use and the recording lets you hear how each example should sound. Practice the examples slowly at first, gradually increasing tempo. Once you are confident you can play the example evenly without stopping the beat, try playing along with the recording. You will hear a drum beat at the beginning of each example, to lead you into the example and to help you keep time. To play along with the CD your guitar must be in tune with it (see page 240). If you have tuned using an electronic tuner (see below) your guitar will already be in tune with the CD. A small diagram of a compact disc with a number as shown below indicates a recorded example.

23.0 ◄────── CD Track Number

ELECTRONIC TUNER

The easiest and most accurate way to tune your guitar is by using an **electronic tuner**. An electronic tuner allows you to tune each string individually to the tuner, by indicating whether the notes are sharp (too high) or flat (too low). If you have an electric guitar you can plug it directly in to the tuner. If you have an acoustic guitar, the tuner will have an inbuilt microphone. There are several types of electronic guitar tuners but most are relatively

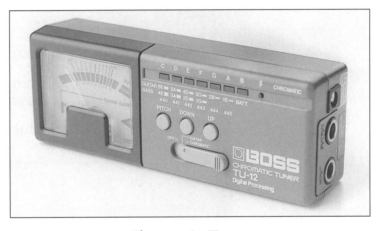

Electronic Tuner

inexpensive and simple to operate. Tuning using other methods is difficult for beginning guitarists and it takes many months to master, so we recommend you purchase an electronic tuner, particularly if you do not have a guitar teacher or a friend who can tune it for you. Also if your guitar is way out of tune you can always take it to your local music store so they can tune it for you. Once a guitar has been tuned correctly it should only need minor adjustments before each practice session.

TUNING YOUR GUITAR

Before you commence each lesson or practice session you will need to tune your guitar. If your guitar is out of tune everything you play will sound incorrect even though you are holding the correct notes. On the accompanying CD the **first track** contains the **six strings of the guitar**. For a complete description of how to tune your guitar, see page 240.

 1. 6th String
E Note (Thickest string)

 5th String
A Note

 4th String
D Note

 3rd String
G Note

 2nd String
B Note

 1st String
E Note (Thinnest string)

ELECTRIC GUITARS

As far as playing goes, electric and acoustic guitars have much in common. Many of the techniques are the same, and both types contain a body, neck, head, bridge, nut and tuning keys. The main difference is the way the sound is produced. Electric guitars are very quiet unless they are plugged into an amplifier, as they do not have a large sound hole and body to create the sound. When plugged in, however, electric guitars can be played much louder than acoustic guitars. The photos below show the two most common types of electric guitar - the **solid body electric** and the **hollow body electric**.

The **solid body electric** is commonly used in Metal, Rock, Blues and Pop Music. Famous solid body guitars are the **Gibson Les Paul** and the **Fender Stratocaster**.

The **hollow body electric** (semi acoustic) is most commonly used in Jazz and Blues music.

SOLID BODY ELECTRIC   HOLLOW BODY ELECTRIC
(semi acoustic)

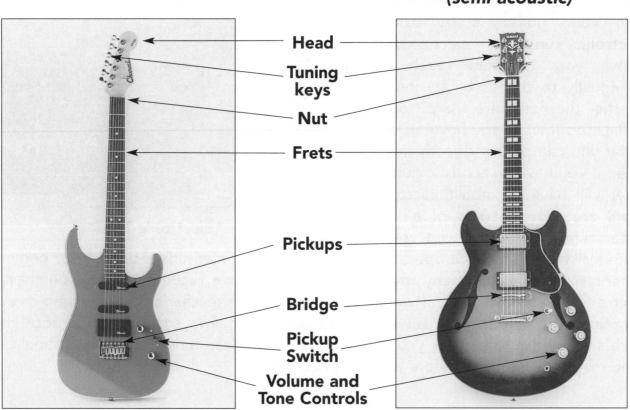

Head
Tuning keys
Nut
Frets
Pickups
Bridge
Pickup Switch
Volume and Tone Controls

ELECTRIC GUITAR PICKUPS

Electric guitars have **pick-ups** (a type of inbuilt microphone) and need to be played into an **amplifier** (amp) to be heard. There are two basic types of pickups which produce different types of sounds. The classic Fender Guitars such as the **Stratocaster** and the **Telecaster** contain **single coil pickups** which produce a clear, crisp sound which is excellent for rhythm playing. Both guitars are also capable of producing biting trebly lead sounds. The most popular Gibson solid body **Les Paul**, and hollow body models such as the **335** contain **double coil pickups**. These produce a fatter, more chunky sound than single coil pickups. Many more recent guitars such as the solid body electric shown above contain a combination of single and double coil pickups.

AMPLIFIERS

There are two basic styles of amplifiers, as shown below. A **combo** amp (combined amplifier and speaker) is usually best for beginners as it is smaller and easier to carry around. The other type is a **stack**, which consists of an amplifier "head" and a separate speaker box containing up to four speakers. Stacks are mostly used by bands playing in large venues.

There are also two different types of sound generation systems in amplifiers. One is the **valve** or vacuum tube amplifier, and the other is the **solid state** or transistor amplifier. Valve amplifiers have traditionally been the most popular because of their ability to produce a clear crisp sound without losing warmth or depth of tone and for their ability to provide fine grades of overdriven sounds. Small valve amps also produce great natural distortion sounds when turned right up. This is more difficult to achieve with larger amplifiers, mainly because by the time you turn the amp up enough to get the desired tone it's just too loud! In recent years there have been many advances in amplifier design and manufacture and there are now a variety of both valve and solid state amplifiers which produce great sounds. If you haven't been playing for long, it is probably best to go for a fairly versatile one which is capable of producing a variety of sounds suitable for several styles of music. As with guitars, try out several amps before deciding.

TYPES OF AMPLIFIERS

COMBO
(combined amp and speaker)

STACK
(separate amp head and speaker)

Once you plug your electric guitar into an amplifier you can produce many different sounds with it. These will be demonstrated later in the book. For now all you need to do is plug your guitar into the input socket on the amplifier and turn up the volume controls on both.

UNDERSTANDING THE CONTROL KNOBS

To get the best sounds out of your guitar and amplifier, you will need to understand the **volume and tone controls** and how they work. Some guitars have only one volume control which works for all the pickups and others have separate volume controls for each pickup. Examples of these are shown below.

 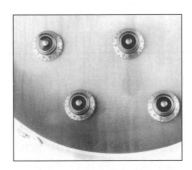

Amplifiers may have one or two volume controls. Amps with a single volume control are very straightforward to use: you simply turn the knob until you have the required volume. Amps with two volume controls are capable of producing more different sounds, specifically-various amounts of distortion. Usually the controls on these amps are called **volume** and **master volume**, as shown below. To start with, set your master volume higher than the other volume to get your basic sound.

Notice the **treble**, **middle** and **bass** controls on the amp control panel shown above. These are **tone controls** which alter the type of sound coming out of the amplifier. The names of the controls refer to the sound frequencies they can alter. Treble refers to high frequencies, bass refers to low frequencies and middle refers to those in between. There are also amplifiers which have extra tone controls like high mid and low mid, and sometimes "presence" which refers to higher middle frequencies. Experiment with the controls until you can hear how they work and work out what settings you like. This is a very personal thing and everyone has their own favorite settings. If you are having trouble hearing how the tone controls work, try setting two of them to 0 and the other to 10, and then gradually bring the dial back down. Then try swapping between them, then try various combinations. Tone controls on a guitar consist of a single knob which is numbered **1** to **10**. The higher the number, the higher the frequency. Once again, experiment to find the types of tones you prefer. The most suitable settings will vary depending on the musical context.

STRINGS

It is important to have the correct set of strings fitted to your guitar, especially if you are a beginner. Until you build enough strength in your hands to fret the chords cleanly, light gauge or low tension strings are recommended. A reputable music store which sells guitar strings should be able to assist with this. It is important to change your strings regularly, as old strings go out of tune easily and are more difficult to keep in tune. In time, you may wish to experiment with heavier string gauges as they generally produce a stronger tone.

LESSON ONE

HOW TO READ MUSIC

Good guitarists are able to move freely between chords and single notes. To do this well, you need to understand how the notes relate to the chords; and this in turn requires a basic knowledge of music theory. The first step is learning to read music.

There are two methods used to write guitar music: the **traditional music notation** method (using music notes, ♩) and **tablature.** Both are used in this book but you need only use one of them. Most guitarists find tablature easier to read. However, it is important to learn to read traditional music notation as well. Nearly all sheet music is written in traditional notation. Even if you don't read well, you will need a basic knowledge of how rhythms are written.

TABLATURE

Tablature is a method of indicating the position of notes on the fretboard. There are six "tab" lines, each representing one of the six strings of the guitar. Study the following diagram.

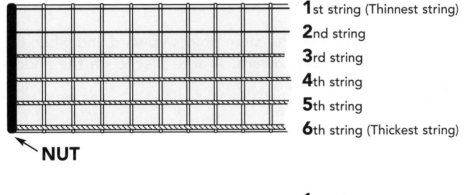

1st string (Thinnest string)
2nd string
3rd string
4th string
5th string
6th string (Thickest string)

NUT

THE LEFT HAND

The left hand fingers are numbered as such:

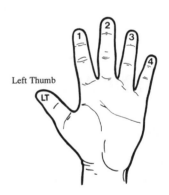

Left Thumb

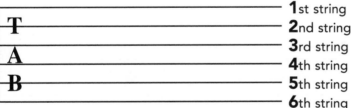

1st string
2nd string
3rd string
4th string
5th string
6th string

When a number is placed on one of the lines, it indicates the fret location of a note e.g.

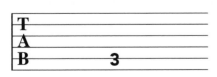

This indicates the open (unfretted) 3rd string (a G note).

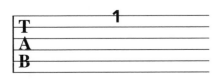

This indicates the 3rd fret of the 5th string (a C note).

This indicates the 1st fret of the 1st string (an F note).

MUSIC NOTATION

The musical alphabet consists of **7** letters:

A   B   C   D   E   F   G

Music is written on a **staff**, which consists of 5 parallel lines. Notes are written on these lines and in the spaces between them.

MUSIC STAFF

The **treble** or **'G' clef** is placed at the beginning of each staff line. This clef indicates the position of the note G.

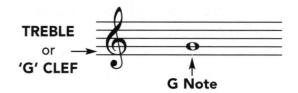

TREBLE
or ⟶
'G' CLEF

G Note

Notehead

The **head** of a note indicates its position, on the staff, e.g.:

This is a G note

This is an E note

When the note head is below the middle staff line the stem points upward and when the head is above the middle line the stem points downward. A note placed on the middle line (**B**) can have its stem pointing either up or down.

LEARNING THE NOTES ON THE STAFF

To remember the notes on the lines of the staff, say:

Every **G**ood **B**oy **D**eserves **F**ruit.

The notes in the spaces spell:
F A C E

Extra notes can be added above or below the staff using short lines, called **leger lines**.

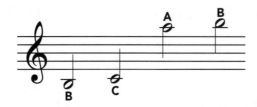

THE QUARTER NOTE

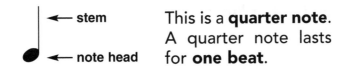

← stem

← note head

This is a **quarter note**.
A quarter note lasts
for **one beat**.

THE OPEN STRINGS OF THE GUITAR

The term "**open string**" means a string with no left hand fingers pressed down (unfretted). When correctly tuned, the open strings of the guitar correspond to the notes **E A D G B** and **E** from low to high, as shown below. Notice that the open **4th** string **D** note is in the space below the staff, while the low **A** and **E** notes are on leger lines below the staff. Don't worry if you can't recognize these notes yet, they will all be introduced as the book progresses. An easy way to remember the names of the open strings (from high to low) is to say **E**aster **B**unny **G**ets **D**inner **A**t **E**aster.

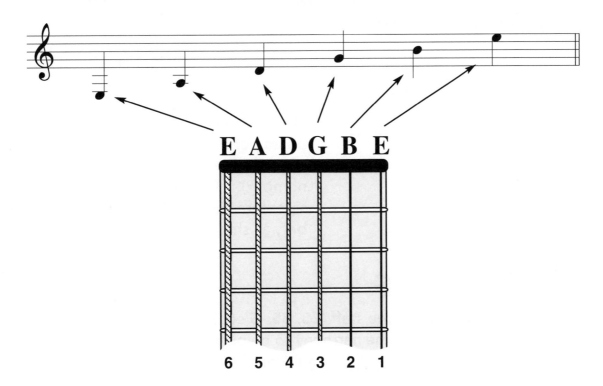

Here is an exercise to help you recognize the notes which represent the open strings of the guitar. Name the notes out loud as you play each one. All the notes here are quarter notes, which last for one beat each. However, don't worry about the timing at this stage; just make sure you are playing the correct notes.

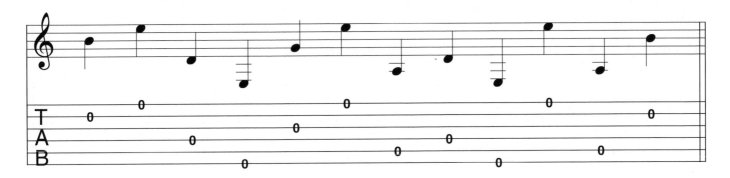

BAR LINES

In most music, **bar Lines** are drawn across the staff, dividing the music into sections called **bars** or **measures**. A **double bar line** signifies either the end of the music, or the end of an important section of it.

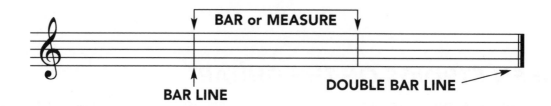

TIME SIGNATURES

At the beginning of each piece of music, after the treble clef, you will see two numbers. These numbers are called the **time signature**.

**Time Signature
(Four Four time)**

4 – this indicates 4 beats per bar.

4 – this indicates that each beat is worth a quarter note.

The time signature indicates the number of beats per bar (the top number) and the type of note receiving one beat (the bottom number). This means that the $\frac{4}{4}$ time signature indicates **four quarter notes per bar**, as shown in example 2.0.

CHORD SYMBOLS

Notice letters and symbols above the staff (**E5, B5, G** etc.) in the following example. These are **chord symbols** which indicate the harmony to be played by accompanying instruments such as a second guitar or a keyboard. You will learn how to play chords in lesson 7.

 **2.0**

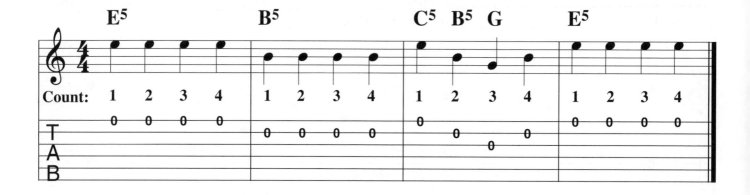

LESSON TWO

GETTING YOUR HANDS MOVING

Most activities involving our hands (e.g. catching a ball or holding a knife and fork) use the whole hand rather than individual finger movements. However, playing musical instruments requires a variety of specific actions from individual fingers. It takes quite a bit of training before the fingers become reliably accurate every time you play. When training the hands and fingers, it is best to separate them wherever possible, and zero in on the exact movement you are trying to perfect. In this lesson you will learn some examples which use essential movements for both the left and right hands.

RIGHT HAND TECHNIQUE

USING A PICK

The most common way of playing the electric guitar is with a **pick** (or **plectrum**). Picks come in various sizes and thicknesses. Generally the thinner ones work better for rhythm playing and the thicker ones are better for lead playing. You may need to experiment with several picks before deciding which one suits you best. The traditional picking grip is to hold the pick between the thumb and the last joint of the index finger.

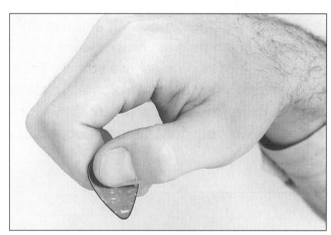

Hold pick with thumb and first finger.

RIGHT HAND POSITION

There are two basic right hand positions when using a pick. The first is to keep the fingers of the right hand closed, and the second to open the hand across the face of the guitar. Try both positions and decide which one you are most comfortable with.

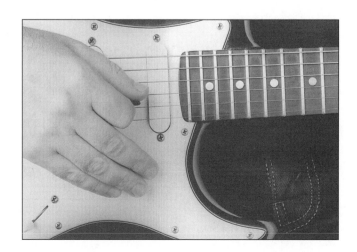

To help keep the right hand steady when picking, try bracing the fourth finger on the face of the guitar as shown in the photo. Note that while this position is helpful in picking situations it is not used when strumming.

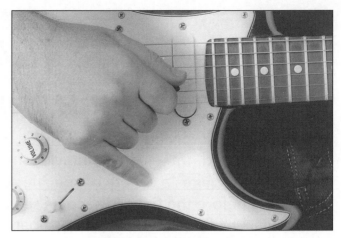

Brace fourth finger

PICKING THE OPEN STRINGS

To pick the strings, use a downward motion of the pick (called a **downstroke** and indicated by the symbol **V**), and use only the tip of the pick to strike the string, as shown in the diagram below. Shown below is a picking exercise designed to help you gain control of picking notes on all of the strings. Take it slowly at first and be sure to keep all the notes even in both tempo and volume. To develop a good sense of timing right from the start, it is important to use a metronome (or drum machine) every time you practice. It also helps to tap your foot on each beat and count out loud as you play.

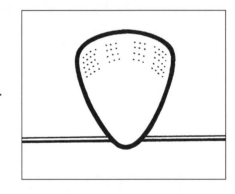

Use the tip of the pick to play the string.

 **2.1**

This exercise involves all the **open** (unfretted) **strings** played as quarter notes. Count 1 2 3 4 1 2 3 4 etc. as you play, using all downstrokes. The two dots before the double bar at the end are a **repeat sign**. This indicates that you play the piece again from the beginning.

Repeat Sign

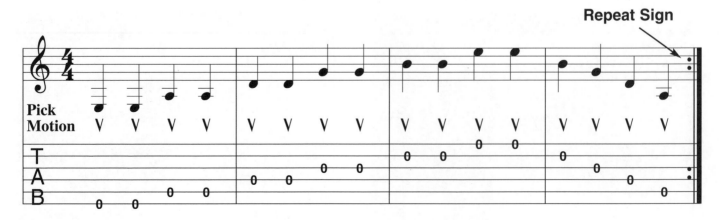

LEFT HAND TECHNIQUE

FINGER PLACEMENT

All notes must be fretted with the tips of the fingers and positioned as close as practical to the fretwires.

Fingertips as close as practical to fretwires.

LEFT HAND POSITION

There are two basic positions for the left hand. In most cases the thumb should be positioned behind the neck of the guitar with the fingers evenly arched over the fretboard. When using techniques such as the bend, release bend, vibrato etc. you may find it more comfortable to have the thumb in a higher position, wrapped over the top of the fretboard.

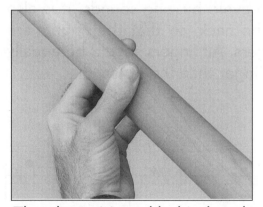

Thumb positioned behind neck.

Thumb positioned over the neck.

NOTES ON THE FRETBOARD

The notes on the guitar fretboard change alphabetically one fret at a time. You will recall that the musical alphabet is made up of seven letters: **A B C D E F G.**

The distance between most of the letters is called a tone (or whole step). From A to B is a tone, from D to E is a tone etc. There are even smaller steps between these letters called half steps (also called semitones). They are written as follows: **A** A♯ **B C** C♯ **D** D♯ **E F** F♯ **G** G♯. These are the 12 notes used in all western music.

Notice that there are no steps between B-C and E-F; the distance between these notes is already a semitone. The signs following the non-bold letters are called sharps. Flat signs can also be used, giving: **A** A♭ **G** G♭ **F E** E♭ **D** D♭ **C B** B♭.

THE OPEN POSITION

The same note can often be played in more than one place on the guitar fretboard. To avoid confusion, the fretboard can be divided into **positions** consisting of groups of **four frets** to go with the **four fingers** of the left hand. The lowest fret of the group of four determines the name of the position. E.g. if the first finger is at the first fret, the other fingers follow naturally at frets 2, 3 and 4. This is described as the **first position**. If all the fingers were moved up one fret (first finger at the 2nd fret) this would be called **second position**, etc. When using the **open strings** as the lowest notes, you are playing in the **open position**. This consists of the open strings and the first three frets; as shown in the photograph below.

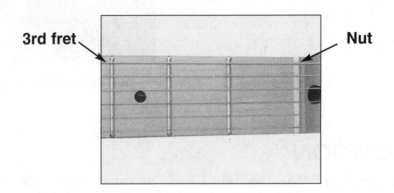

For the following exercise it is important to pay careful attention to the use of the left hand fingers. Do not worry about the note names for now, just follow the TAB. Remember to place the tips of the fingers close to the fretwire to avoid buzzing sounds. It is also important to keep the palm of the hand parallel to the neck, so that the fingers are stretched. This helps develop **independence** of the fingers. All fingers should be equally strong, that is, it should not be easier to play with one finger than the other.

CD 1 2.2

LESSON THREE

NOTES ON THE FIRST STRING

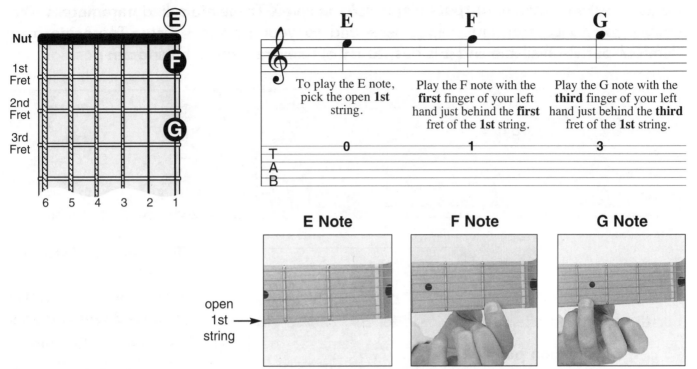

As a general rule:

Play notes on the **first** fret with your **first** finger.

Play notes on the **second** fret with your **second** finger.

Play notes on the **third** fret with your **third** finger.

The following example uses the notes **E**, **F** and **G** on the first string. As you move from **F** (1st fret) to **G** (3rd fret) leave your first finger on the **F** note. This will create a smoother sound when you return from **G** to **F**. Remember to play on the tips of your fingers and use only downstrokes with the pick. Listen carefully as you play and make sure your notes sound clear and even. To help you develop a good sense of time, **always use a metronome** and tap your foot on each beat. There are two ways to practice this exercise: one is to **name the notes out loud** as you play and the other is to **count** as you play. Use both these methods until the exercise becomes easy.

3.0

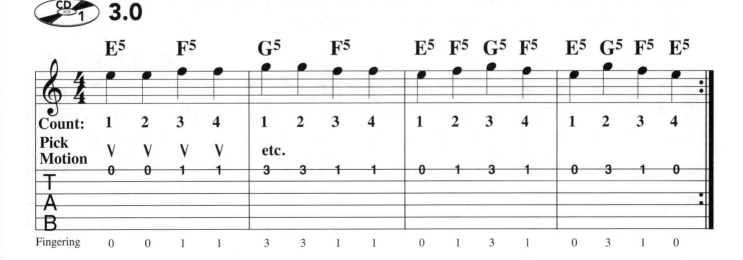

OVERDRIVE AND DISTORTION

One of the most popular sounds in **electric guitar** playing is **distortion**. This is achieved by **overdriving** an amp (turning the pre-amp volume up and the master volume down) or by using a distortion pedal. Pedals have a variety of controls, but usually include **drive** or **distortion** (to control the amount of distortion), **tone** (amount of treble or bass frequencies) and **level** or **output** (overall volume level). These are called **parameters**. They enable you to control and shape the sound to your personal taste. There are many different pedals available and it is best to try out several before buying one.

Distortion pedal

To achieve distortion sounds with an amp, turn your master volume **down** and your pre-amp volume **up**.

 **3.1**

Here is another example using the notes E, F and G on the first string. It has been recorded using an overdrive sound. Set your amp or use a pedal to get an overdrive sound you like and then try playing along with the recording.

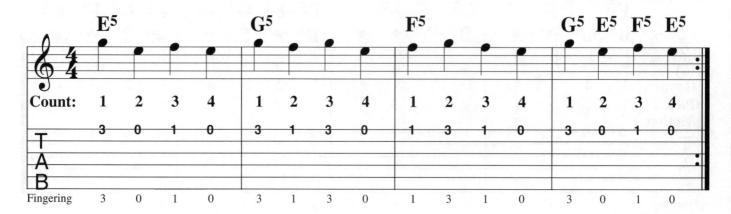

NOTES ON THE SECOND STRING

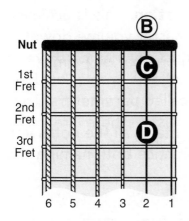

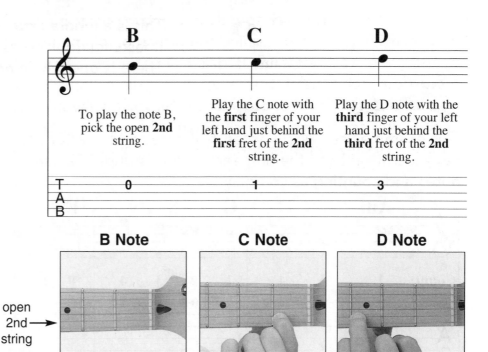

To play the note B, pick the open **2nd** string.

Play the C note with the **first** finger of your left hand just behind the **first** fret of the **2nd** string.

Play the D note with the **third** finger of your left hand just behind the **third** fret of the **2nd** string.

Notes written above the middle line of a staff usually have their stems going down. Notes written below the middle line of the staff usually have their stems going up. The stem for the **B note** can go up or down.

open 2nd string

B Note   **C Note**   **D Note**

THE HALF NOTE

One of the ways expression is created in music is by using notes of different values (lengths). Music is like a language, there are short sounds, longer sounds, emphasised sounds and silences. These will all be introduced in the course of the book.

This is a **half note**. It has a value of **two** beats.
There are **two** half notes in one bar of ⁴⁄₄ time.
One half note is equal to two quarter notes.

Count: 1   2

CD 1 3.2

The following example contains both quarter notes and **half notes**. Remember to count out loud as you play until you can play the example easily and evenly. Once again, it has been recorded using an overdriven sound. You can choose to use either a clean sound or an overdriven sound for any example.

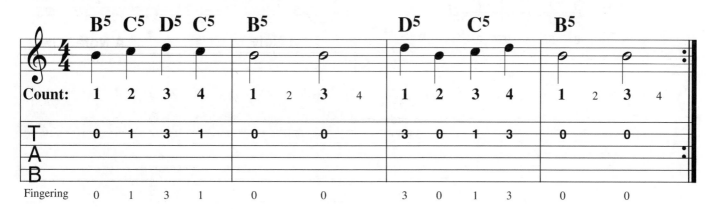

THE WHOLE NOTE

O

This is a **whole note**.
It lasts for **four** beats.

Count: **1** 2 3 4

There is **one** whole note in one bar of $\frac{4}{4}$ time.

 **4.0**

This example uses whole notes, half notes and quarter notes. It contains all the notes you have learnt on both the first and second strings. Remember to practice both naming the notes and counting as you play.

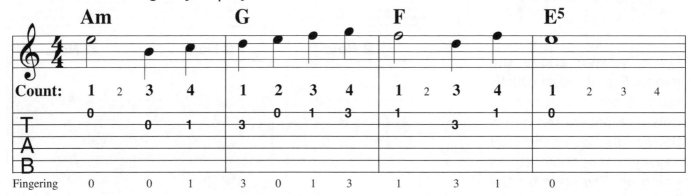

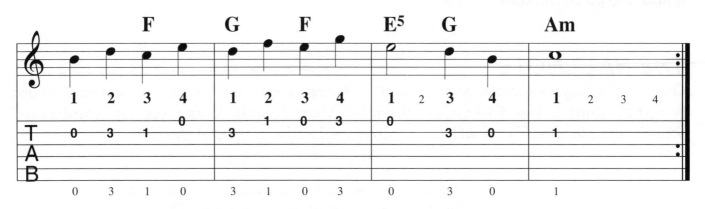

NOTES ON THE THIRD STRING

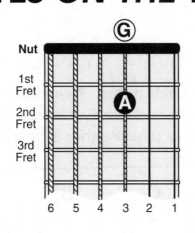

Nut

1st Fret

2nd Fret

3rd Fret

6 5 4 3 2 1

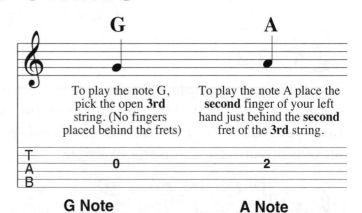

G   **A**

To play the note G, pick the open **3rd** string. (No fingers placed behind the frets)

To play the note A place the **second** finger of your left hand just behind the **second** fret of the **3rd** string.

G Note   **A Note**

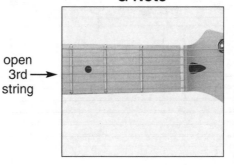

open 3rd → string

THE OCTAVE

Although there are only seven different letters in the musical alphabet, it is possible to find higher and lower versions of them at various places on the fretboard. The distance between any note and its next higher or lower repeat is called an **octave** You already know two **G** notes–the open 3rd string and the third fret of the 1st string. These two G notes are an octave apart. The following example makes use of both these G notes.

4.1

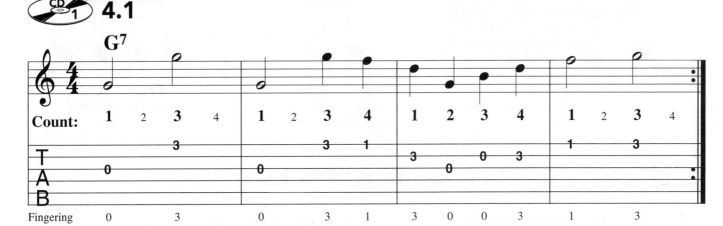

THE DOTTED HALF NOTE

A **dot** written after a note extends its value by **half**. A dot after a half note means that you hold it for **three** beats.

Count: 1 2 3

4.2

To finish this lesson, here is an example which makes use of all the notes and note values you have learnt so far. Remember to count as you play and be sure that all your notes are clear and even. This one has been recorded faster than previous examples. Take it slowly at first and gradually work up your speed until you can play along with the recording.

LESSON FOUR

THE EIGHTH NOTE

 This is an **eighth note**. It lasts for half a count. There are eight eighth notes in one bar of $\frac{4}{4}$ time

Count: 1

 Count: 1   **+**
Two eighth notes joined together.

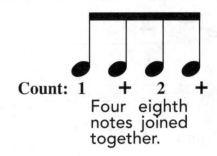 Count: 1   **+**   2   **+**
Four eighth notes joined together.

 **5.0**   *How to Count Eighth Notes*

Count:	1	+	2	+	3	+	4	+
Say:	1	and	2	and	3	and	4	and
TAB	0	0	0	0	0	0	0	0

ALTERNATE PICKING

All the examples you have played so far have involved a downward pick motion, indicated by a Ⅴ. When playing eighth notes, a down (Ⅴ) and up (Λ) picking technique is commonly used. This is called **alternate picking**, and is essential for the development of speed and accuracy. The technique involves using a down pick **on** the beat (the number count) and an up pick **off** the beat (the 'and' count). Practice example 12 using alternate picking until you can do it comfortably and then try the following example which uses alternate picking for eighth notes and downstrokes for all the quarter and half notes. It is a good idea to practice the first two bars and last two bars separately at first, as the picking is quite different in these two sections.

 **5.1**

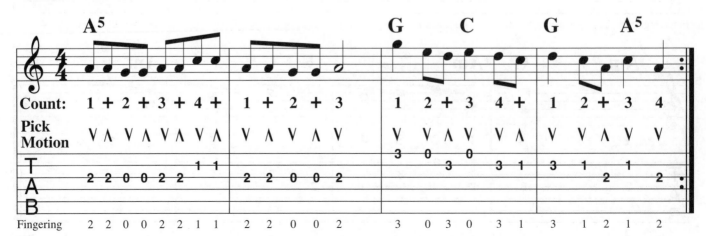

Here are some more examples to help you become comfortable using eighth notes. Remember to use alternate picking and count out loud as you play along with your metronome. Practice each one slowly until you can play it smoothly and evenly. Gradually increase the speed on your metronome until you can play at the same tempo (speed) as the recording.

6.0

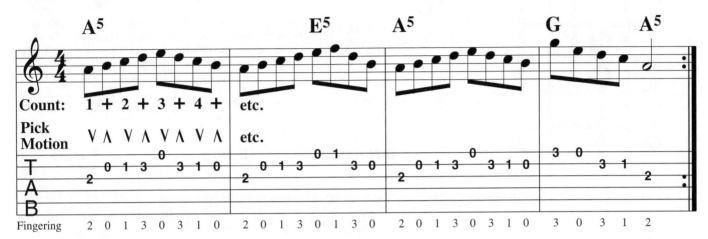

6.1

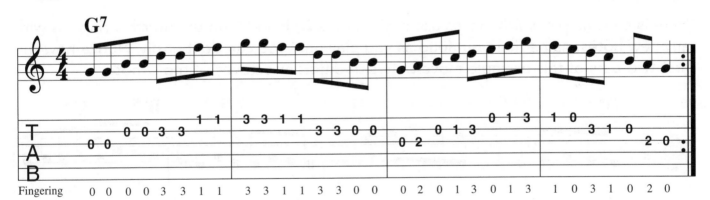

6.2

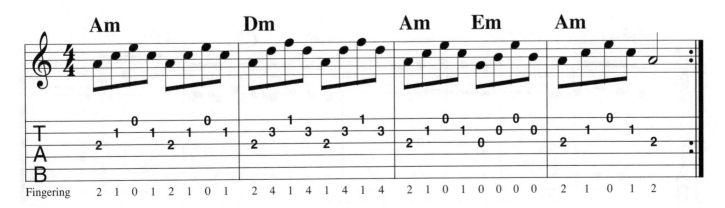

LESSON FIVE

NOTES ON THE FOURTH STRING

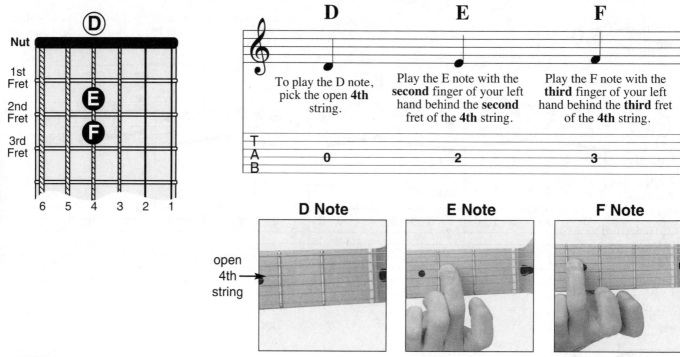

D	E	F
To play the D note, pick the open **4th** string.	Play the E note with the **second** finger of your left hand behind the **second** fret of the **4th** string.	Play the F note with the **third** finger of your left hand behind the **third** fret of the **4th** string.

D Note   **E Note**   **F Note**

CD 1 **7.0**

Here is an example which makes use of the notes **D**, **E** and **F** on the fourth string. As with any new notes, name them out loud as you play until you can do it easily. Notice how the first two bars of this example move between different octaves of the **D** note.

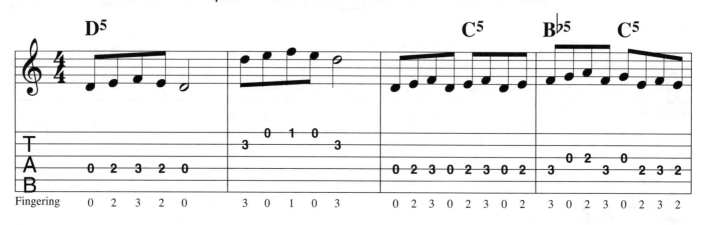

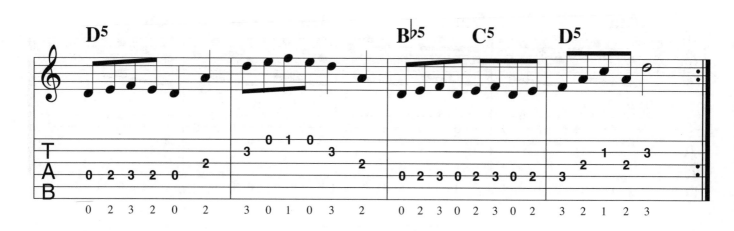

NOTES ON THE FIFTH STRING

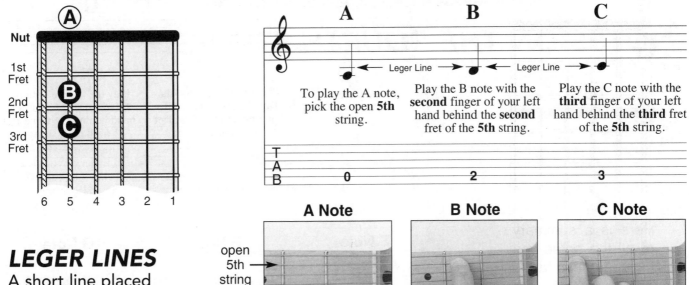

LEGER LINES

A short line placed beneath the staff is called a **Leger Line.**

CD 1 **7.1**

This example makes use of the notes **A**, **B** and **C** on the fifth string. It begins the same as the previous example but moves between different octaves of the **A** note instead of **D**. As before, name the notes out loud until you are totally comfortable with them. Notice how the low notes alternate with the higher octave of the **A** note in bars 3 and 4. The 2nd finger should remain on the high **A** note throughout these two bars, while the notes **B** and **C** are played by the 1st and 3rd fingers. Take care with the picking in these bars also. The low notes are all downstrokes, while the high **A** notes are all upstrokes.

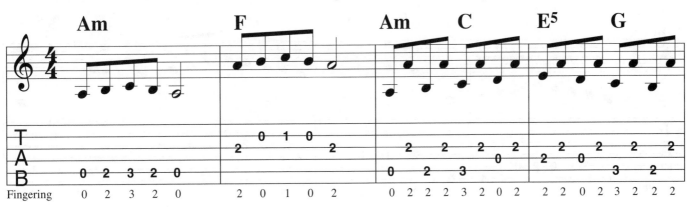

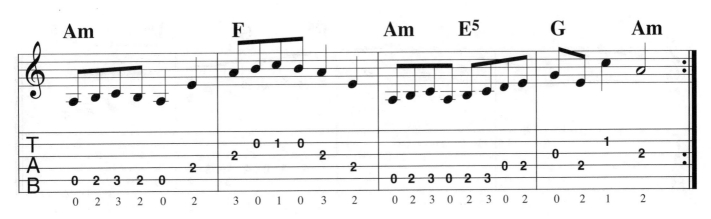

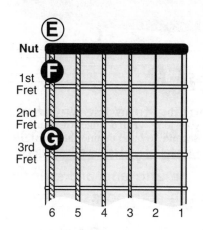

NOTES ON THE SIXTH STRING

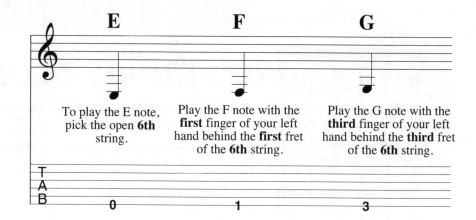

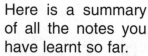

Here is a summary of all the notes you have learnt so far.

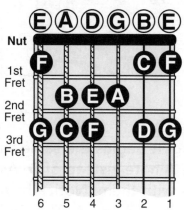

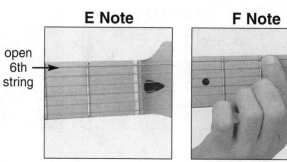
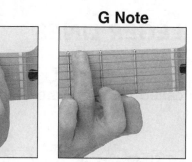

E Note   **F Note**   **G Note**

open 6th string

7.2

The example below uses these three new notes along with all the other notes you have learnt. Notice that the notes on the sixth string are lower versions of the notes on the first string and require extensive use of leger lines in the written music.

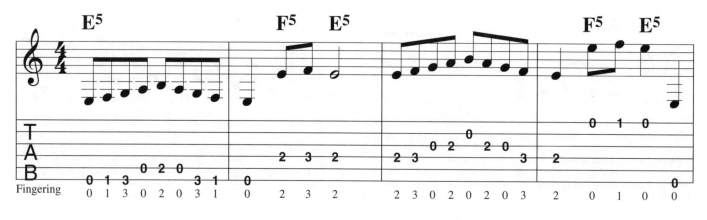

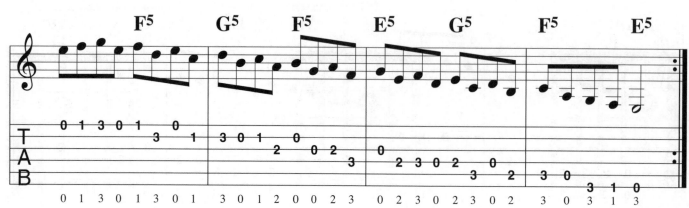

LESSON SIX

PLAYING TWO STRINGS TOGETHER

Everything you have played so far has involved picking one string at a time. However, as a guitar player, it is important to be able to play one, two, three, four, five or six strings together at any given moment. Two notes played together are called **double stops**. The example below uses the 1st and 2nd strings together and then the 2nd and 3rd strings together. **All the notes here are played with downstrokes** (even the 8th notes). As with all examples, make sure all the notes are clear and even.

 8.0 **(All Downstrokes)**

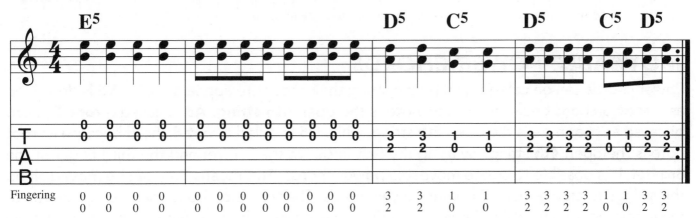

POWER CHORDS

The term "chord" usually applies to three or more notes played together. However, in Rock and several other styles of music, two notes played together are often called chords as well. This especially applies to the formations shown below which are called **Power Chords**, or **fifth chords**. The **symbol** for these chords consists of a **letter name** and the **number 5** (E5, A5, D5, etc). The **letter name** (also known as the **root note**) refers to the first note of the chord. E.g. the root note of an **A5** chord is **A**. The **5** refers to the other note which is a **5th interval above the root note**. An interval is the distance between two notes. Intervals will be discussed in a later lesson. For now all you need to know is the root note of the chord and the fingering.

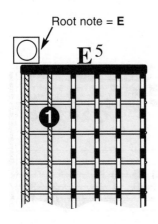

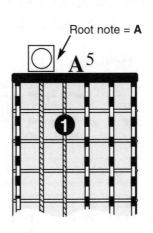

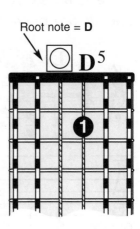

The example below uses the power chord shapes shown on the previous page. Notice that the root notes of these chords are simply the open **A**, **D**, and **low E** strings. All you have to do to change between these chords is move your first finger between the 5th, 3rd and 4th strings. Use all downstrokes with the pick as you play this example.

8.1

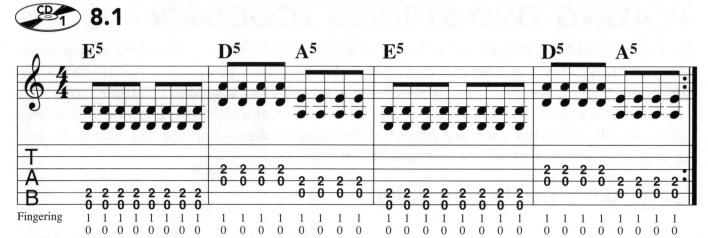

MOVEABLE POWER CHORDS

Power chords can be categorized by the string their root note appears on, i.e. **E5** is described as a **root 6** chord because it's **root note** is the open **6th string**. A5 is called a **root 5** chord because its root note is the open **5th** string, while **D5** is called a **root 4** chord because its root note is the open **4th** string. By using the first finger at the 1st fret and the third finger at the 3rd fret, it is possible to create moveable power chords. This means they can be moved along the strings to create many different power chords. The transition from open power chords to moveable power chords is shown in the diagrams below. The root 5 moveable chord below is called **A♯5** or **B♭5** as it is a **semitone** (one fret) **higher than A** and a semitone **lower** than **B**.

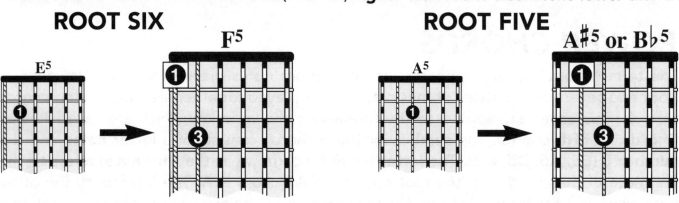

8.2

Here is an exercise for changing between open and moveable power chords. The open chords are played here with the open string and 2nd finger.

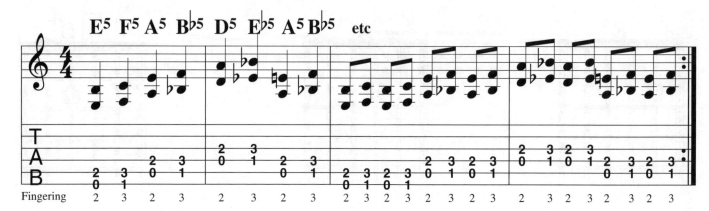

RIGHT HAND DAMPING

When playing power chords, it is common to damp the strings slightly with the right hand. This results in a tighter, more chunky sound. Rest the heel of the hand on the strings at the bridge and then pick the strings you want to sound. It may take a bit of practice to get the desired sound: it all depends on the exact position of the right hand and the amount of pressure used on the strings. Here is an example.

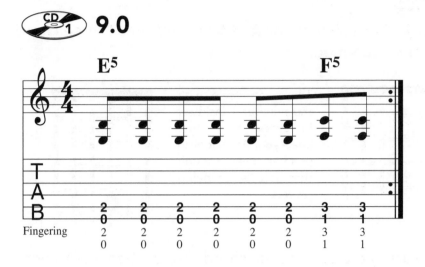

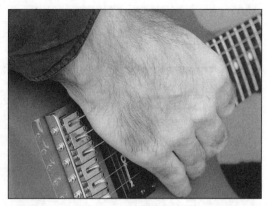

Rest heel of right hand on strings near bridge

A power chord can be formed on **any** root note by selecting the note with the 1st finger and then adding the 3rd finger two frets up on the next (higher) string. Because the formation remains the same regardless of where on the fretboard the chord is played, you don't need to think about the name of the higher note. As long as you know the root note, you can easily find the right chord. The following example uses various root 5 and root 6 power chords built on notes you have already learnt, along with **A5** played as a **root 6** chord at the **5th fret** and **D5** played as a **root 5** chord at the **5th fret**.

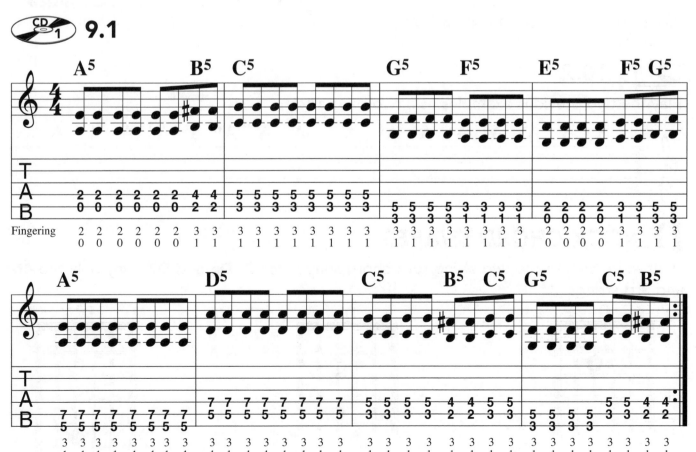

ROCK 'N' ROLL CHORDS

When playing Rock'n'Roll or Blues styles, guitarists commonly use power chords with one note being the root note, and the other alternating between the 5th, 6th and flattened 7th degrees. These chords can be referred to as Rock'n'Roll chords, or simply **Rock chords**.

A ROCK CHORD SHAPES

Written below are the two string Rock chord shapes for **A**, **A6** and **A7**. In all three chord shapes only the 5th and 4th strings are strummed.

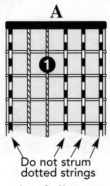

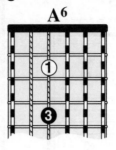

The open circle with the number 1 inside it indicates that you keep your 1st finger in position even though that note is not being played.

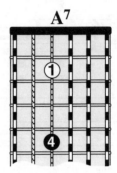

Play the following chord progression using the above rock chord shapes. Use eighth note strums and only play the 5th and 4th strings. Use only down strums as this sounds better when playing the Rock chords in the following examples.

 **10.0**

 **10.1**

 **10.2**

Play the two previous examples as a two bar pattern.

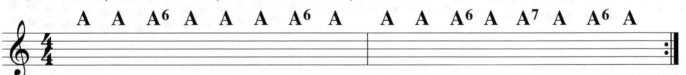

D ROCK CHORD SHAPES

Written below are the two string rock chord shapes for **D**, **D6** and **D7**. Play only the **4th** and **3rd** strings.

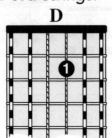

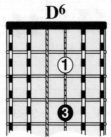

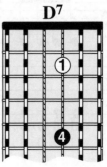

Play the following two bar chord progression using the **D** rock chord shapes. Use only downward eighth note strums playing the 4th and 3rd strings only.

 **10.3**

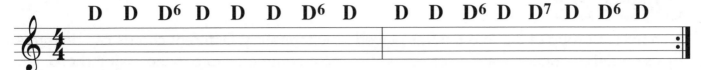

D D D⁶ D D D D⁶ D   D D D⁶ D D⁷ D D⁶ D

E ROCK CHORD SHAPES

Written below are the two string rock chord shapes for **E**, **E6** and **E7**. Play only the **6th** and **5th** strings.

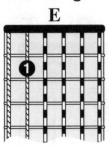
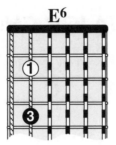
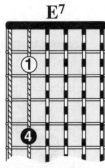

Play the following two bar chord progression using the above rock chord shapes. Use only downward eighth note strums.

 10.4

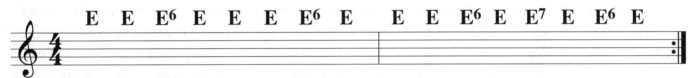

E E E⁶ E E E E⁶ E   E E E⁶ E E⁷ E E⁶ E

TWELVE BAR BLUES

12 Bar Blues is a chord progression which repeats every 12 bars. It can be played in any key and is a standard musical form in Rock as well as Blues and Jazz. 12 bar Blues sounds great when played using the Rock Chords you have just learnt, as demonstrated in the following example.

 11. 12 Bar Blues in the key of A

LESSON SEVEN

CHORDS

A **chord** is a group of 3 or more notes played simultaneously. Different chords can be formed by using different combinations of notes. The most common chord is the **major chord**.

Chords are learnt with the help of a **chord diagram**. This is a grid of horizontal and vertical lines representing the strings and frets of the guitar. A chord diagram will show you exactly where to place your left hand fingers in order to play a particular chord. The diagram on the left here here shows the most common fingering for a **C major** chord.

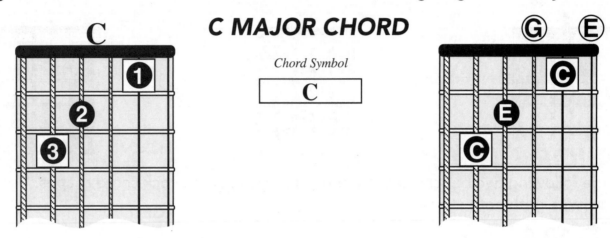

C MAJOR CHORD

Chord Symbol

C

If you look at the diagram on the right, you can see that the C major chord contains the notes **C**, **E** and **G**. The chord takes its name from the first note of the chord. This note is called the **root note** of the chord. Any major chord is usually described by its **letter name** only, so a **C major** chord would usually be called a **C** chord. Although this chord contains more than three notes, there are still only three different notes, because notes C and E occur twice in this fingering.

To play the **C** chord, play **the first 5 strings** with the pick using one downward motion. This is called a **strum**. Hold the pick lightly and strum from the wrist. Keep your wrist relaxed. If any notes buzz or sound muffled, you may have to press harder with one or more fingers. Make sure your fingers are just behind the fret.

CHORD SYMBOLS

Chords are indicated by a **chord symbol** above the music notation. In the case of major chords, the symbol consists only of the letter name of the chord. E.g. a **C chord** is indicated by the **letter C**, an **A chord** is indicated by the letter **A**, a **B♭** chord is indicated by the symbol **B♭**, etc.

RHYTHM NOTATION

As well as traditional music notation and tablature, guitar music sometimes uses **rhythm notation**. This is similar to traditional notation, except that the notes have a diagonal line instead of a notehead. This tells you that instead of playing individual notes, you will be strumming chords. The names of the chords to be played are written above the notation, as shown in the example on the following page.

STRUMMING

When playing chords lasting for whole, half or quarter notes, downward strums are used. However, when strumming eighth notes, it is common to use **alternate strumming**, which is similar to alternate picking. All the notes **on** the beat (the **number** part of the count) are **downstrums**, while the notes **between** the beats (the **and** (**+**) part of the count) are **upstrums**. example 12 uses alternate strumming in the final bar. Remember to keep your wrist relaxed regardless of which direction you are strumming.

12.

MAJOR CHORD FORMATIONS

Most chord formations are closely related to the **five basic major chord shapes** which are shown below. To remember the 5 shapes, think of the word **CAGED**.

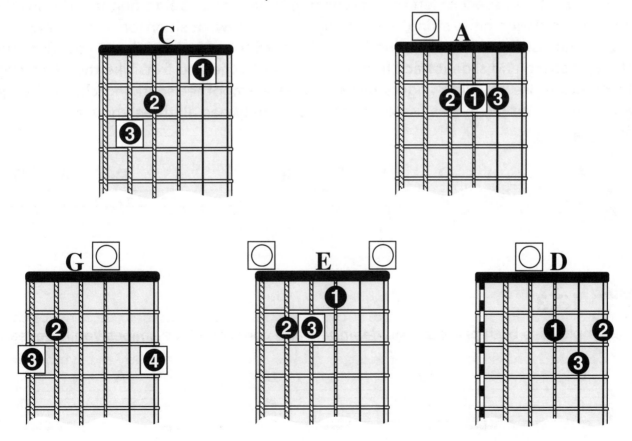

Practice changing between all of these shapes—C to A, C to G, C to E, C to G, A to E, D to G etc, **slowly with your metronome** until you have them memorized and can instantly move from one chord to any other chord.

Once you can remember the shapes for the chords, try the following progressions.

PIVOT AND GUIDE FINGERS

Where common notes occur between chords (e.g. 2nd finger in C chord and A chord—as in the following example), keep the finger down when changing. This is called a **pivot finger**. It will result in a smoother sound.

Another important aspect of left hand technique is the use of **guide fingers**. This involves keeping your finger on a string and sliding it to a new position on that string when changing chords. E.g. when changing from a **D** chord to an **A** chord, keep your 3rd finger on the 2nd string and slide it back from the 3rd fret to the 2nd fret. Like the pivot finger technique, the use of guide fingers helps to create smoother sounding chord changes. The following example makes use of guide fingers between all three chords.

This example uses both **pivot** and **guide** fingers and contains all the shapes you have learnt.

LESSON EIGHT

RESTS

Rests are used to indicate specific periods of silence. Below are three different rest values–the **quarter rest** worth **one** beat of silence, the **half rest** worth **two** beats of silence and the **whole rest** worth a **whole bar** of silence. Small counting numbers are placed under rests. Note that the half rest sits on top of the middle line of the staff, while the whole rest hangs below the fourth line.

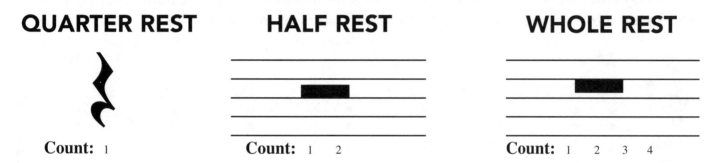

QUARTER REST	HALF REST	WHOLE REST
Count: 1	Count: 1 2	Count: 1 2 3 4

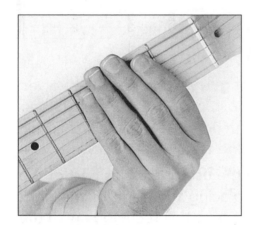

When a rest comes after you have played a note, you must stop the note sounding i.e. stop the strings vibrating. This can be done by placing your left hand fingers lightly across all the strings. Do not press too hard as this will produce a new note. This **muting** technique is also useful to stop previously played notes sounding at the same time as a new note is played.

 **14.0**

Here is an example which uses all three rests shown above. Remember that a rest indicates **silence**. Don't be lazy with the way you mute the strings. Be sure that there are absolutely no sounds still ringing when a rest is indicated. A rest may refer to your part only or the whole band. Notice how the rest the final bar here leaves room for the drums on the recording. It is also important to count along with your metronome and tap your foot on each beat regardless of whether a note or a rest appears in the music. This way you will develop a solid and confident sense of time.

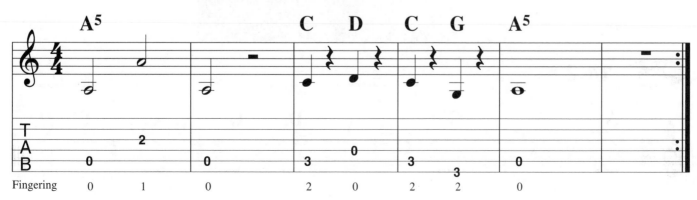

THE EIGHTH REST

 This symbol is a **eighth rest.** It indicates **half a beat** of silence.

 **14.1**

Try this example which makes use of eighth rests with power chords. Listen to the recording and notice how the rests help drive the rhythm forward. Count carefully at first and be sure to tap your foot only on the beats and not in between.

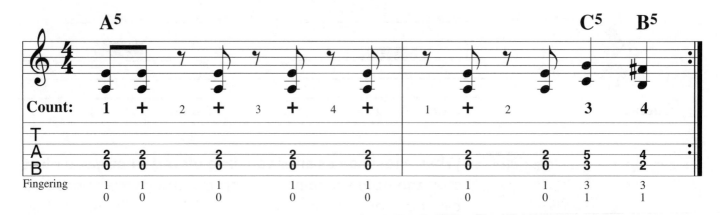

RESTS WITH CHORD PLAYING

A strummed rhythm can often be made more interesting by the use of rests as part of the pattern. When playing chords, rests are often achieved by placing the edge of the right hand over the strings (as shown in the photograph below). Practice this technique with the following example.

 **14.2**

LESSON NINE

IDENTIFYING EIGHTH NOTE RHYTHMS

There is a simple system for identifying any note's position in a bar by naming notes off the beat according to which beat they come directly after. The system works as follows. Within a bar of continuous eighth notes in $\frac{4}{4}$ time, there are **eight** possible places where notes could occur. The first beat is called **one** (1), the next eighth note is called the "**and of one**", then comes beat **two**, the next eighth note is called the "**and of two**", then beat **three**, followed by the "**and of three**", then beat **four**, followed by the "**and of four**" which is the final eighth note in the bar. These positions are shown in the notation below.

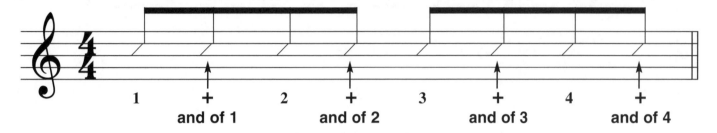

This system is particularly useful if you are having trouble with the timing of a rhythm. You simply identify where the notes occur in relation to each beat and then count them slowly until you have memorized the rhythm.

 **15.0**

In the first bar of this example, the notes occur on beat **1**, then the **and of two**, **three**, and the **and of 3**. In the second bar, the notes occur on the **and of 1**, the **and of 3** and the **and of 4**. Even though there are many rests here, it is important to keep a constant eighth note strumming motion going in the air just above the strings throughout the example. This is sometimes called "playing air" and is a good way to keep time.

 **15.1**

Here is another example which uses eighth rests. Try analyzing it in the manner shown above and then learn it from memory. Remember to count out loud as you play.

PERCUSSIVE STRUMMING

An important rhythm technique used in many styles of music is the **Percussive Strum**. This is achieved by forming a chord shape with the left hand and placing it on the strings, but **not** pressed down on the frets. A percussive strum is indicated by using an **X** in place of a notehead. This technique can be applied to anything from a two note power chord to a bar chord covering all six strings. Listen to the following example on the recording to hear what the percussive strum should sounds like when applied to Root 5 power chords.

CD 1   16.0

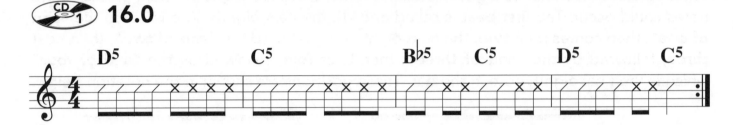

DEVELOPING RHYTHMIC CONTROL

To become a good rhythm player it is essential to have control over where in the bar you place notes or chords and where you leave spaces. One way to improve this ability is to take each subdivision of the beat i.e., eighth notes, triplets or sixteenth notes, and practice moving each one to all possible positions within a single beat and then within a bar. To keep the feel of the basic subdivision, use percussive strumming in place of rests. The next example contains exercises using eighth notes. Play the exercises as written at first, then try swinging all the eighth notes. **Remember to use your metronome, count out loud and tap your foot evenly on the beat.**

CD 2   16.1

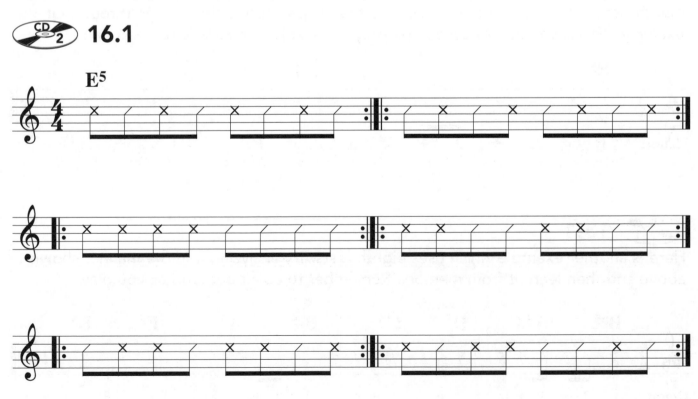

ACCENTS

A simple power chord rhythm can be made to sound 'heavier' by applying an **accent** to some of the strums within the rhythm. An accent is achieved by playing the strum a little louder or stronger. An accent is often shown as a small wedge (>) above or below the note, as shown below.

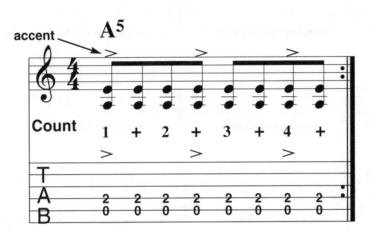

17.0

17.1

The following example applies the accent to a simple chord progression that uses the open power chords **A5**, **D5**, and **E5**.

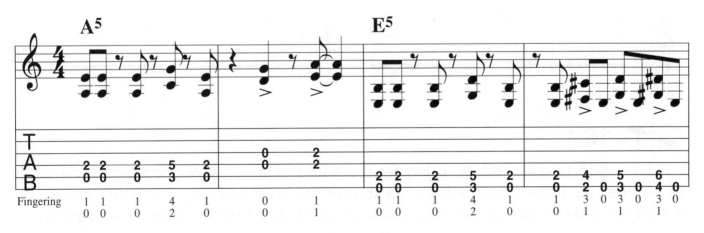

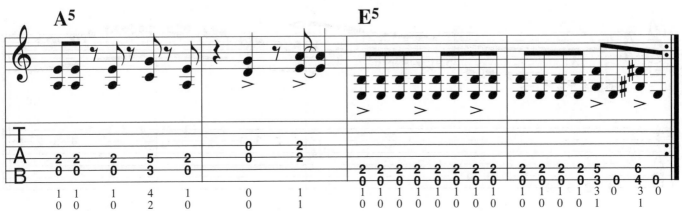

A good way to gain control of accents is to take a systematic approach similar to the earlier percussive strumming exercises and practice accents on all possible eighth note positions within a bar individually, and then in combinations, as shown below.

18.0

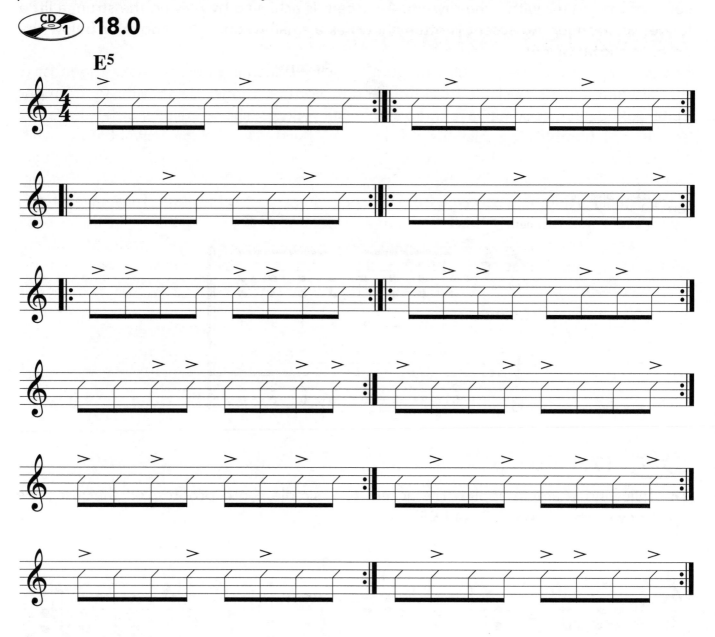

18.1

It is also important to work on using accents with single notes. A good way to do this is to use the four finger exercise from the start of the book and play it in eighth notes, first accenting all the notes on the beat, and then all the notes off the beat, as shown here.

LESSON TEN

USING THE GUITAR PICKUPS

Another important aspect of electric guitar playing is learning how to make the most of the different sounds available from the various pickup settings. These will vary from one guitar to the next, as some have three **single coil pickups** (shown below), others have two double coil **humbucking pickups** (often called humbuckers–also shown below) while others have various combinations of these two basic types. Single coil pickups originally came from Fender guitars like the **Stratocaster**. They have a bright, crisp and sometimes cutting quality. Humbuckers came from Gibson guitars like the **Les Paul**. They have a fatter more beefy sound. Today there are many companies making variations on these basic pickup types. Each one has it's own sound and everyone has their own preference. Many professional guitarists use more than one guitar, each with different pickups, to give them different sounds for different songs, especially when recording.

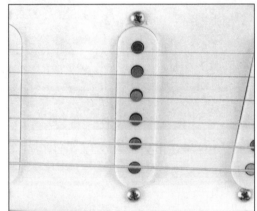

Single coil pickup

Double coil "Humbucker"

 **19.0**

The following example demonstrates the sound of the two basic types of pickups. The first time through the example is played on a guitar with single coil pickups; the second time it is played on a guitar with double coil humbuckers. Listen to the CD to hear the different tonal qualities.

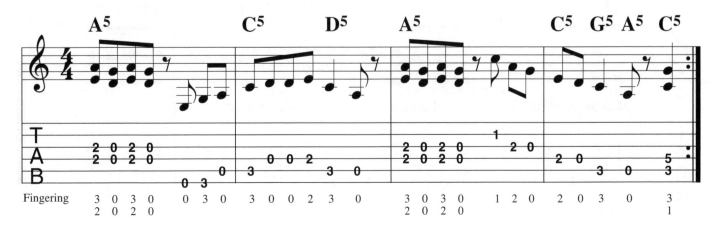

PICKUP SELECTOR SWITCHES

As well as the type of pickups used, it is possible to get a variety of tones out of a guitar by selecting different pickup positions. This could mean using the neck pickup only, the bridge pickup only or a combination of pickups. The pickup position is selected with the **pickup selector switch**. The type of switch varies from one guitar to the next, but once again there are two basic types. On Fender style guitars (usually single coil) there are usually three pickups and a five–way selector switch which allows you to use any of the three pickups individually, or an "in between" position involving either the neck and middle pickups, or the bridge and middle pickups. On Gibson style guitars there are usually two double coil humbuckers and a three–way selector switch to choose either pickup individually or both combined. Both types of selector switches are shown below. These days many guitars have extra pickup possibilities and extra switches. Only the basic types are dealt with here.

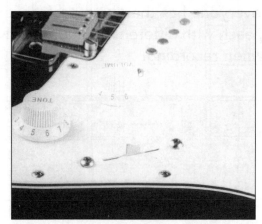

Fender style 5 way switch

Gibson style 3 way switch

Guitarists often change pickup settings in the middle of a song, or solo to get a different tonal effect. The best time to do this is where a **rest** occurs in the music. All you do is stop picking or strumming and move your hand to alter the pickup selector switch before resuming playing. The following example is an exercise designed to help you gain control of switching pickups between phrases. Change the pickup settings where the rests occur and keep counting in time with your metronome and tapping your foot as you play the example so as to keep your timing even.

 19.1   Changing Pickup Settings

LESSON ELEVEN

MINOR CHORDS

Another common chord type is the minor chord. Minor chords are often described as having a "sadder" or more intense sound than major chords. Shown below are three basic minor chord shapes. As with previous chords, memorize each shape and then practice changing between them. Once you are comfortable with them, try example 20.0 which uses all three shapes.

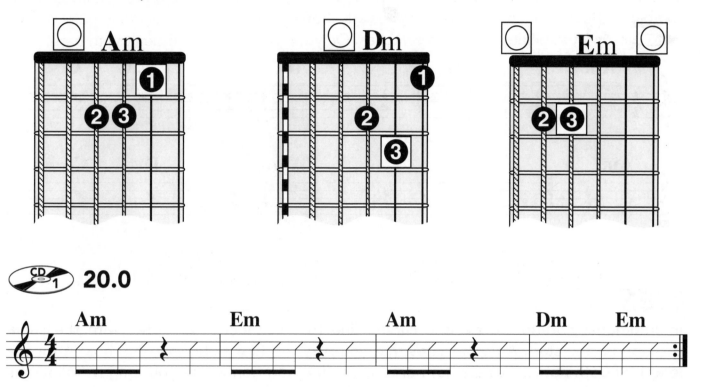

20.0

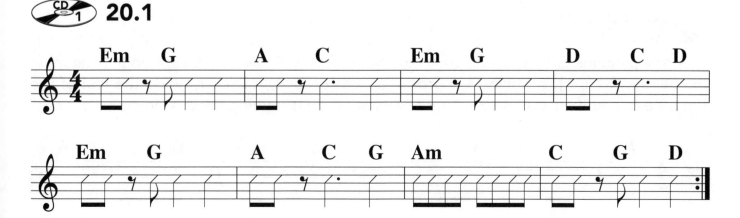

VISUALIZING

Most people have trouble changing chords smoothly at first. One way to overcome this is to practice the changes with your eyes closed and visualize each new shape in your mind before you change to it. This helps to make sure you really know the shapes from memory and gets you into the habit of thinking ahead as you play. Try this technique with the following example, which contains almost all the chord shapes you have learnt so far.

20.1

46

STACCATO

It is not always desirable to leave a chord ringing once it has been played. In electric guitar playing it is common to cut the sound of a chord off as soon as it has been played, making the rhythm very crisp. The technique of cutting chords or notes shorter than their written value is called **staccato**. With chords containing open strings, staccato is usually achieved by placing the side of the right hand across all the strings immediately after strumming the chord. Staccato is indicated by placing a **dot** directly above or below the intended note or chord.

TIES

In traditional notation, a **tie** is a curved line that connects two notes with the **same** position on the staff. A tie indicates that you play the **first** note only, and hold it for the length of both notes. Ties are not necessary in Tab notation where you can just follow the count. Here is an example which uses ties. Count carefully as you play.

This one contains ties, rests and staccato chords. You will have to disrupt your strumming momentum where the staccato chords and rests occur, but keep it going the rest of the time. Keep counting evenly regardless of what your strumming hand is doing.

LESSON TWELVE

ARPEGGIOS

An **arpeggio** is a chord played one note at a time. The following example demonstrates a **C** chord played first as a chord (strummed) and then as an arpeggio (picked). Playing chords as arpeggios is a common way of creating guitar parts in a band situation.

 **23.0**

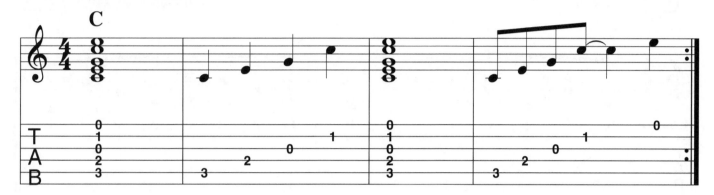

Here is an example which makes use of arpeggios. Hold down the chord shapes indicated as much as possible except when playing notes which are not in the chords (e.g. the B note at the end of bar 2). Take care with your picking and make sure all your notes are clear and even.

 **23.1**

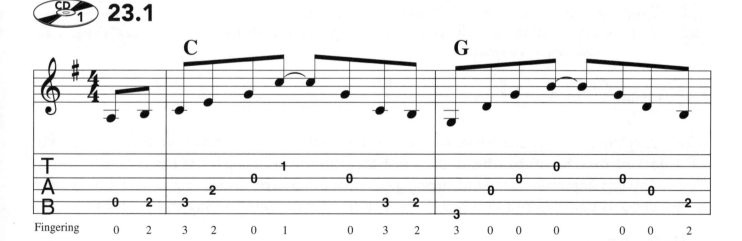

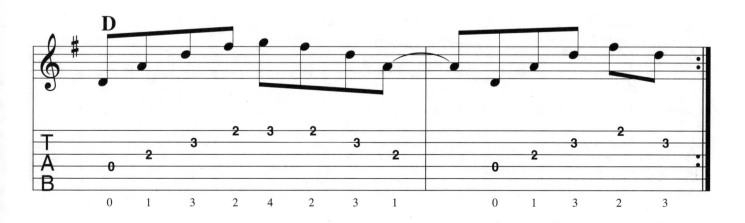

PLAYING TWO STRINGS WITH THE FIRST FINGER

The following example uses both eighth and quarter rests. The first finger plays both the 3rd and 4th strings, as shown in the accompanying photo. Instead of playing on the tip, the last segment of the finger is **flattened** across both strings. This technique is very common in electric guitar playing.

 23.2

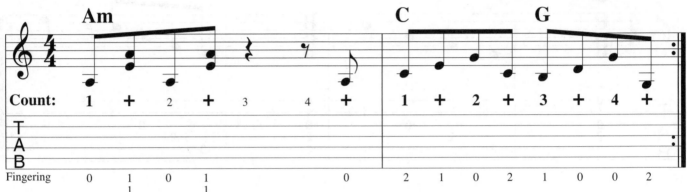

THE SIX EIGHT TIME SIGNATURE

$\begin{smallmatrix}6\\8\end{smallmatrix}$ This is the **six eight** time signature.
There are six eighth notes in one bar of $\begin{smallmatrix}6\\8\end{smallmatrix}$ time.
The six eighth notes are divided into two groups of three.

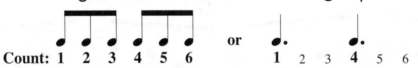

When playing $\begin{smallmatrix}6\\8\end{smallmatrix}$ time there are **two** beats within each bar with each beat having the value of a **dotted quarter note** (this is different to $\begin{smallmatrix}4\\4\end{smallmatrix}$ time where each beat is a quarter note). The following example combines arpeggios of open chords and power chords in $\begin{smallmatrix}6\\8\end{smallmatrix}$ time. In the second bar, the 2nd and 3rd fingers slide up two frets to play the **D** and **F♯** notes.

 **23.3**

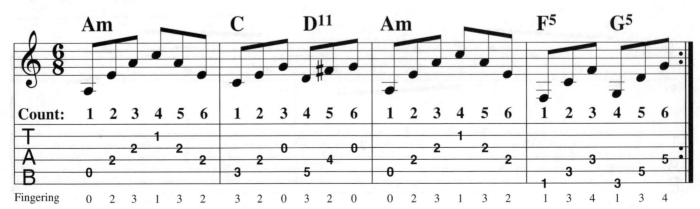

LESSON THIRTEEN

LEARNING ALL THE NOTES

So far you have learnt the open strings of the guitar and all the **natural** notes in the first three frets. However, if you want to be a good musician, it is necessary to learn **all** the notes on the fretboard and also know how to read them. This means learning the notes called **sharps** and **flats** which occur in between some of the natural notes.

TONES AND SEMITONES

A **semitone** is the smallest distance between two notes used in western music. On the guitar, notes which are a semitone apart are **one fret** apart (e.g. the note C on the 3rd fret 5th string is one semitone above the note B at the second fret). This could also be reversed i.e. the note **B** is one semitone (one fret) below the note **C**. Notes which are a **tone** (two semitones) apart, are **two frets** apart. An example of this would be the notes F and G on the sixth string or the first string. Check these on the diagram below and on your guitar.

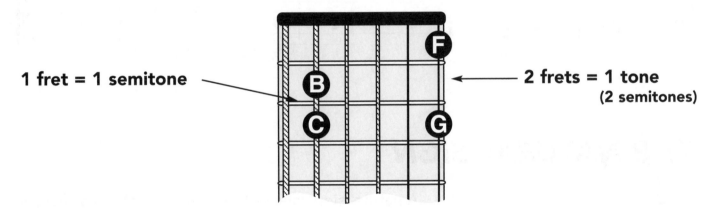

1 fret = 1 semitone

2 frets = 1 tone
(2 semitones)

SHARPS

A **sharp sign(♯)** placed **before** a note, raises the pitch of that note by **one semitone (one fret)**. To play a sharp note picture the normal note (the **natural** note) on the fretboard and then place your next finger on the next fret. Try these examples:

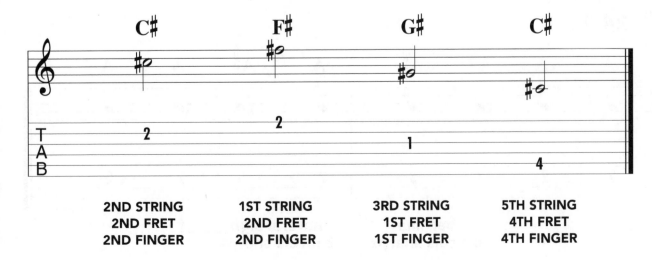

2ND STRING	1ST STRING	3RD STRING	5TH STRING
2ND FRET	2ND FRET	1ST FRET	4TH FRET
2ND FINGER	2ND FINGER	1ST FINGER	4TH FINGER

THE CHROMATIC SCALE

Using sharps you can now play five new notes, which occur between the seven natural notes you already know. The following exercise uses all twelve notes which occur within one octave of music. It is an example of a **Chromatic Scale**. Chromatic scales consist entirely of **semitones** (i.e. they move up or down one fret at a time) and the start and finish notes are always the same (this is called the **keynote** or **tonic**). The chromatic scale uses **all twelve notes** used in western music and can begin on **any** note. Note that in the example below, there are no sharps between **B** and **C**, or **E** and **F**. This is because they are a semitone apart and there is no room for an extra note between them. Play the exercise slowly and steadily, making sure you use the correct fingering.

 **24.0**

THE NATURAL SIGN

 This is a **natural** sign.

A natural sign cancels the effect of a sharp or flat for the rest of that bar, or until another sharp or flat sign occurs within that bar.

A sharpened note stays sharp until either a **bar line** or a **natural sign** (♮) cancels it as in the following example.

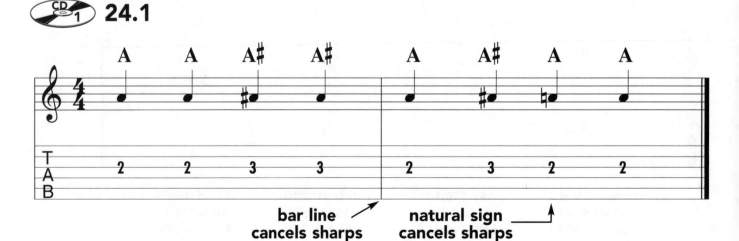 **24.1**

bar line cancels sharps

natural sign cancels sharps

 **25.**

Now play this example which makes use of both sharp and natural signs. Play it slowly at first and say the name of each note out loud as you play it.

To improve your knowledge of sharps and natural signs, find each of the following notes on the fretboard of your guitar. Write the name of each note above or below the note if necessary.

FLATS

A **Flat** (♭) does the opposite of a sharp. Placed immediately **before** a note, it **lowers** the pitch of that note by one semitone.

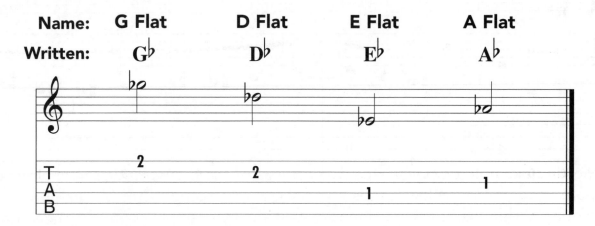

As with sharps, flats are cancelled by a bar line or by a natural sign.

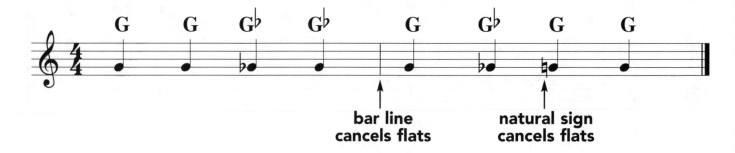

The use of sharps and flats means that the same note can have two different names. For example, F# is the same note as G♭ and G# is also A♭. These are referred to as **enharmonic** notes. The following diagram outlines all of the notes in the **first position** on the guitar (including both names for the enharmonic notes). The first position consists of the open string notes and the notes on the first **four** frets.

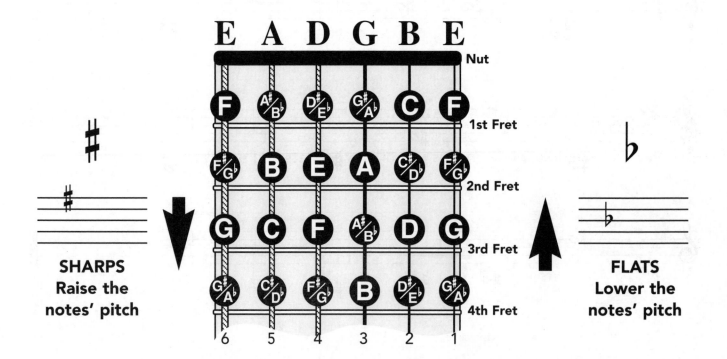

Here is an exercise to improve your knowledge of flats. Once again, write the names above or below the notes and then find them on the guitar.

The following example demonstrates two octaves of the **E chromatic scale**. Notice that sharps are used as the scale ascends and flats as it descends. This is common practice when writing chromatic passages in music. As with any example containing new notes, it is important to name the notes out loud as you practice this scale.

26.0   E Chromatic Scale in Open Position

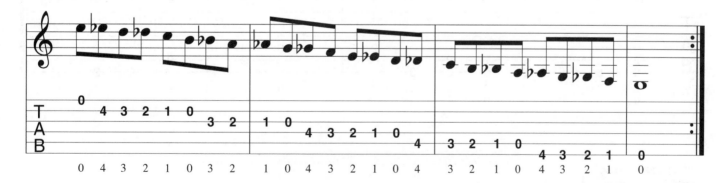

26.1

Now play this example which makes use of sharps, flats and naturals.

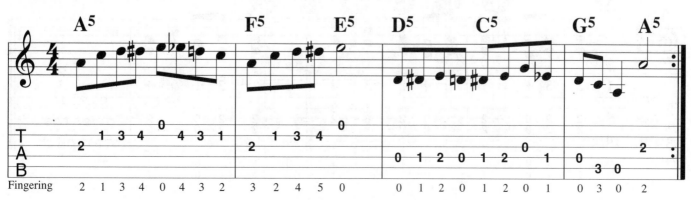

LESSON FOURTEEN

SYNCOPATION

When ties are used to connect eighth notes, an "off the beat" feel is created. This is called **syncopation**. When a chord change is anticipated by half a beat, it is described as giving the rhythm a **push**. These things are demonstrated in the following example.

 **27.0**

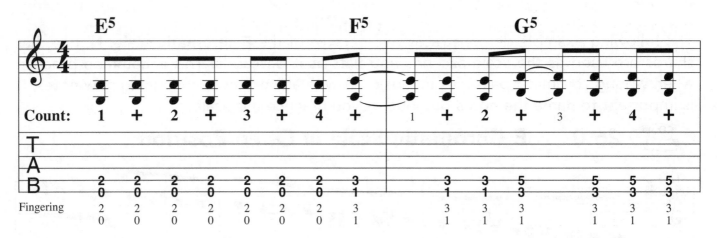

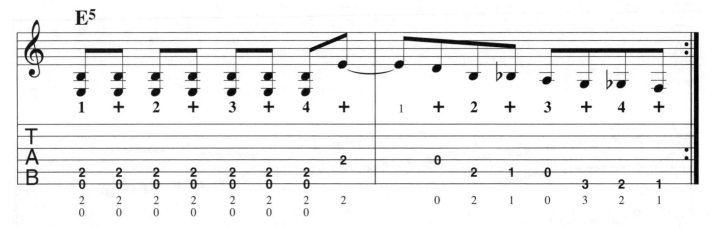

 **27.1**

This example uses both rests on the beat and ties on the beat to create syncopation. Notice once again the use of the first finger across the 3rd and 4th strings at the 2nd fret.

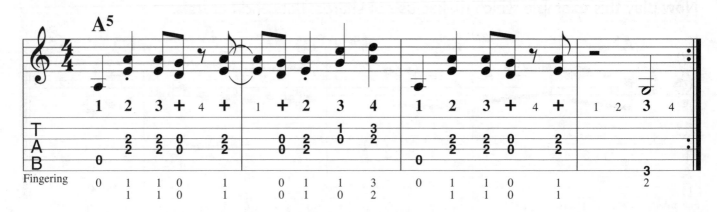

THE COMMON TIME SIGNATURE

 This symbol is called **common time**. It means exactly the same as $\frac{4}{4}$. The next example uses the common time signature.

THE LEAD-IN

Sometimes a song does not begin on the first beat of a bar. Any notes which come before the first full bar are called **lead-in notes** (or pick-up notes). When lead-in notes are used, the last bar is also incomplete. The notes in the lead-in and the notes in the last bar add up to one full bar. Here is an example.

 **28.0**

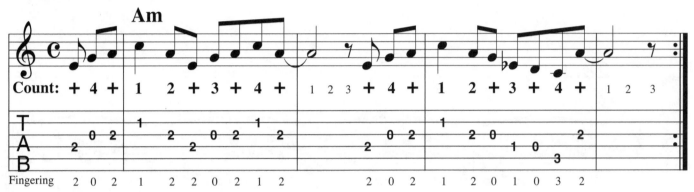

RIFFS

A **riff** is a short pattern of notes (usually one or two bars long) which repeats throughout a verse or section of a song. A riff can also be varied to fit a chord progression. The use of riffs is common in many styles of music including Rock, Metal, Blues, Jazz and Funk. Many of the examples you have already learnt are riffs. Here is another example. There are also several more on the following pages.

 **28.1**

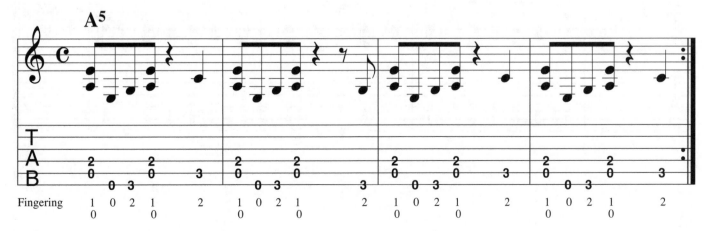

Here are some more riffs. Learn them and then make up some of your own based on the ideas presented here. Don't worry about the notes too much, just experiment until you find something that sounds good and then memorize it.

28.2

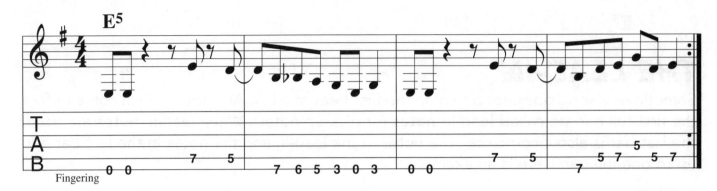

28.3

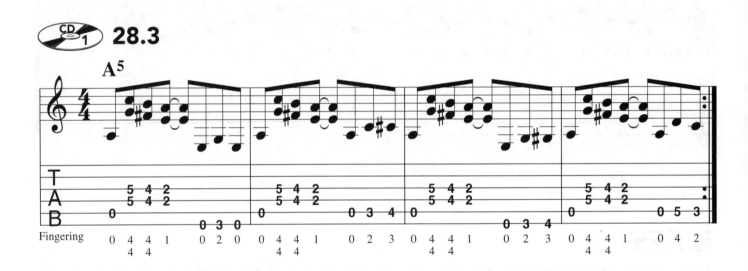

28.4

The following 12 bar Blues contains a riff which is altered to fit each new chord as it occurs. As with previous examples, play it slowly at first and gradually increase the tempo.

 **29.**

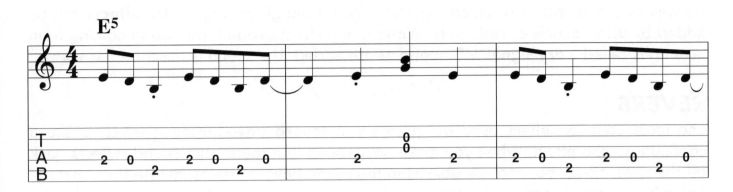

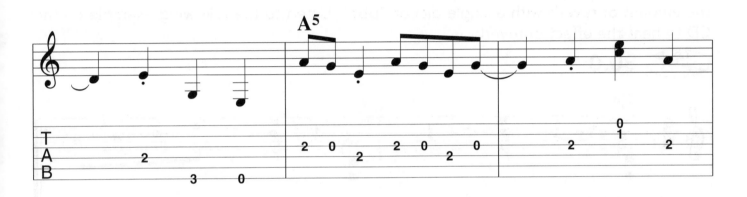

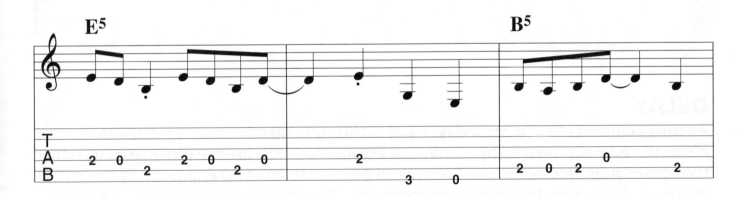

LESSON FIFTEEN

USING GUITAR EFFECTS

As well as the sound of an electric guitar played through an amp, extra **effects** can be added by using pedals or rack units. Without any effects added, the sound coming from an amp is called a **dry signal**. When effects are added, the sound is described as **wet**.

REVERB

The most common effect used by guitarists is **reverb** (reverberation) which is like a continuous echo effect. When you make any sound in a room, that sound reflects back off the walls, floor, roof and any objects in the room. Reverb effects imitate these natural reflections. Like distortion, the amount of reverb can be controlled and shaped by the controls on the pedal or unit. Many amps have reverb units built into them and you control the amount of reverb with a single dial or "**pot**". Listen to the following example on the CD to hear the effect of reverb.

 **30.0**

DELAY

Another common effect is the **delay**. Delay is closely related to reverb; but the difference is that the echoes produced by a delay unit are distinct and a precise distance apart rather than continuous. Because of this, delays can be used to create guitar parts by timing the delays to fit in with the tempo of the music. This is demonstrated in the following example. Once again, listen to the CD to hear the effect. This example uses a new F chord shape which is shown in the diagram below.

30.1

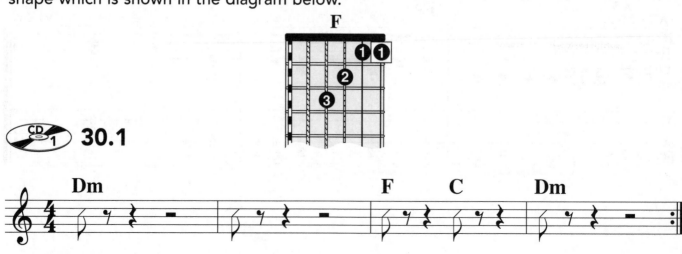

CHORUS

Another effect related to delay is the **chorus**. This creates a feeling of space and movement within the sound. A chorus unit delays the sound, changes it to become less regular and also adds slight pitch fluctuations, then mixes the effected signal with the original dry signal. As with all effects, the best way to understand the chorus is to experiment with the various parameter controls on your particular unit. The example below demonstrates the effect of the chorus.

 **30.2**

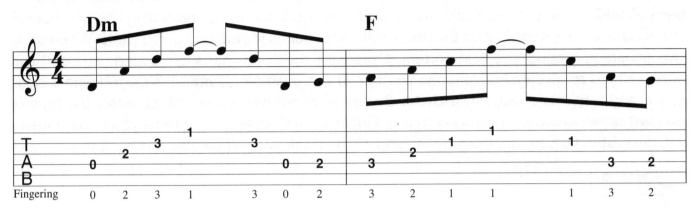

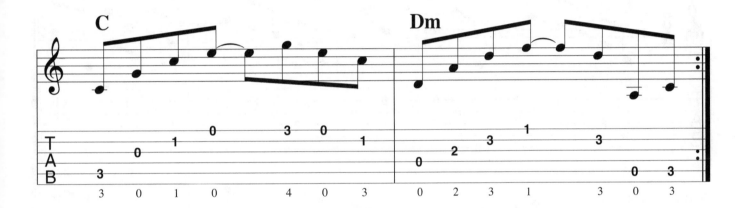

FLANGER

There are many other effects which can be used to alter the sound of the guitar. Space doesn't allow us to cover them all, but ask other guitarists or staff at a music store to demonstrate them for you. One unit which can create a variety of sounds is the **flanger**. A common effect produced by a flanger is sometimes described as like a jet taking off. Listen to the following example on the CD to hear a flanging effect.

 **30.3**

THE THREE FOUR TIME SIGNATURE

This is the **three four** time signature. It tells you there are **three** quarter note beats in each bar.

The next example demonstrates two guitar parts played along with a rhythm section in ¾ time. The basic beat subdivisions (quarter notes, eighth notes, triplets and sixteenth notes) work exactly the same in ¾ time as they do in 4 time. The notation here shows the bass and drum parts as well as the guitars. Watch the notation as you listen to the recording and see how all the parts work together. Notice the use of different sounds for the two guitar parts. When using two guitars in a band, this is important. Otherwise the guitar parts can sound "muddy" and become hard to distinguish from one another. In this example, **Guitar 1** is played with a clean sound and a chorus effect, while **Guitar 2** uses an overdriven sound. Most times, the type of part will determine the best sound to use. Guitar 2 uses notes and rhythms you haven't learnt yet. Just listen to it for now, but by the end of the book you will be able to play it too.

CD 1 31.

SECTION 2
Scales, Keys, Chord Types

LESSON SIXTEEN

THE MAJOR SCALE

The **major scale** is a series of **8** notes in alphabetical order that has the familiar sound:

Do   Re   Mi   Fa   So   La   Ti   Do

Thus the **C major scale** contains the following notes.

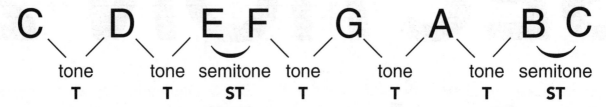

	C	D	E F	G	A	B C
	tone	tone semitone	tone	tone	tone semitone
	T	**T**	**ST**	**T**	**T**	**T**	**ST**

The distance between each note is two frets except for **E F** and **B C** where the distance is only one fret. A distance of two frets is a **tone**, indicated by **T**. A distance of one fret is a **semitone**, indicated by **ST**.

The following example demonstrates one octave of the **C** major scale.

 **32.0**

The diagram below shows all the natural notes in the open position. They are all notes of the C major scale, even though the lowest note of the pattern is E and the highest note is G. The key note **C** occurs twice and is indicated with a square around it. This pattern can be described as the full open position fingering of the C major scale. These notes have been used to play thousands of melodies ranging from Classical music to Folk and Country, to Jazz, to classic Rock songs.

C MAJOR SCALE IN OPEN POSITION

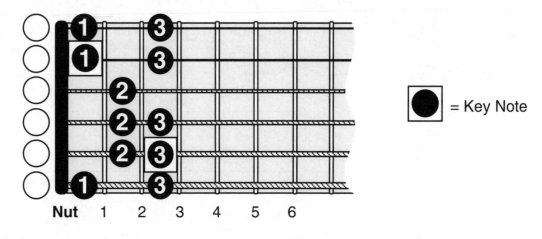

Here are the notes from the diagram written in standard music notation and tablature.

32.1

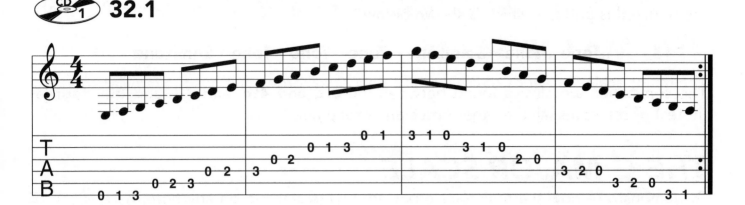

It is not necessary to always start and finish on the note C. Depending on which chords you are playing over, it may sound best to start on **any** of the notes in the scale. E.g. if you were playing over a **C** chord followed by a **D minor** chord you could play the scale starting on **C** for the **C chord** but start on **D** for the **D minor** chord, as shown in the following example. This is a **modal** approach to playing scales, which is the way Fusion and Jazz players often use scales. To learn about modal playing, see *Progressive Complete Learn to Play Lead Guitar Manual*.

32.2

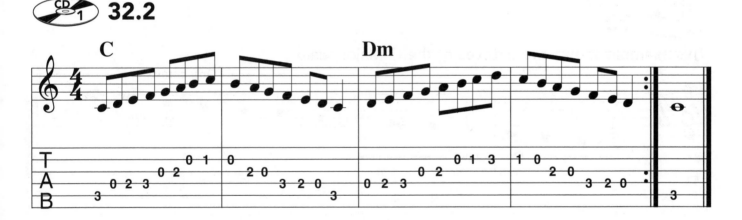

The following example demonstrates a melody created from the C major scale. Once you have memorized the fingering for the scale, experiment with it and create your own melodies.

32.3

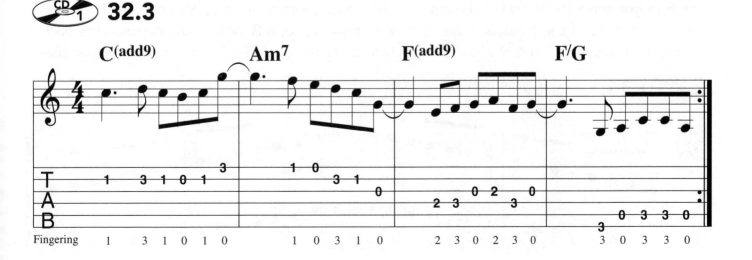

Once you know the pattern of tones and semitones used to create the C major scale, you can build a major scale on any of the twelve notes used in music. It is important to memorize this pattern, which is shown below.

Tone   Tone   Semitone   Tone   Tone   Tone   Semitone

The **semitones** are always found between the **3rd and 4th**, and **7th and 8th degrees** (notes) of the scale. All the other notes are a tone apart.

THE G MAJOR SCALE

To demonstrate how the major scale pattern works starting on any note, here is the **G major scale**. Notice that the 7th degree is F sharp (**F#**) instead of F. This is done to maintain the correct pattern of tones and semitones and thus retain the sound of the major scale (**do re mi fa so la ti do**).

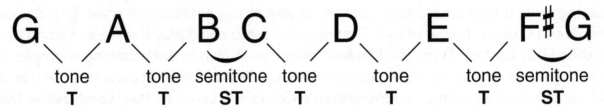

 **33.**

This example shows two octaves of the G Major scale.

THE F MAJOR SCALE

The **F major** scale starts and ends on the note F and contains a B flat (**B♭**) note. Written below are two octaves of the **F major** scale. In the **F major** scale, a **B♭** note must be used instead of a B note in order to keep the correct pattern of tones and semitones for the major scale.

 **34.**

LESSON SEVENTEEN

MORE ABOUT MAJOR SCALES

Once you know the pattern of tones and semitones used to create the C major scale, you can build a major scale on **any** of the twelve notes used in music. It is important to memorize this pattern, which is shown below.

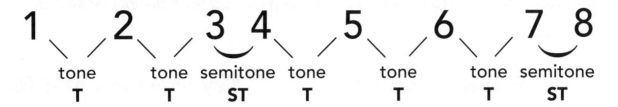

The **semitones** are always found between the **3rd and 4th**, and **7th and 8th** degrees of the scale. All the other notes are a tone apart. By simply following the pattern of tones and semitones, it is possible to construct a major scale starting on any note. The scale will be named by the note it starts on. The following example demonstrates three more major scales.

KEYS AND KEY SIGNATURES

The **key** describes the note around which a piece of music is built. When a song consists of notes from a particular scale, it is said to be written in the **key** which has the same notes as that scale. The key signature is written at the start of each line of music, just after the clef.

The number of sharps or flats in any key signature depends on the number of sharps or flats in the corresponding major scale. The major scales and key signatures for the keys of **F** and **G** are shown below. Without sharps and flats, these scales would not contain the correct pattern of tones and semitones which gives the major scale its distinctive sound.

G Major Scale

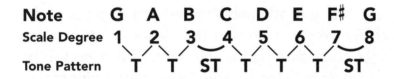

Key Signature of G Major

The **G major** scale contains one sharp, F♯, therefore the key signature for the key of **G major** contains one sharp, F♯.

F Major Scale

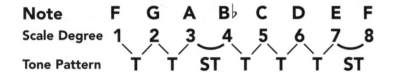

Key Signature of F Major

The **F major** scale contains one flat, B♭, therefore the key signature for the key of **F major** contains one flat, B♭.

Some scales contain sharps while others contain flats because there has to be a separate letter name for each note in the scale. E.g. the G major scale contains F♯ instead of G♭ even though these two notes are identical in sound. If G♭ was used, the scale would contain two notes with the letter name G and no note with the letter name F. In the key of F major, the note B♭ is chosen instead of A♯ for the same reason. If A♯ was used, the scale would contain two notes with the letter name A and no note with the letter name B.

The charts on the following page contain the **key signatures** of all the major scales used in music, along with the number of sharps or flats contained in each key. Because there are 12 notes used in music, this means there are 12 possible starting notes for major scales (including sharps and flats). Note that some of the keys will have sharps or flats in their name, e.g. F♯ major, B♭ major, E♭ major, etc. Keys which contain sharps are called sharp keys and keys which contain flats are called flat keys.

The key signatures for all the major scales that contain sharps are:

	G Major	D Major	A Major	E Major	B Major	F♯ Major
Sharps	F♯	F♯ C♯	F♯ C♯ G♯	F♯ C♯ G♯ D♯	F♯ C♯ G♯ D♯ A♯	F♯ C♯ G♯ D♯ A♯ E♯

The sharp key signatures are summarised in the table below.

*The new sharp **key** is a fifth interval * higher*

Key	Number of Sharps	Sharp Notes
G	1	F♯
D	2	F♯, C♯
A	3	F♯, C♯, G♯
E	4	F♯, C♯, G♯, D♯
B	5	F♯, C♯, G♯, D♯, A♯,
F♯	6	F♯, C♯, G♯, D♯, A♯, E♯

*The new sharp **note** is a fifth interval higher*

Written below are the key signatures for all the major scales that contain flats.

	F Major	B♭ Major	E♭ Major	A♭ Major	D♭ Major	G♭ Major
Flats	B♭	B♭E♭	B♭E♭A♭	B♭E♭ A♭D♭	B♭E♭ A♭D♭G♭	B♭E♭ A♭D♭G♭C♭

The flat key signatures are summarised in the table below.

*The new flat **key** is a fourth interval higher*

Key	Number of Flats	Flat Notes
F	1	B♭
B♭	2	B♭, E♭
E♭	3	B♭, E♭, A♭
A♭	4	B♭, E♭, A♭, D♭
D♭	5	B♭, E♭, A♭, D♭, G♭,
G♭	6	B♭, E♭, A♭, D♭, G♭, C♭

*The new flat **note** is a fourth interval higher*

* An **interval** is the distance between two notes. Intervals are named by the number of letters they are apart, e.g. C to G is a fifth. Intervals are discussed in detail in lesson 22.

THE KEY CYCLE

There are many reasons why you need to be able to play equally well in every key. Bands often have to play in keys that suit their singer. That could be **F#** or **D♭** for example. Keyboard players tend to like the keys of **C**, **F** and **G**, while **E** and **A** are fairly common keys for guitar. Horn players like flat keys such as **F**, **B♭** and **E♭**. Apart from this, Jazz tunes often contain many key changes in themselves. For these reasons, you need to learn how keys relate to each other so you can move quickly between them.

One way to do this is to use the **key cycle** (also called the **cycle of 5ths** or **cycle of 4ths**). It contains the names of all the keys.

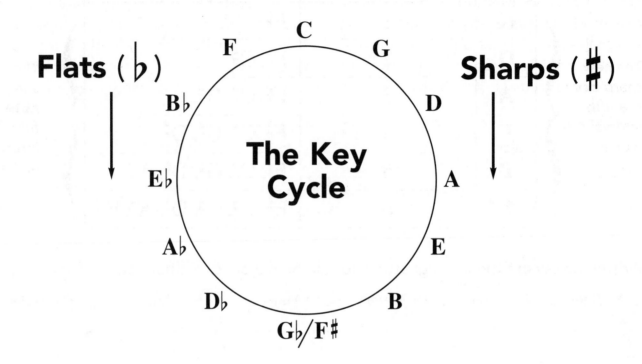

To help memorize the key cycle, think of it like a clock. Just as there are 12 points on a clock, so there are 12 keys. **C** is at the top and contains no sharps or flats. Moving around clockwise you will find the next key is **G**, which contains one sharp (**F#**). The next key is **D**, which contains two sharps (**F#** and **C#**). Progressing further through the sharp keys, each key contains an extra sharp, with the new sharp being the 7th note of the new key, and the others being any which were contained in the previous key. Therefore the key of A would automatically contain **F#** and **C#** which were in the key of D, plus **G#** which is the 7th note of the A major scale. When you get to **F#** (at 6 o'clock), the new sharp is called **E#** which is enharmonically the same as **F**. Remember that **enharmonic** means two different ways of writing the same note - ie, **F#** = **G♭**. Thus the key of **F#** contains six sharps, while the key of **G♭** contains six flats – all of which are exactly the same notes.

If you start at **C** again at the top of the cycle and go anti-clockwise you will progress through the flat keys. The key of **F** contains one flat (**B♭**), which then becomes the name of the next key around the cycle. In flat keys, the new flat is always the 4th degree of the new key. Continuing around the cycle, the key of **B♭** contains two flats (**B♭** and **E♭**) and so on. **Practice playing all the notes around the cycle both clockwise and anticlockwise.** Once you can do this, play a **major scale** starting on each note of the cycle, as shown on the following page.

MAJOR SCALES IN ALL KEYS

The following example demonstrates one octave of the major scale, ascending and descending in every key, and moving anticlockwise around the key cycle. The scales are shown here **without tablature** to help improve your music reading. There is a vast amount of written music which does not contain tablature. If you can't read notation, it means a large proportion of the music in the world is unavailable to you. However, if you can read music well, it is easy to learn a new style or music written for **any** instrument (not just guitar).

You already know all the notes contained in these scales and they can all be played in the open position or first position. Learning scales may not seem as interesting as playing melodies, but a little effort at this stage will pay off later on, regardless of the style of music you are playing. Memorize the notes of each scale and then try playing it with your eyes closed while visualizing how the notation for the scale would look. Once you have learnt all the scales, you will be able to read music better, play melodies confidently in any key and be able to improvise in any key much more easily. Practice these scales with your metronome to make sure you maintain an even tempo through all the fingerings.

CD 1 — 35.

LESSON EIGHTEEN

HOW TO LEARN A NEW KEY

To become a good musician, it is essential to learn how to play fluently in any key. Once you know what notes are in the scale of a key you are not familiar with, the next step is to transfer the knowledge to your instrument until you can instantly find any note of the scale on the fretboard.

Let's take the key of **D major** as an example. The notes of the scale are written below. Notice that there are two sharps in this key – **F♯** and **C♯**.

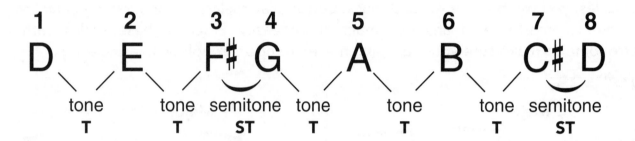

36.0

This example shows the fingering for all octaves of the notes of the D major scale in the open position. Learn it from memory and then play it with your eyes closed, naming each note as you play and visualising the notation in your mind. Once you can do this, name the scale degrees as you play instead of the note names. The degrees are written here between the notation and the tablature.

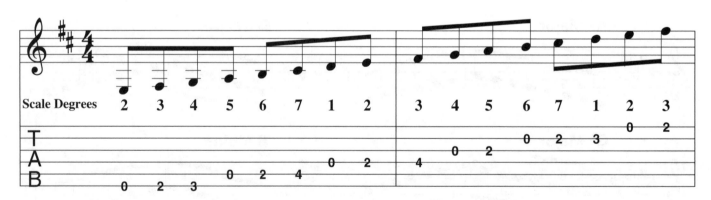

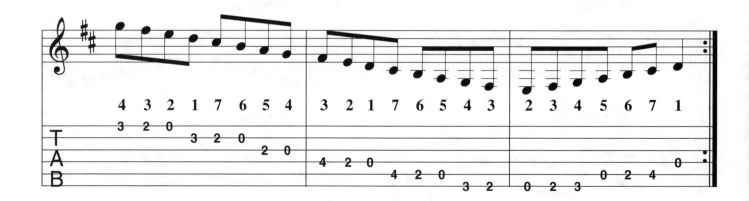

Once you are confident you can instantly find any note of the scale you are working on, try playing some sequences with the notes of the scale. Once again, work towards memorizing each new pattern and then play it with your eyes closed while naming first the notes and then the scale degrees. Here are some sequences to practice.

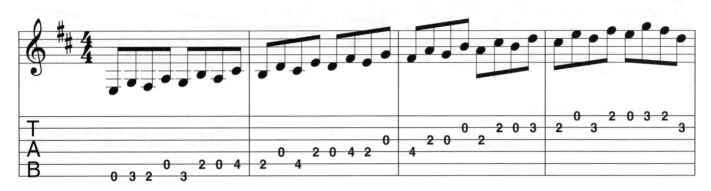

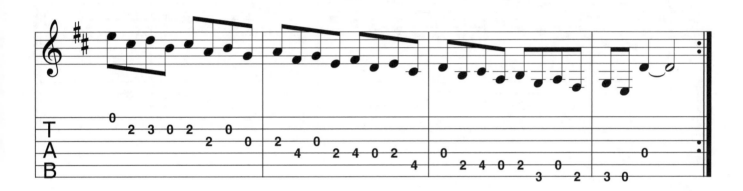

Practice this pattern descending as well as ascending.

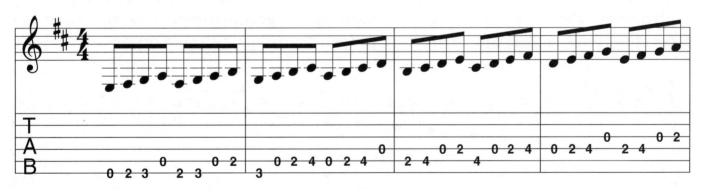

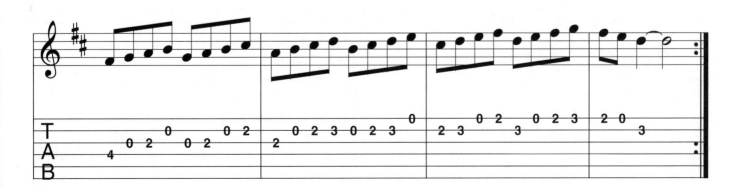

It is also a good idea to practice scales using and sequences using different rhythms. Here is one which uses a quarter note on the first beat and eighth notes for the rest of the bar. Continue the pattern all the way up to G on the first string and then back down again.

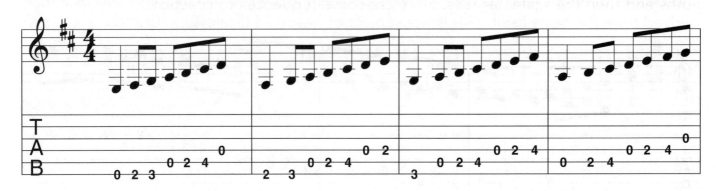

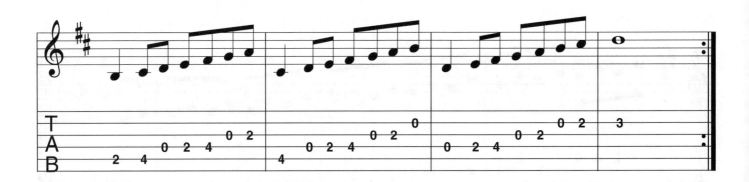

 **36.1**

This example runs through the fingering for the D major scale using a rhythm containing eighth rests. Take it slowly at first and count along with your metronome as you play. If you work consistently on this type of exercise, you will develop a much stronger sense of timing.

37. Song For D

Here is a song in the key of **D major**. Listen to how the accompaniment fits with the melody and creates different feelings when moving between major and minor. These chords are all derived from the scale itself. This is the subject of lesson 25 (Scale Tone Chords).

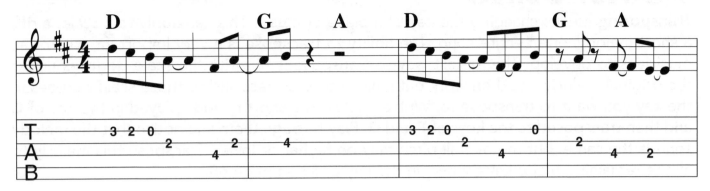

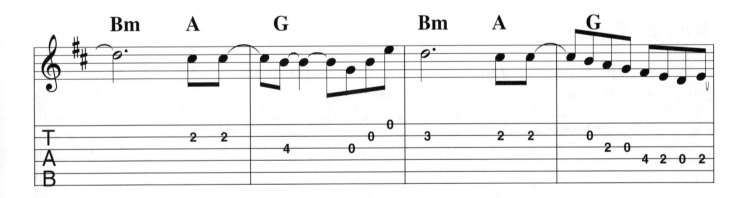

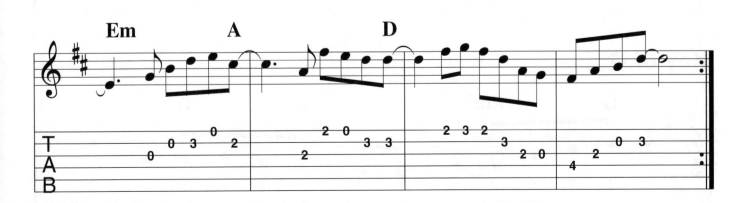

LESSON NINETEEN

TRANSPOSING

Transposing means changing the key of a piece of music. This can apply to a scale, a riff, a short melody, or an entire song. The ability to transpose is a very important skill for all musicians to develop. The easiest way to transpose is to write the **scale degrees** under the original melody and then work out which notes correspond to those scale degrees in the key you want to transpose to. Written below is a short melody played in the key of **C** and then transposed to the keys of **F** and **G**. Play through them and notice that the melody sounds the same, but the overall pitch may be higher or lower. Transpose this melody to all the remaining major keys shown in the key cycle on page 68.

38.   Key of C

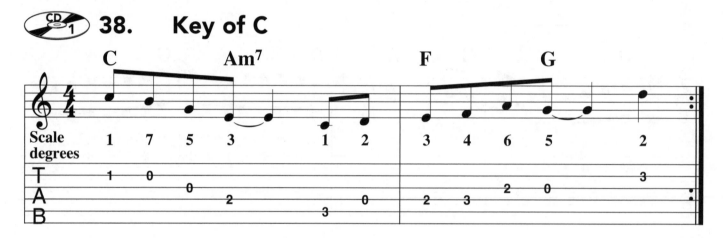

Key of F

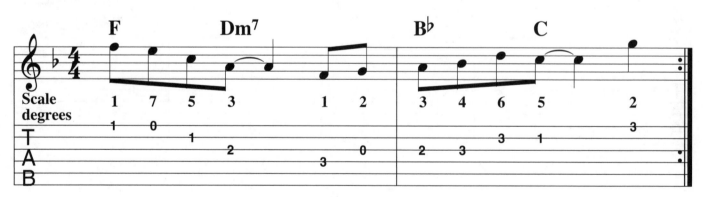

Key of G

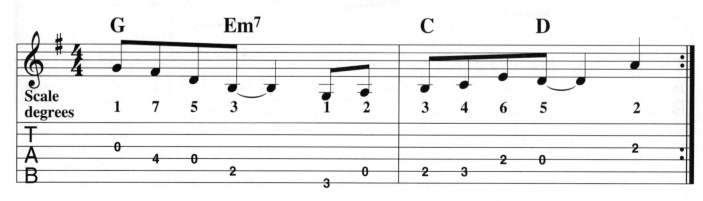

Here is the song from the previous lesson transposed to the key of **E**. Learn it in this key and then transpose it to all the other keys. You should make a habit of transposing everything you learn to as many keys as possible. You should aim to eventually be able to play any song in any key at a moment's notice. This is essential for professional guitarists, as they are often working with different singers, horn players, keyboard players, etc, all of whom may prefer to play any song in their own favorite key. If the guitarist they are working with doesn't know how to play in that key, they will call someone else instead.

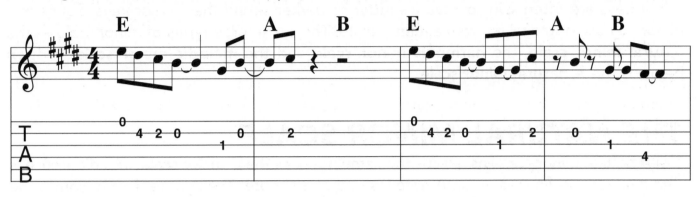

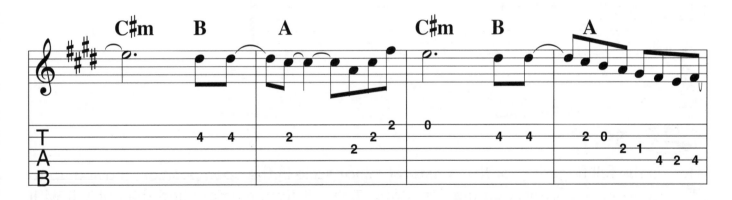

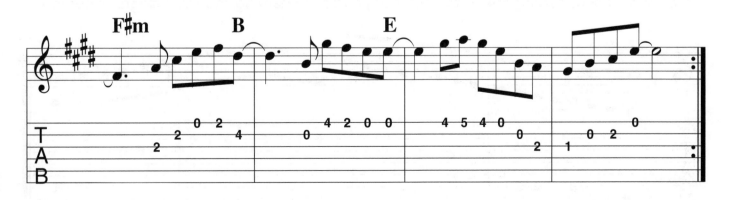

LESSON TWENTY

MINOR KEYS AND SCALES

Apart from major keys, the other basic tonality used in western music is a **minor key**. Minor keys are often said to have a sadder or darker sound than major keys. Songs in a minor key use notes taken from a **minor scale**. There are three types of minor scale — the **natural minor scale**, the **harmonic minor scale** and the **melodic minor scale**. Written below is the **A natural minor** scale.

THE NATURAL MINOR SCALE

The A natural minor contains exactly the same notes as the C major scale. The difference is that it starts and finishes on an **A** note instead of a C note. The A note then becomes the key note. To highlight the difference, the degrees of the scale as they would relate to the A major scale are written under the note names. Notice the **flattened 3rd**, **6th and 7th**.

CD 1 39.0

CD 1 39.1

Here is the full fingering for the **A natural minor** scale in the open position, moving up to the high A at the 5th fret on the first string. Learn it from memory and then play it with your eyes closed, naming the notes out loud, and then naming the scale degrees out loud.

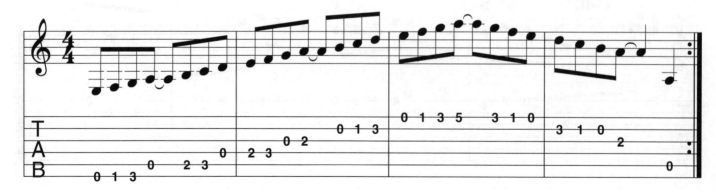

 **40.**

Here is a melody in the **key of A minor** which is derived from the **A natural minor scale**. Learn it and then try making up your own melodies based on the ideas presented here. The natural minor scale is frequently used in lead guitar playing and is demonstrated in more detail with moveable fingerings in lesson 53.

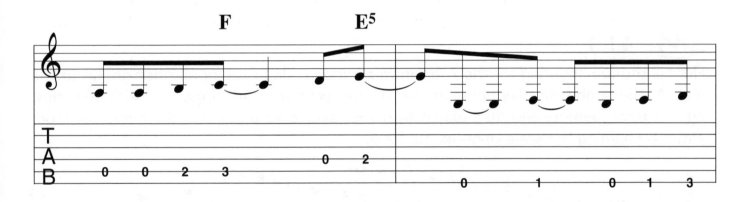

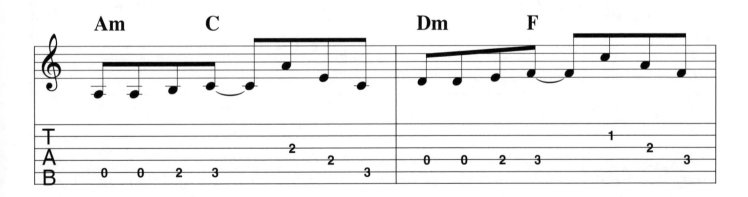

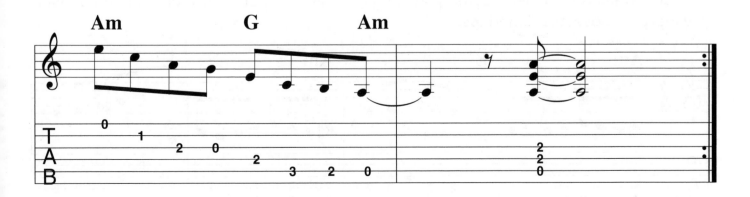

THE HARMONIC MINOR SCALE

The harmonic minor scale has a distance of 1½ tones between the **6th** and **7th** degrees. The **raised 7th degree** is the only difference between the harmonic minor and the natural minor. This scale is often described as having an "Eastern" sound.

41.0   A Harmonic Minor

41.1

Here is the full fingering for the **A harmonic minor** scale in the open position, up to the high **A**. Remember to play notes at the 4th fret with your 4th finger. As with all scales, learn it from memory and then play it with your eyes closed, naming the notes out loud, and then naming the scale degrees out loud.

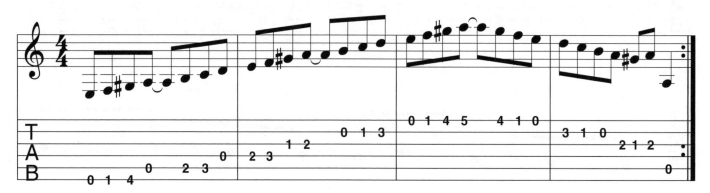

42.

The following example is derived from the notes of the A harmonic minor scale. This scale is used extensively in Metal guitar playing and is demonstrated further in lesson 55 with a variety of moveable fingerings.

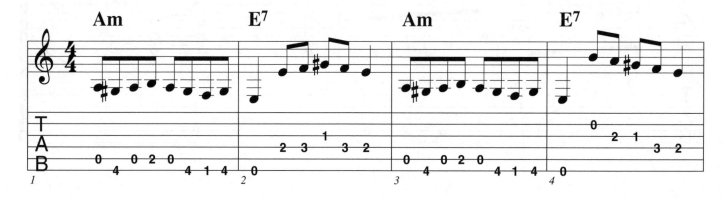

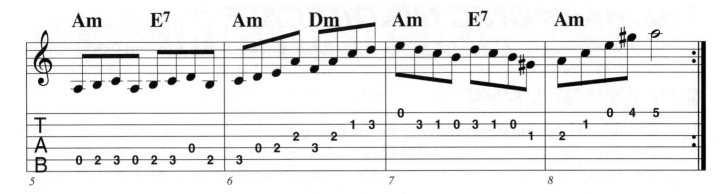

THE MELODIC MINOR SCALE

In Classical music, a **melodic minor** scale has the **6th** and **7th** notes sharpened when ascending and returned to natural when descending. However, in Jazz and other more modern styles, the melodic minor descends the same way it ascends. An easy way to think of the ascending melodic minor is as a major scale with a flattened third degree.

43.0   **A Melodic Minor**

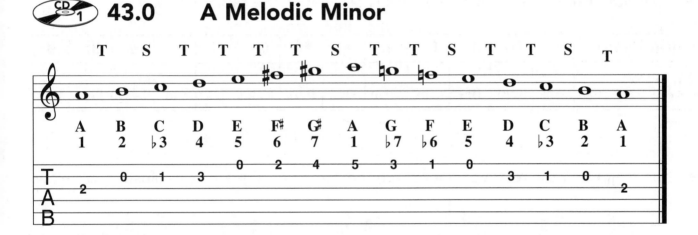

 **43.1**

Here is the full fingering for the A **melodic minor** scale in the open position, up to the high **A**.

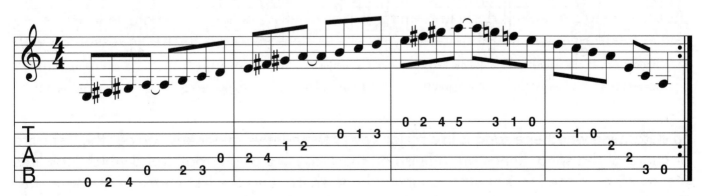

LESSON TWENTY ONE

RELATIVE KEYS

if you compare the **A natural minor** scale with the **C major** scale you will notice that they contain the same notes; the only difference is that they start on a different note. Because of this, these two scales are referred to as "relatives"; **A minor** is the **relative minor** of **C major** and vice versa.

Major Scale: C Major

Relative Minor Scale: A Natural Minor

The harmonic and melodic minor scale variations are also relatives of the same major scale, e.g. the **A harmonic** and **A melodic minor** scales are all relatives of **C major**.

For every major scale (and ever major chord) there is a relative minor scale which is based upon the **6th note** of the major scale. This is outlined in the table below.

MAJOR KEY (I)	C	D♭	D	E♭	E	F	F#	G♭	G	A♭	A	B♭	B
RELATIVE MINOR KEY (VI)	Am	B♭m	Bm	Cm	C#m	Dm	D#m	E♭m	Em	Fm	F#m	Gm	G#m

Both the major and the relative minor share the same key signature, as illustrated below.

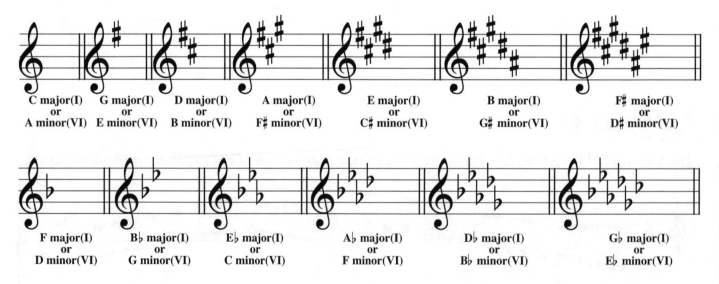

To determine whether a song is in a major key or the relative minor key, look at the last note or chord of the song. Songs often finish on the root note or the root chord which indicates the key. E.g., if the key signature contained one sharp, and the last chord of the song was **Em**, the key would probably be **E minor**, not **G major**. Minor key signatures are always based on the natural minor scale. The sharpened 6th and 7th degrees from the harmonic and melodic minor scales are not indicated in the key signature. This usually means there are accidentals (temporary sharps, flats or naturals) in melodies created from these scales.

44.

This example keeps alternating between the relative keys of **C major** and **A minor**. The arpeggio style of playing used here is particularly effective when playing a Rock ballad.

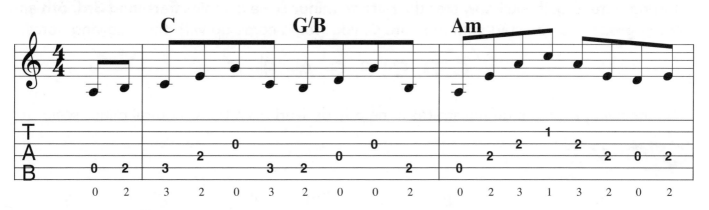

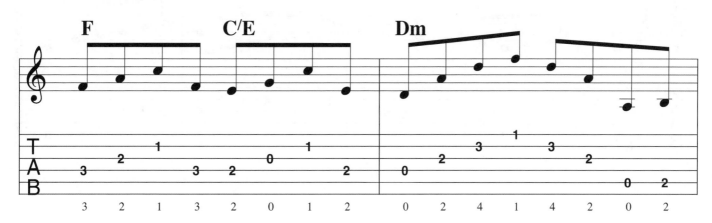

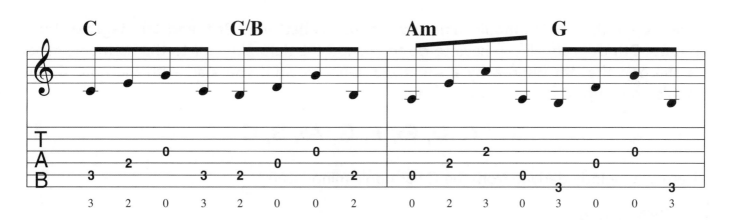

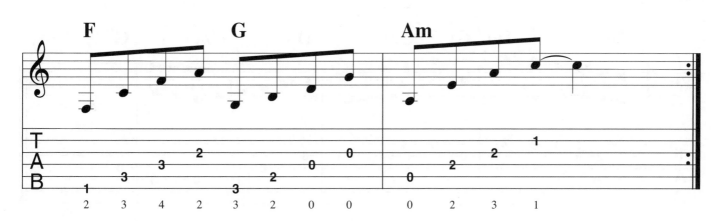

LEARNING MINOR SCALES IN ALL KEYS

By simply following the formula for each type of minor scale, either by scale degrees or pattern of tones and semitones, it is possible to create any of the minor scales from any starting note. E.g. if you know that the **natural minor** scale contains **flattened 3rd, 6th and 7th degrees** and you start with the note **C**, you would come up with the following notes:

C, D, E♭, F, G, A♭, B♭, C

The following example demonstrates a melody derived from the C natural minor scale.

CD 1 **45.0**

If you know that the **harmonic minor** scale contains **flattened 3rd, and 6th degrees**, but a **natural 7th degree**, all you have to do to change the natural minor to the harmonic minor is **sharpen the 7th degree by a semitone**. Once again if you start with the note **C**, you would come up with the following notes -

C, D, E♭, F, G, A♭, B, C

Here is a melody derived from the C harmonic minor scale.

CD 1 **45.1**

To change the harmonic minor to an **ascending melodic minor** you need to **sharpen the 6th degree by a semitone**. Starting with the note **C**, you would come up with the following notes:

C, D, E♭, F, G, A, B, C

The Classical form of the descending melodic minor is identical to the natural minor. To become familiar with the notes of minor scales in all keys, it is important to **write out the three types of minor scales starting on each of the 12 notes of the chromatic scale**.

The following example is a melody derived from the C melodic minor scale.

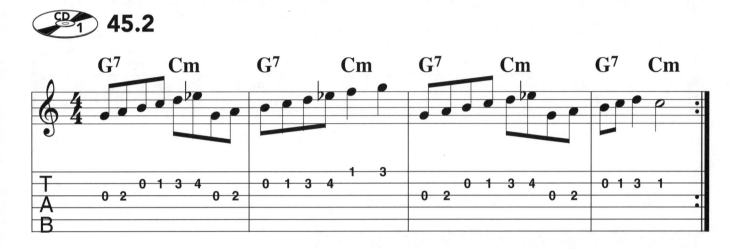

It is also important to be able to transpose melodies in minor keys. The process is the same as for major keys - write the scale degrees under the melody notes and then work out what notes those degrees equate to in the key you want to transpose to. Just say you wanted to transpose the previous example to the key of **A minor**. First write out the notes of the melodic minor scale in that key as shown here.

A, B, C, D, E, F♯, G♯, A

Then work out the degrees of the melody and write them out again in the key of A minor as shown in the following example.

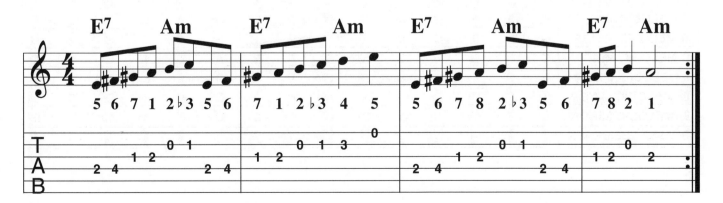

Here is the same example transposed to **F minor**. The key signature of F minor contains **four flats**, but the sixth and seventh degrees of the melodic minor are raised, so the notes **D** and **E** will be **naturals**. Remember to learn the notes of the scale first:

F, G, A♭, B♭, C, D♮, E♮, F

Then work out the degrees of the melody and write them out again in the key of **F minor**.

TABLE OF MINOR SCALES

Here is a table which shows the notes of the melodic minor scale in all twelve keys. Remember that the **descending melodic minor is the same as the natural minor**. To work out the notes for the **harmonic minor**, simply **flatten the 6th** degree of the ascending melodic minor.

	T	S	T	T	T	T	S	T	T	S	T	T	S	T
A MELODIC MINOR*	A	B	C	D	E	F#	G#	A	G♮	F♮	E	D	C	B	A
E MELODIC MINOR*	E	F#	G	A	B	C#	D#	E	D♮	C♮	B	A	G	F#	E
B MELODIC MINOR*	B	C#	D	E	F#	G#	A#	B	A♮	G♮	F#	E	D	C#	B
F# MELODIC MINOR*	F#	G#	A	B	C#	D#	E#	F#	E♮	D♮	C#	B	A	G#	F#
C# MELODIC MINOR*	C#	D#	E	F#	G#	A#	B#	C#	B♮	A♮	G#	F#	E	D#	C#
G# MELODIC MINOR	G#	A#	B	C#	D#	E#	G	G#	F#	E♮	D#	C#	B	A#	G#
D# MELODIC MINOR	D#	E#	F#	G#	A#	B#	D	D#	C#	B♮	A#	G#	F#	E#	D#
D MELODIC MINOR*	D	E	F	G	A	B♮	C#	D	C♮	B♭	A	G	F	E	D
G MELODIC MINOR*	G	A	B♭	C	D	E♮	F#	G	F	E♭	D	C	B♭	A	G
C MELODIC MINOR	C	D	E♭	F	G	A♮	B♮	C	B♭	A♭	G	F	E♭	D	C
F MELODIC MINOR	F	G	A♭	B♭	C	D♮	E♮	F	E♭	D♭	C	B♭	A♭	G	F
B♭ MELODIC MINOR	B♭	C	D♭	E♭	F	G♮	A♮	B♭	A♭	G♭	F	E♭	D♭	C	B♭
E♭ MELODIC MINOR	E♭	F	G♭	A♭	B♭	C♮	D♮	E♭	D♭	C♭	B♭	A♭	G♭	F♭	E♭
ROMAN NUMERALS	I	II	III	IV	V	VI	VII	VIII	VII	VI	V	IV	III	II	I

LESSON TWENTY TWO

INTERVALS

An **interval** is the distance between two musical notes. **All melodies and chords are made up of a series of intervals**. Intervals are measured in numbers, and are calculated by counting the number of letter names (**A B C D E F G A**) between and including the notes being measured. Within an octave, intervals are: **Unison** (two notes of the same pitch played or sung together or consecutively), **2nd, 3rd, 4th, 5th, 6th, 7th** and **Octave** (two notes an octave apart). Thus **A** to **B** is a **2nd** interval, as is B to C, C to D etc. **A** to **C** is a **3rd** interval, **A** to **D** is a **4th**, **A** to **E** is a **5th**, **A** to **F** is a **6th**, **A** to **G** is a **7th** and **A** to the next **A** is an **octave**.

Intervals may be **melodic** (two notes played consecutively) or **harmonic** (two notes played at the same time). Hence two people singing at the same time are said to be singing in harmony.

INTERVAL QUALITIES

Different intervals have different qualities, as shown below:

Quality	Can be applied to
Perfect	Unisons, 4ths, 5ths and Octaves
Major	2nds, 3rds, 6ths and 7ths
Minor	2nds, 3rds, 6ths and 7ths
Augmented	All intervals
Diminished	All intervals

Interval qualities can be best explained with the aid of a chromatic scale. If you look at the one below, it is easy to see that since **intervals are measured in semitones**, they may begin or end on a sharp or flat rather than a natural note.

Perfect intervals are **4ths**, **5ths** and **octaves**. If you **widen** a perfect interval by a semitone it becomes **augmented** (added to). E.g. if you add a semitone to the perfect 4th interval **C** to **F**, it becomes the **augmented 4th interval C** to **F#**. Notice that the letter name remains the same–it is not referred to as C to G♭.

If you **narrow** a perfect interval by a semitone it becomes **diminished** (lessened). E.g. if you lessen the perfect 5th interval **D** to **A** by a semitone, it becomes the **diminished 5th interval D to A♭**. Again, the letter name remains the same–it is not referred to as D to G#.

Major intervals (2nds, 3rds, 6ths and 7ths) become minor if narrowed by a semitone and **minor** intervals become major if widened by a semitone. A **diminished** interval can be created by narrowing a perfect or minor interval by a semitone. An **augmented** interval can be created by widening a perfect or major interval by a semitone.

INTERVAL DISTANCES

In summary, here is a list of the distances of all common intervals up to an octave, measured in semitones. Each new interval is one semitone further apart than the previous one. Notice that the interval of an octave is exactly twelve semitones. This is because there are twelve different notes in the chromatic scale. Notice also that the interval which has a distance of six semitones can be called either an augmented 4th or a perfect 5th. This interval is also often called a **tritone** (6 semitones = 3 tones).

Minor 2nd - One semitone

Major 2nd - Two semitones

Minor 3rd - Three semitones

Major 3rd - Four semitones

Perfect 4th - Five semitones

Augmented 4th or Diminished 5th - Six semitones

Perfect 5th - Seven semitones

Minor 6th - Eight semitones

Major 6th - Nine semitones

Minor 7th - Ten semitones

Major 7th - Eleven semitones

Perfect Octave - Twelve semitones

The following example demonstrates all of the common intervals ascending within one octave, starting and ending on the note **C**.

46.

FINDING INTERVALS ON THE FRETBOARD

A good musician can instantly play any interval from any note either harmonically (at the same time) or in ascending or descending order. The diagrams below show the most common ways of playing intervals on the guitar. Learn them one at a time and listen carefully to the sound of each interval as you play it.

Minor 2nd
(One Semitone)

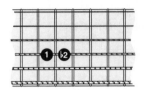 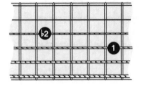 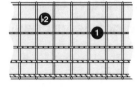

Major 2nd
(Two Semitones)

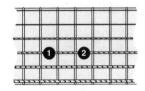 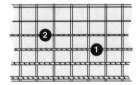 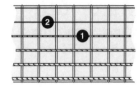

Minor 3rd
(Three Semitones)

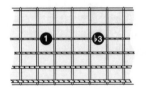 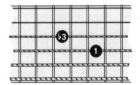 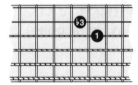

Major 3rd
(Four Semitones)

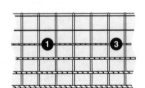 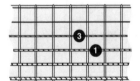 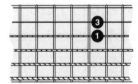

Perfect 4th
(Five Semitones)

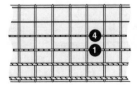 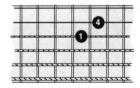

Tritone -Aug 4th or Dim 5th
(Six Semitones)

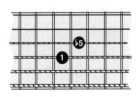 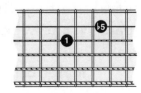

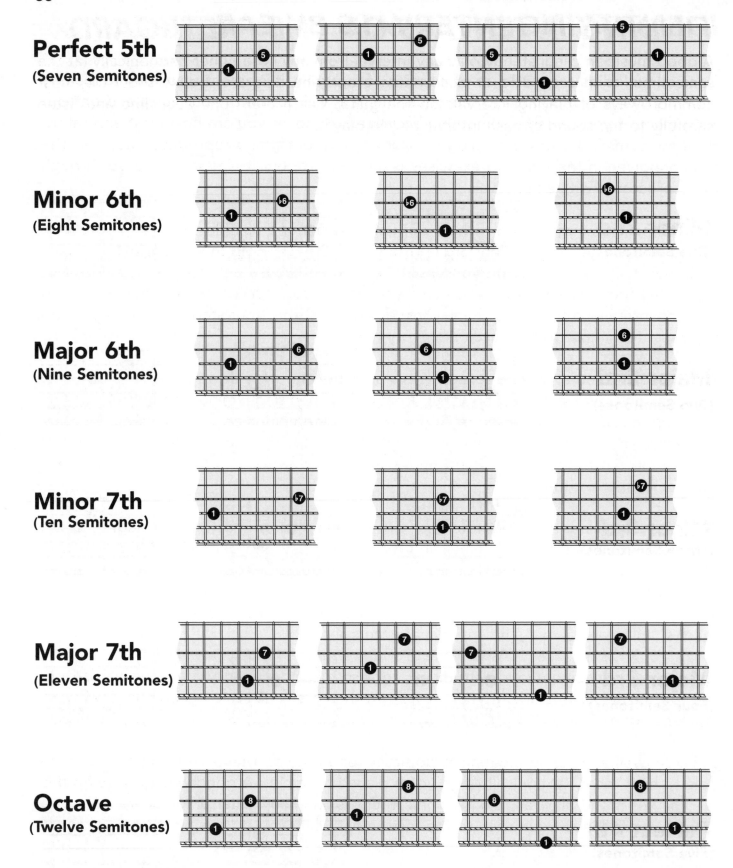

Perfect 5th
(Seven Semitones)

Minor 6th
(Eight Semitones)

Major 6th
(Nine Semitones)

Minor 7th
(Ten Semitones)

Major 7th
(Eleven Semitones)

Octave
(Twelve Semitones)

These diagrams show only the most common ways of playing intervals on the guitar, but they are not the only patterns. You should also work on playing every possible interval on each individual string. This is easier than it sounds. All you have to do is work out how many frets apart the interval is: e.g. a perfect 4th is five frets apart, a minor 6th is eight frets apart, etc.

IDENTIFYING INTERVALS BY EAR

Since **all melodies are made up of a series of intervals**, it is essential to learn to identify intervals by ear and be able to reproduce them at will both with your voice and on your instrument. If you can sing something accurately, it means you are hearing it accurately. Here are some ways of developing your ability to identify and reproduce intervals. The example given in the first two exercises is a minor 3rd, but it is essential to go through these processes with **all** intervals.

1.   Choose an interval you wish to work on (e.g. minor 3rds). Play a starting note (e.g. C) and sing it. Then sing a minor 3rd up from that note (E♭). Hold the note with your voice while you test its accuracy on your instrument. Then choose another starting note and repeat the process. Keep doing this until you are accurate every time. The next step is to sing the interval (in this case a minor 3rd) downwards from your starting note. Again, do this repeatedly until you are accurate every time.

2.   Sing the same interval consecutively upwards and then downwards several times. E.g. start on C and sing a minor 3rd up from it (E♭). Then sing a minor 3rd up from E♭ (G♭). Then another minor third up from G♭ (B♭♭ - which is enharmonically the same as A). Then up another minor 3rd (C an octave higher than the starting note). Once you can do this, reverse the process (Start on C and sing a minor 3rd down to A, then another minor 3rd down and then another, etc).

3.   Play and sing a starting note (e.g. C) and then think of it as the first degree of the chromatic scale - sing "one". Now sing the flattened second degree of the scale - sing "flat two". This note is a minor 2nd up from your C note (a D♭ note). Then sing the C again ("one"). Then sing the second degree of the scale (a D note - sing "two"). Next, sing your C Note again ("one"). Continue in this manner all the way up the chromatic scale until you reach C an octave above. The entire sequence goes: 1, ♭2, 1, 2, 1, ♭3, 1, 3, 1, 4, 1, ♭5, 1, 5, 1, ♭6, 1, 6, 1, ♭7, 1, 7, 1, 8, 1. As with the previous exercises, once you can do this accurately (check your pitches on your instrument), reverse the process and sing downwards from the top of the scale, working your way down the chromatic scale again. The downward sequence goes 1(8), 7, 1, ♭7, 1, 6, 1, ♭6, 1, 5, 1,♭ 5, 1, 4, 1, 3, 1, ♭3, 1, 2, 1, ♭2, 1, 1, 1(8).

4.   As well as hearing intervals melodically (one note at a time), it is important to be able to hear them harmonically (two notes played together). A good way to develop this is to have a friend play random harmonic intervals on either guitar or keyboard while you identify them. Keep your back to the instrument while you do this, so that you cannot identify the intervals by sight.

It is important to work at these things regularly until they become easy. Don't get frustrated if you can't hear intervals accurately at first. Most people have trouble with this. If you work at it for several months, you will see a dramatic improvement in your musical hearing, and will be able to improvise much more freely as well as being able to work out parts off CDs more easily.

LESSON TWENTY THREE

UNDERSTANDING CHORDS

As you learnt in Lesson 7, a **chord** is a group of three or more notes played simultaneously. Different types of chords can be formed by using different combinations of notes. The most basic type of chord contains three different notes and is called a **triad**. The most common triads are **major chords**. All major chords contain three notes taken from the major scale bearing the same letter name as the chord. These three notes are the **1** (first), **3** (third) and **5** (fifth) degrees (notes) of the major scale, so the **chord formula** for the major chord is:

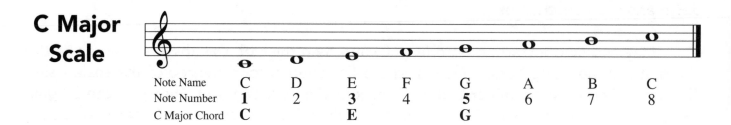

Chord Symbol

| C |

1   3   5

The C Major Chord

Notes in Chord

C	E	G
1	**3**	**5**

The **C major chord** is constructed from the **C major scale**. Using the above chord formula on the C major scale below, you can see that the **C** major chord contains the notes **C**, **E** and **G**.

C Major Scale

Note Name	C	D	E	F	G	A	B	C
Note Number	**1**	2	**3**	4	**5**	6	7	8
C Major Chord	**C**		**E**		**G**			

Once you have the correct notes for a **C** chord they can be arranged in any order. As long as the notes are still C, E and G, you still have a C chord. E.g. a C chord could be played C E G, or E G C, or G C E, or even G E C. These various arrangements of the notes within a chord are called **inversions**. It is also possible to **double** notes within a chord. E.g. the diagram below shows a common way of playing a C major chord on the guitar. It contains two C notes and two E notes. It is still a C major chord because it only contains notes called C, E and G. **Doubling** notes is common when playing chords on the guitar.

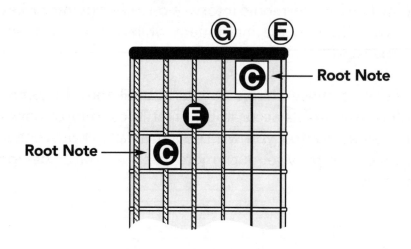

FINGERING VARIATIONS

Here are two more ways of playing a **C** chord in the open position. Listen to the different effects created by changing the order of the notes C, E and G and also doubling different notes within the chord.

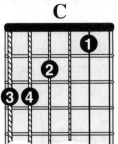
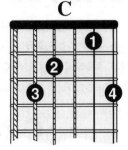

ARPEGGIOS IN ALL KEYS

Like scales, it is important to be able to play chords as arpeggios in every key. The following example demonstrates major arpeggios played around the key cycle. There is no tablature here, but you already know all the notes needed to play these arpeggios.

 **47.**

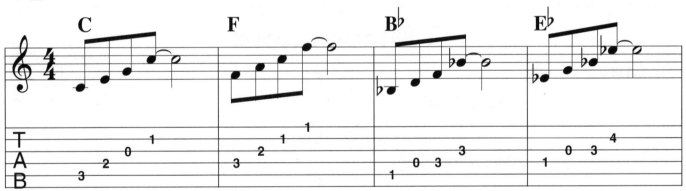

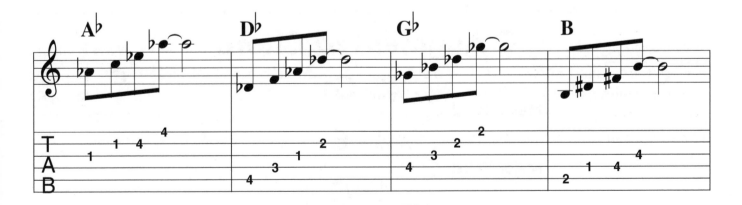

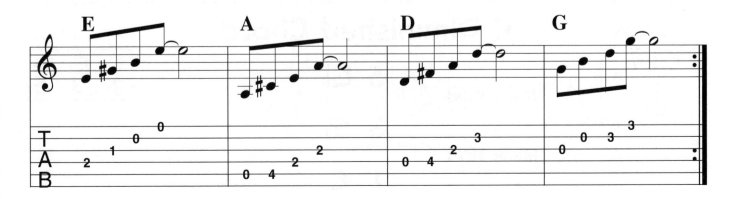

LESSON TWENTY FOUR

CHORD CONSTRUCTION–TRIADS

Chords are usually made up of combinations of major and minor third intervals. As mentioned previously, the simplest chords are made up of three notes. These are called **triads**. There are **four** basic types of triads: **major**, **minor**, **augmented** and **diminished**. Examples of each of these are shown below along with the formula for each one.

C Major Chord

Chord Symbol

C

C	E	G
1	3	5

Notes in Chord

Minor Third — 5 G

Major Third — 3 E

1 C

C Minor Chord

Chord Symbol

Cm

C	E♭	G
1	♭3	5

Notes in Chord

Major Third — 5 G

Minor Third — ♭3 E♭

1 C

C Augmented Chord

Chord Symbol

C+

C	E	G#
1	3	#5

Notes in Chord

Major Third — #5 G#

Major Third — 3 E

1 C

C Diminished Chord

Chord Symbol

Cdim
or
C°

C	E♭	G♭
1	♭3	♭5

Notes in Chord

Minor Third — ♭5 G♭

Minor Third — ♭3 E♭

1 C

For every type of chord there is a corresponding arpeggio. This means there are major, minor, augmented, diminished, dominant seventh and minor seventh arpeggios among others. Shown below is a **C minor arpeggio** which consists of the notes **C**, **E♭** and **G** which are the **root**, **flattened third** and **fifth** of a **C minor chord**.

48.0

48.1

This is a **G minor arpeggio** which consists of the notes **G**, **B♭** and **D**. These are the root, third and fifth of a **G minor chord**.

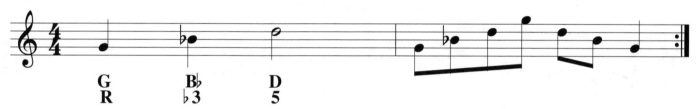

48.1   Minor Arpeggios in all Keys

Here are all the minor arpeggios between **C minor** and **B minor** played chromatically ascending. Try playing them chromatically descending as well. Once again, there is no tablature here, but you already know all the notes needed to play these arpeggios.

AUGMENTED AND DIMINISHED CHORDS

Augmented and diminished chords are not as common as major or minor chords, but it is still important to learn them, as they do occur in many pieces of music as a way of creating tension before resolving to either a major or minor chord. Here are some examples demonstrating these chords. Listen to the CD to hear what they sound like.

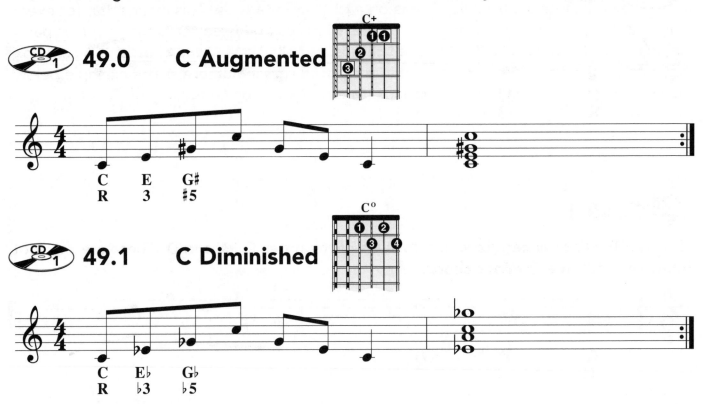

49.0   C Augmented

C   E   G#
R   3   #5

49.1   C Diminished

C   E♭   G♭
R   ♭3   ♭5

 **50.**

Here is an example which makes use of arpeggios of all four types of triads – **major**, **minor**, **augmented** and **diminished**.

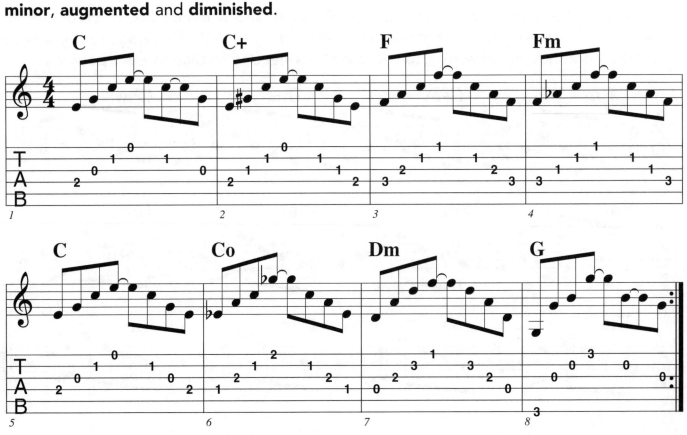

LESSON TWENTY FIVE

SCALE TONE CHORDS

In any key it is possible to build chords on each note of a scale. This means that for every major scale there are **seven** possible chords which can be used for creating guitar parts and harmonising melodies. These seven chords are called **scale tone chords**. It is common practice to describe all the chords within a key with **roman numerals**. The example below demonstrates the seven scale tone triads (three note chords) in the key of C major.

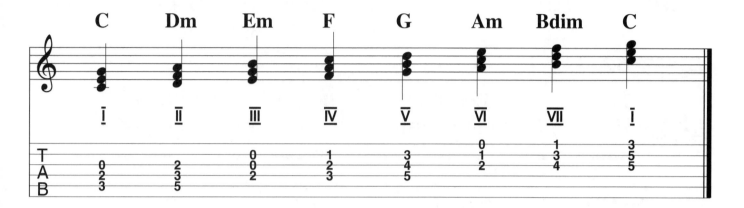

51.

Here are the seven **scale tone triads** in the key of **C** played as arpeggios. The ascending pattern in bars 1 to 4 begins on the **root** of each new chord, while the descending pattern in bars 5 to 8 begins on the **5th** of each new chord. As always, once you can do this in one key, play them in all keys; both around the key cycle and chromatically ascending and descending.

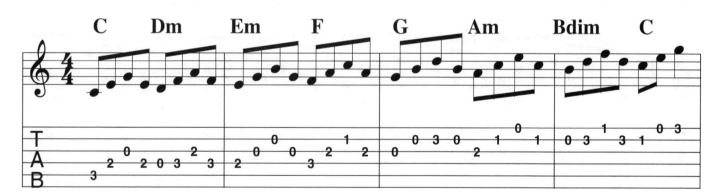

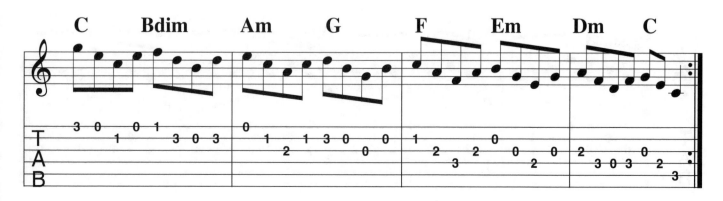

Once you know the notes for any of these chords, you can use any fingering you like to play them. This may involve re-arranging the order of the notes or doubling some of the notes, but as long as the chord shape you are playing contains only the three note names involved in that particular chord, you are still playing the right chord. The following example demonstrates a common progression in the key of C. By analyzing the progression in terms of chord numbers, it is easy to transpose to other keys or use other fingerings. This progression would be described as Ī IIĪ IV̄ V̄ IIĪ VĪ IĪ V̄. The chord shapes used on the recording are shown below.

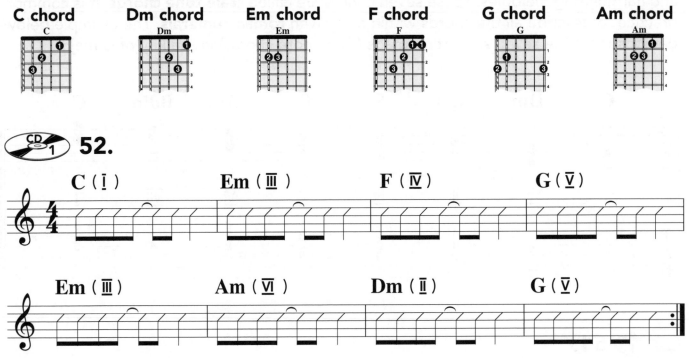

52.

53.

Here is the **same progression** played on a classical guitar as a picked arpeggio pattern. As you can see, there are many ways of playing any chord progression.

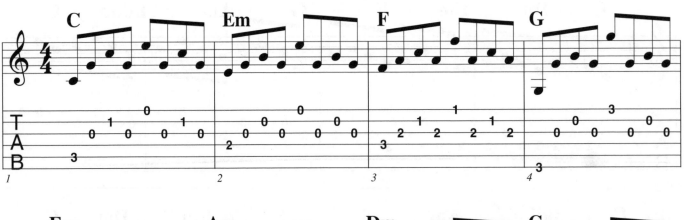

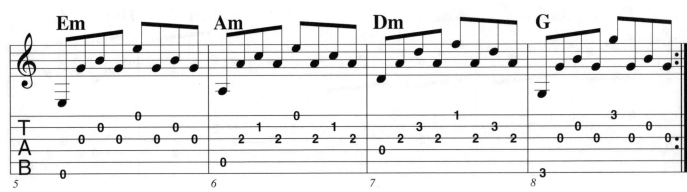

MAJOR KEY TRIAD PATTERN

If you go through and analyse all of the scale tone chords in the key of C major you come up with the following pattern:

Ī	**Major**	**(C Major Chord)**
ĪĪ	**Minor**	**(D Minor Chord)**
ĪĪĪ	**Minor**	**(E Minor Chord)**
ĪV	**Major**	**(F Major Chord)**
V̄	**Major**	**(G Major Chord)**
V̄Ī	**Minor**	**(A Minor Chord)**
V̄ĪĪ	**Diminished**	**(B Diminished Chord)**

This pattern remains the same regardless of the key. For **any major key**, Chord Ī is **always** major, chord ĪĪ is always minor, chord ĪĪĪ is always minor, etc. The only thing that changes from one key to the next is the letter names of the chords. This can be demonstrated by looking at the scale tone triads for the key of **G major** which are shown below.

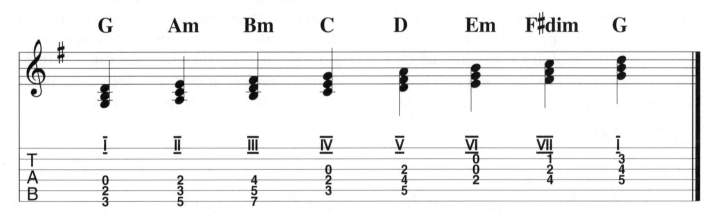

By simply following the roman numerals and remembering which chords are major, minor, etc, it is easy to transpose chords from one key to another. Here is the progression from example 52 transposed to the key of **G**. Try picking it in the manner of example 53.

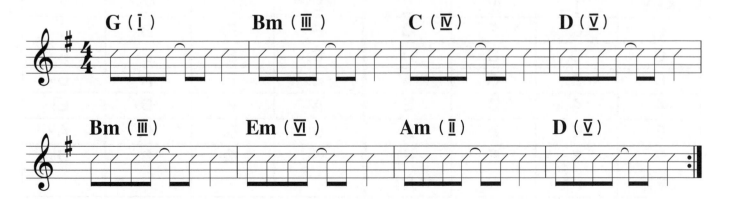

PRIMARY CHORDS

In any key there are some chords which are more commonly used than others. The three most common chords are Ī, ĪV and V̄. These are called the **primary chords**. With these three chords, it is possible to harmonize (accompany with chords) any melody in the key, because between them they contain every note of the scale, as shown below in the key of **C**.

C Major Scale   C D E F G A B C

Primary Triads

```
 G      C      D
 E      A      B
 C      F      G
 Ī      ĪV     V̄
```

HARMONIZING MELODIES

To harmonize a melody, you simply play a chord which contains a note from that melody on the **first beat of each bar**. In time, you could also add another chord on the **third** beat of the bar. There is always more than one chord which could be used, but some sound better than others. The more songs you learn and analyze, the easier it becomes to find the right chords to play. If you look at the scale and chords above, you will notice that the notes **C** and **G** appear in more than one of the chords. This means that if you were harmonizing a melody in the **key of C**, you could try both chords wherever one of these notes appear on the first beat of a bar. The following example shows a melody in C major harmonized with chords Ī, ĪV and V̄. Learn it and then transpose it to all the other keys.

CD 1 54.

The table below shows the primary chords in all twelve major keys.

PRIMARY TRIADS IN ALL MAJOR KEYS

KEY	Ī	ĪV	V̄	KEY	Ī	ĪV	V̄
C	C	F	G	F	F	B♭	C
G	G	C	D	B♭	B♭	E♭	F
D	D	G	A	E♭	E♭	A♭	B♭
A	A	D	E	A♭	A♭	D♭	E♭
E	E	A	B	D♭	D♭	G♭	A♭
B	B	E	F♯	G♭	G♭	C♭	D♭
F♯	F♯	B	C♯				

Although most melodies can be harmonized using only chords $\underline{\text{I}}$, $\underline{\text{IV}}$ and $\underline{\text{V}}$, it is also common to use one or more of the remaining chords ($\underline{\text{II}}$, $\underline{\text{III}}$, $\underline{\text{VI}}$ and $\underline{\text{VII}}$) to create a different feeling. These other chords are called **secondary chords**. As with primary chords, the secondary chord chosen for the harmony in any given bar should contain the melody note which occurs on the first or third beat of that bar (wherever the chord changes). Here is the melody from the previous example harmonized with both primary and secondary chords. Once again, learn it and then transpose both the melody and the chords to all the other keys.

 **55.**

COMMON PROGRESSIONS

One of the best ways to become familiar with chords in all keys is to take a simple progression and transpose it to all of the keys. This may be slow at first, but the more you do it, the easier it gets. Here are some common progressions to learn and transpose. Remember to practice them in different ways, e.g. as strummed chords and picked as arpeggios.

$$\underline{\text{I}} \ \underline{\text{IV}} \ \underline{\text{V}} \ \underline{\text{I}} \qquad \underline{\text{I}} \ \underline{\text{VI}} \ \underline{\text{IV}} \ \underline{\text{V}} \qquad \underline{\text{II}} \ \underline{\text{V}} \ \underline{\text{I}} \qquad \underline{\text{I}} \ \underline{\text{VI}} \ \underline{\text{II}} \ \underline{\text{V}} \qquad \underline{\text{I}} \ \underline{\text{IV}} \ \underline{\text{VII}} \ \underline{\text{III}} \ \underline{\text{VI}} \ \underline{\text{II}} \ \underline{\text{V}}$$

SCALE TONE TRIADS IN ALL KEYS

Scale Note:	$\underline{\text{I}}$	$\underline{\text{II}}$	$\underline{\text{III}}$	$\underline{\text{IV}}$	$\underline{\text{V}}$	$\underline{\text{VI}}$	$\underline{\text{VII}}$	$\underline{\text{VIII}}$ ($\underline{\text{I}}$)
Chord Constructed:	major	minor	minor	major	major	minor	dim	major
C Scale	C	Dm	Em	F	G	Am	B°	C
G Scale	G	Am	Bm	C	D	Em	F#°	G
D Scale	D	Em	F#m	G	A	Bm	C#°	D
A Scale	A	Bm	C#m	D	E	F#m	G#°	A
E Scale	E	F#m	G#m	A	B	C#m	D#°	E
B Scale	B	C#m	D#m	E	F#	G#m	A#°	B
F# Scale	F#	G#m	A#m	B	C#	D#m	E#° (F°)	F#
F Scale	F	Gm	Am	B♭	C	Dm	E°	F
B♭ Scale	B♭	Cm	Dm	E♭	F	Gm	A°	B♭
E♭ Scale	E♭	Fm	Gm	A♭	B♭	Cm	D°	E♭
A♭ Scale	A♭	B♭m	Cm	D♭	E♭	Fm	G°	A♭
D♭ Scale	D♭	E♭m	Fm	G♭	A♭	B♭m	C°	D♭
G♭ Scale	G♭	A♭m(G#m)	B♭m	C♭ (B)	D♭	E♭m	F°	G♭

CHORD SHAPES

Here is a chart of some basic fingerings for major, minor and diminished chords. With the chords shown here you should be able to work out how to play the seven scale tone chords in each of the major keys. Learn the chords outlined by a box first, as these are the easiest and most practical. Although the other shapes are all useful, in many cases bar chords can be used instead. These will be discussed in later lessons. All the boxed chords sound particularly good on acoustic guitars and for fingerpicking. Remember that there is always more than one fingering for a chord, so experiment with doubling notes in these chords or re-arranging the order of the notes.

Major Chords

Minor Chords

Diminished Chords

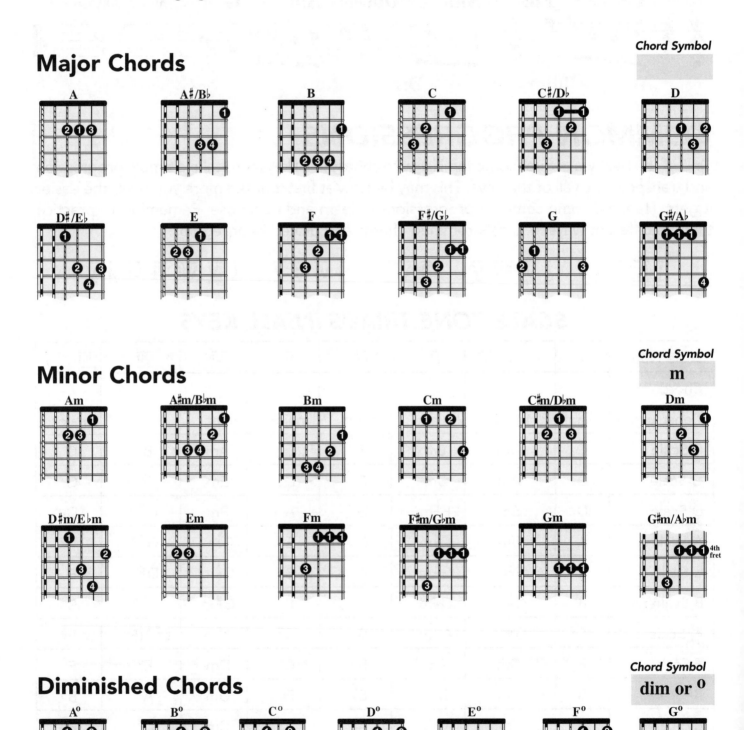

LESSON TWENTY SIX

MINOR KEY SCALE TONE TRIADS

As you learnt in Lesson 21, to find the relative minor of any major key, you start on the **6th** degree of the major scale. The example below shows the scale tone triads for the key of **A minor**, the chords derived from the **natural minor** scale. As you will see, the chords are exactly the same as those contained in the key of C major. The only difference is the starting and finishing point – because the minor scale starts on **A**, A minor will now be chord Ī instead of V̄Ī.

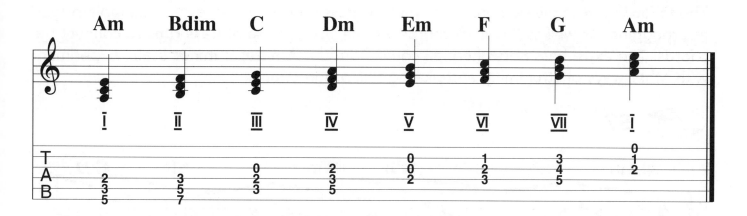

The following progression could be described in two possible ways. All the chords occur in the key of **C major** and also in the key of **A minor**. Because the progression has an obvious minor tonality (sound), musicians would use the second description. Analyze the progression using the roman numerals shown under the chords above, and then experiment with other chord combinations in the key of **A minor**.

56.

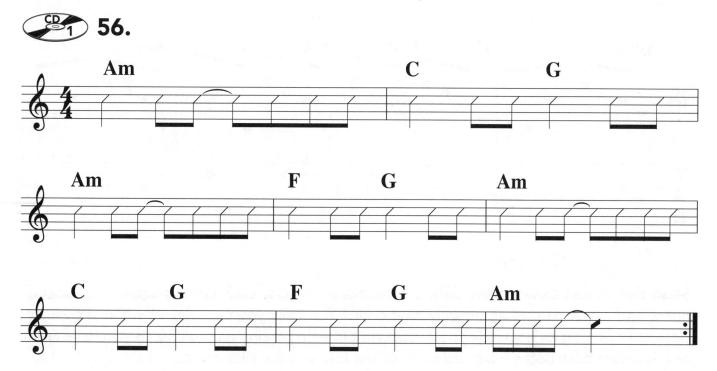

SLASH CHORDS

In the following example, you will notice some new chord symbols. These symbols indicate a chord with a specific bass note under it, and are called **slash chords**. E.g. in bar 2, the chord symbol **G/B** occurs. This indicates a **G** chord played **over** a **B** bass note. In bar 4, the symbol **G/D** indicates a **G** chord over a **D** bass note. In bar 5, the symbol **Am/E** indicates an **A minor** chord with an **E** bass note. Slash chords are often used to create smooth, melodic bass lines and the symbols tell you that a note **other than the root** is played as the bass note of the chord.

BASS RUNS

The following example demonstrates the progression from the previous example played as arpeggios. As well as the slash chords, notice also the use of **bass runs** to connect the chords. The extra bass notes here all come from the **A natural minor** scale. Experiment with other ways of strumming and picking this progression.

 **57.**

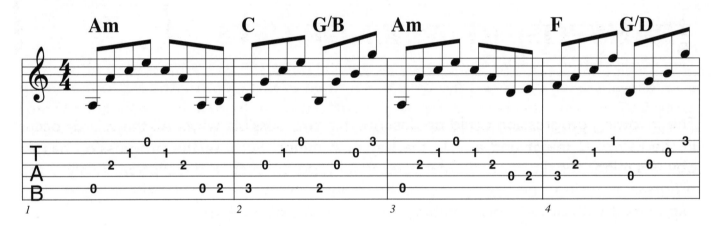

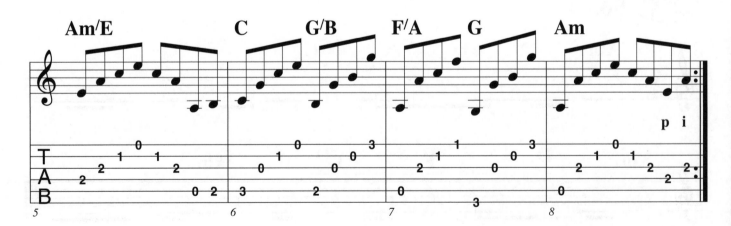

Slash chords can create many different harmonic effects. Each combination has a specific name and often creates an entirely new chord. Basically you can play **any** chord over any bass note as long as it sounds good. Experiment with playing all the chords you have learnt over various bass notes from the scale of the key you are playing in.

CHORDS IN OTHER MINOR KEYS

Written below are the scale tone chords for the key of **E natural minor** which is the relative minor of G major. Once again, the chords will be the same as those of its relative, but the starting note is **E** instead of G so **Em** will be chord Ī.

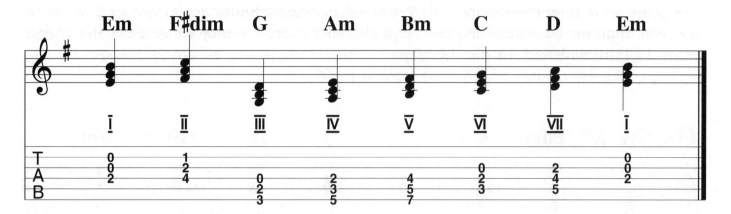

TRANSPOSING IN MINOR KEYS

Like music written in major keys, anything in a minor key can be transposed to other keys. The following example shows the progression from example 56 transposed to the key of **E minor**. Once you have learned the progression in this key, write out the scale tone chords in the remaining eleven minor keys and transpose the progression to those keys as well.

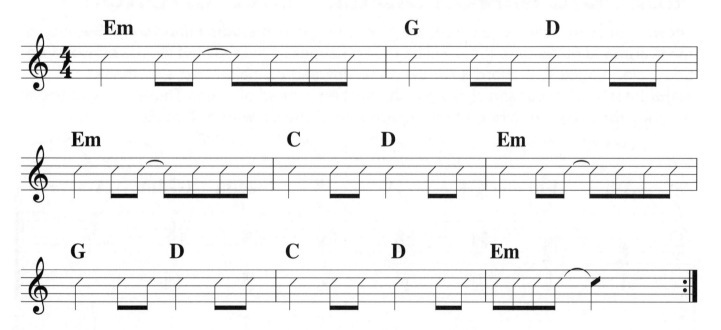

HARMONIC MINOR SCALE TONE CHORDS

Because there are three different minor scales, it is possible to come up with different sets of chords for a minor key by building chords on the notes of each different minor scale. Each variation to the notes of the scale alters the quality of chords built on the scale. The letter names of the chords remain the same, but the chord type may change. Shown below are scale tone chords derived from the **A harmonic minor scale**. Notice that chord III is now **augmented** instead of major, and also that chord V is **major** instead of minor and chord VII is **diminished** instead of major. These changes are all brought about by the raising of the 7th degree of the scale from **G** to **G♯**.

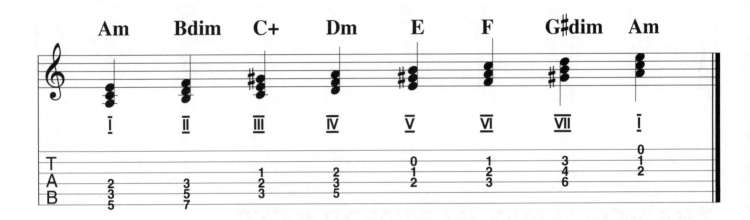

MELODIC MINOR SCALE TONE CHORDS

Shown below are scale tone chords derived from the **A melodic minor scale**. Because of the sharpened 6th degree there will be more changes to the types of chords derived from this scale. Notice that chord II is now **minor** instead of major, and also that chord IV is **major** instead of minor and chord VI is **diminished** instead of major. These changes are all brought about by the raising of the 6th degree of the scale from **F** to **F♯**.

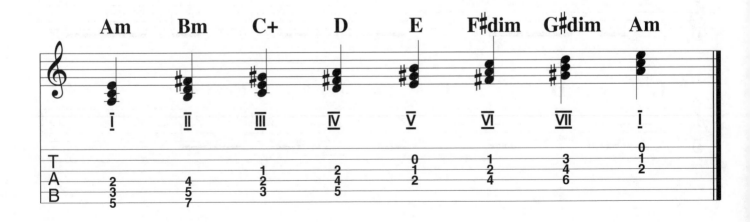

When playing music in minor keys, it is common to use chords from all three types of minor scales. A good example of this is the song **House of the Rising Sun**. The chords to this song are written below in arpeggio style in the key of **A minor**. Look through the chords and see which ones come from each type of minor scale. Once you have done this, transpose it to several other keys.

 58. House of the Rising Sun

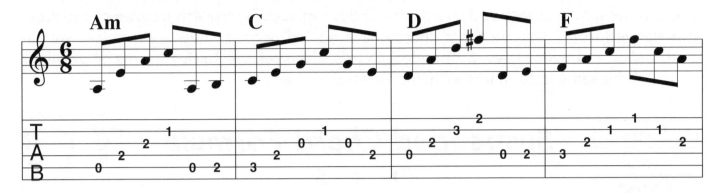

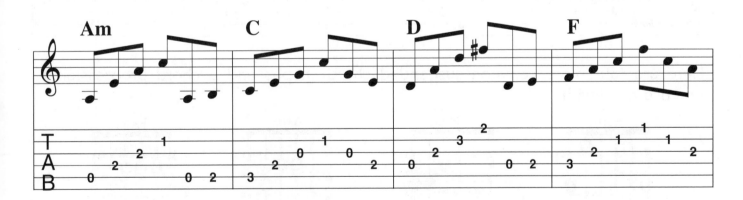

LESSON TWENTY SEVEN

SUSPENDED CHORDS

Major, minor, augmented and diminished chords are all triads – three note chords. Another useful type of triad is the **suspended chord**, such as the **Csus** you learnt in the previous lesson. In suspended chords, the 3rd is replaced by the **4th degree** of the scale it is derived from. Because these chords have no 3rd degree, they work equally well in both major and minor keys. Suspended chords often resolve back to a major or minor chord of the same letter name as demonstrated below.

Chord Symbol

Csus

or

Csus^4

Suspended Chord Formula

1   4   5

Notes in Chord

C	F	G
1	4	5

Suspended chords often resolve back to a major or minor chord of the same letter name as demonstrated below.

CD 1 **59.0**

Here are four more common suspended chord shapes and a chord progression to practice them with.

CD 1 **59.1**

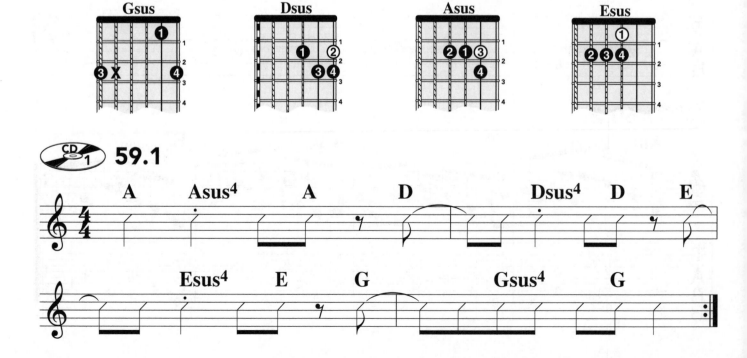

ADD NINE CHORDS

Another useful chord type is the **add nine** (**add9**) chord. These chords are either a major or minor triad with the 9th degree added. The 9th degree is the same as the second degree of the scale, but an octave higher.

Chord Symbol

Cadd⁹

Add Nine Chord Formula

1   3   5   9

Notes in Chord

C	E	G	D
1	3	5	9

CD 1 60.0

Here are some more **add9** chord shapes. Once you have learnt them, use them to play the examples below.

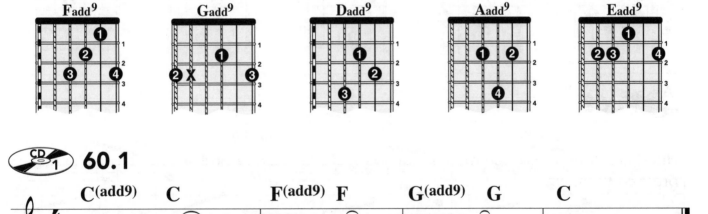

Fadd⁹   Gadd⁹   Dadd⁹   Aadd⁹   Eadd⁹

CD 1 60.1

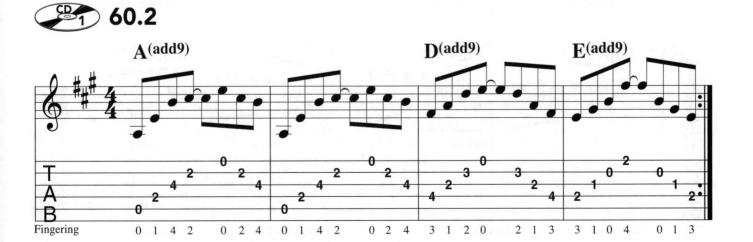

CD 1 60.2

Minor Add Nine Chord Formula

Chord Symbol

Notes in Chord

| Emadd9 |

| 1 | ♭3 | 5 | 9 |

E	G	B	F#
1	3	5	9

61.

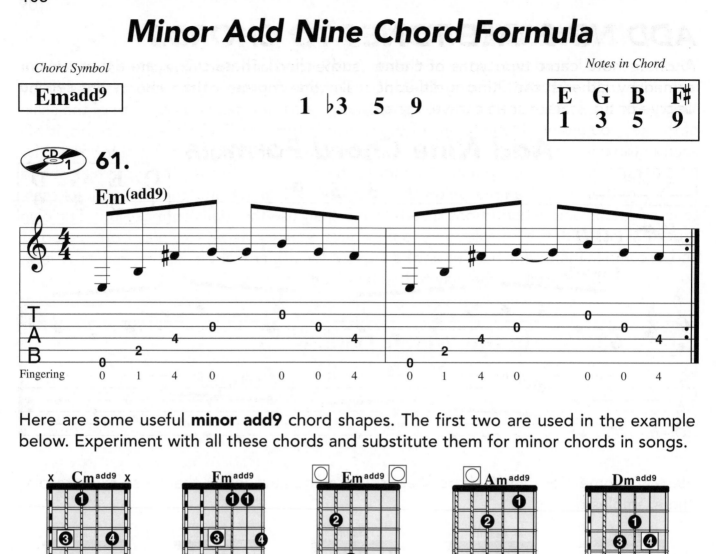

Here are some useful **minor add9** chord shapes. The first two are used in the example below. Experiment with all these chords and substitute them for minor chords in songs.

62.

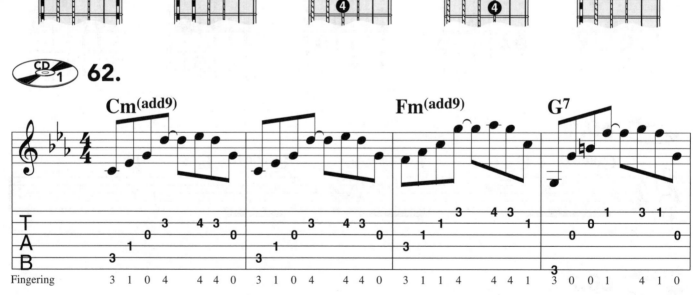

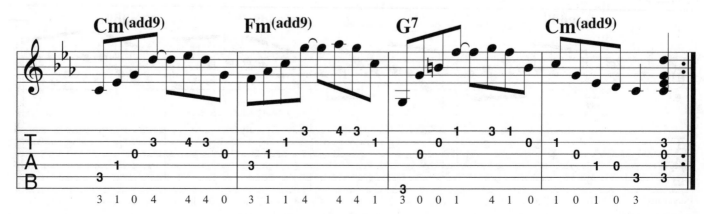

ADDING SCALE TONES TO CHORDS

You have now learnt two types of chords (suspended and add nine chords) which are formed by either substituting a different scale tone for one of the chord tones or by simply adding another scale tone to the existing chord. You can add any note of the scale of the key you are playing in to any of the chords in that key. Each time you do this, it will change the name of the chord, but knowing all these names is not essential for now. The best thing to do is experiment and memorize the notes and chords which you think sound good together. The example below is in the key of **E minor** and contains various scale tone additions and substitutions. Learn it and then use the ideas to make up your own progressions. With the knowledge you now have, you will be able to play both melodies and accompaniments for hundreds of songs and instrumental pieces, as well as writing your own. You are well on the way to becoming an excellent guitarist.

63.   In the Winter Dark

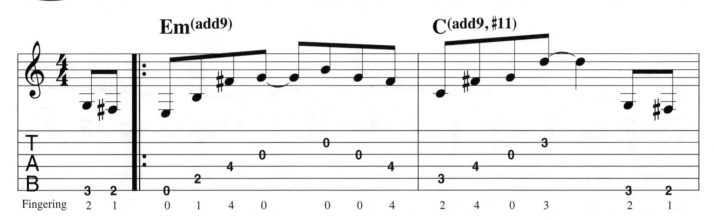

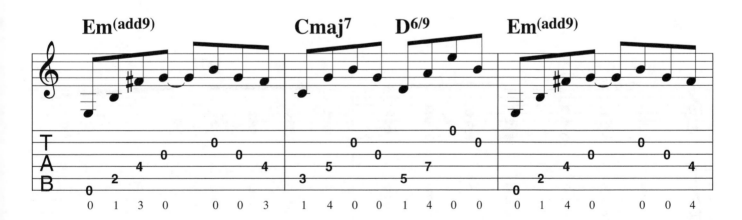

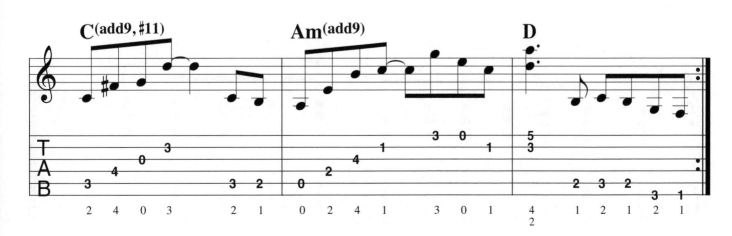

To end this section, here is a Rock rhythm part which makes use of power chords, major chords and double note runs. Although this example is in the key of **A**, it is not strictly in a major or minor key, but makes use of elements of both. This is common in Rock. **Whatever sounds good is ultimately the best thing to play**, regardless of what scale, chord or key it comes from. Experiment with all the sounds you have learnt and have fun with them.

 64. Rattlesnake Rock

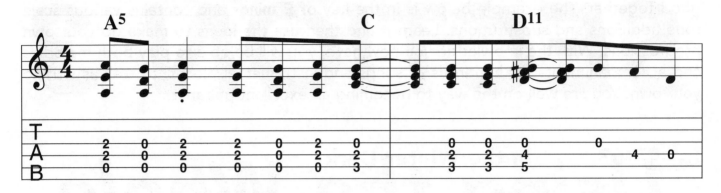

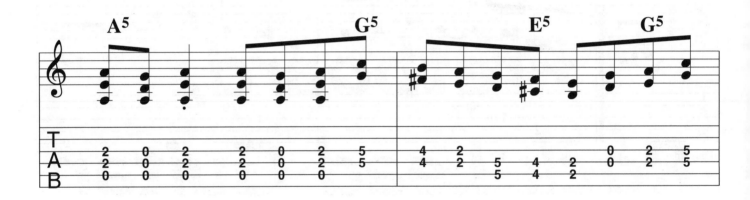

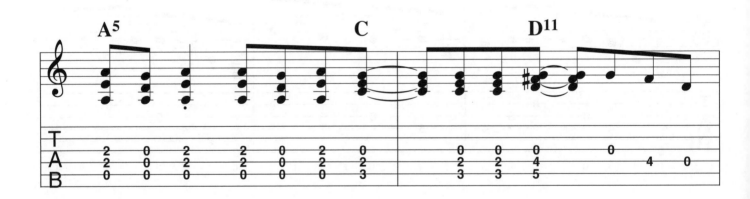

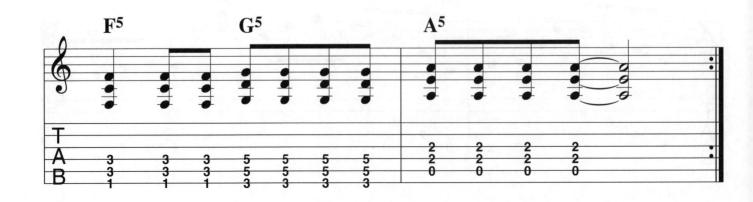

SECTION 3

Using the Whole Fretboard, Rock Lead Guitar

LESSON TWENTY EIGHT

BAR CHORDS

The term "bar chord" means that the first finger acts as a **bar** (sometimes called a **barre**) across all, or some of the strings. The fact that there are no open strings in a bar chord means it is possible to move the one shape to any position on the fretboard and to play in every key. The term "position" refers to the fret your first finger is at. E.g if your first finger is at the **3rd fret**, you are in the **third position**. If your first finger is at the **8th fret**, you are in the **eighth position**. The diagram and photo below demonstrate an **F major** bar chord (played in the **first position**). Notice that this chord is simply an E chord shape played with the 2nd, 3rd and 4th fingers, with a first finger bar behind it.

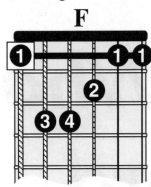

LEFT HAND TECHNIQUE

Bar chords can be difficult to play at first and will require a great deal of practice before they are comfortable to use. Try to keep the first finger of the left hand straight and parallel to the fret. It is also important to keep the other fingers arched and use only the tips of the fingers. The left hand thumb must be kept behind the neck.

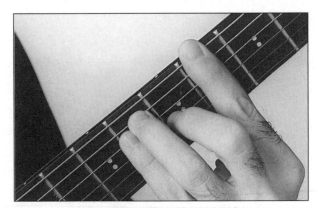

Keep first finger straight.

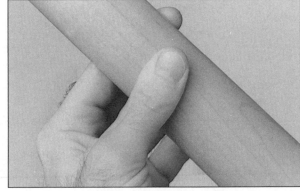

Keep thumb behind neck.

ROOT 6 BAR CHORDS

As with open chords, there are several different types of bar chords, including major, minor and 7th chords. The bar chord shape shown above is referred to as a **root 6** major bar chord because the **root note** (name note) of the chord is on the **6th string**. The root 6 major bar chord can be played at any fret with the name of the chord depending on which note the first finger is fretting on the sixth string. E.g. at the **3rd fret**, this shape would be a **G chord**. At the **5th fret**, it would be an **A chord**, etc.

NOTES ON THE SIXTH STRING

In order to determine exactly where to place your first finger for a particular bar chord it is essential to know the notes on the sixth string from memory. The diagram below shows the notes on the sixth string up to the 13th fret where the **F** note is an octave repeat of the **F** note at the first fret. It is rare to play bar chords any higher than the 12th fret.

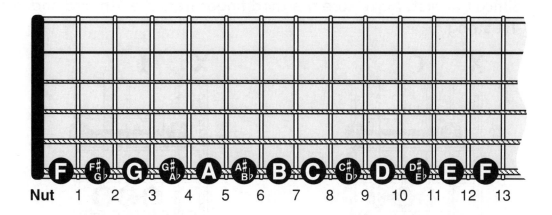

Practice playing bar chords at different frets at random until you can instantly name the chord at any fret. Once you can do this, try the following example, which moves the same shape up and down the neck to form all the chords in the progression.

65.0

PERCUSSIVE STRUMMING WITH BAR CHORDS

In lesson 9 you learned about **percussive strumming**. This technique is commonly used when playing bar chords. As with other chord types, it is achieved by forming a complete chord shape with the left hand and placing it on the strings, but **not** pressed down on the frets. Remember that a percussive strum is indicated by using an **X** in place of a notehead. Listen to the following example on the recording to hear whether you are getting the correct sound. If not, practice it slowly using only quarter notes at first and then move on to eighth notes as shown in the following example.

65.1

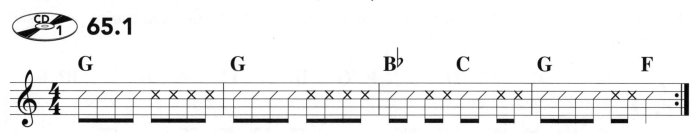

ROOT 5 BAR CHORDS

As the term **root 5** suggests, the root note of these chords can be found on the fifth string, fretted with the first finger bar. Like all bar chords, the same shape can be moved up or down to any position on the fretboard. Below is the basic shape for the root 5 Major bar chord shown in two positions. You will need to have patience with this chord shape, as the combination of the first finger bar and the partial bar with the third finger is particularly difficult at first. Make sure the third finger frets the 4th, 3rd and 2nd strings, but **not** the 1st string.

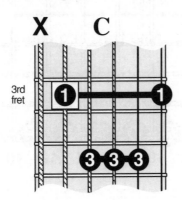

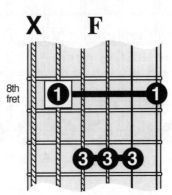

NOTES ON THE FIFTH STRING

To find root 5 bar chords easily, it is essential to know the notes on the 5th string from memory. The diagram below illustrates all notes on the fifth string up to the 13th fret. Try naming a chord and moving to the correct fret. Practice this until you can do it without hesitating or having to think ahead.

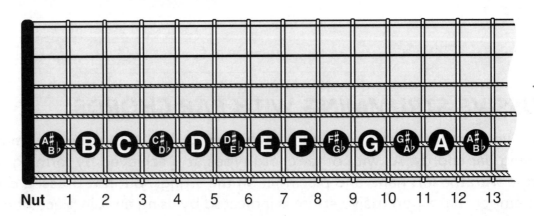

 **66.**

Here is an example which makes use of root 5 bar chords. Notice the use of percussive strumming here.

CHANGING BETWEEN SHAPES

Once you know how to play both root 6 and root 5 bar chords, the next step is learning how to combine them. The exercise below will help you gain control of changing between the two major bar chords. The **G** chord is **root 6** while the **C and D** chords are **root 5**. As you play this example, notice that the chords **G**, **C** and **D** are chords $\bar{I}$, $\bar{IV}$ and $\bar{V}$ in the **key of G**. You could use these chord shapes to play a 12 bar Blues in the key of G. You could also move the chords to other positions on the fretboard and play a 12 bar Blues in any key. This becomes even easier when you learn the following pattern, which applies to all keys.

If **chord $\bar{I}$ is root 6**, then **chord $\bar{IV}$** will be **root 5 at the same fret**, and **chord $\bar{V}$** will be **root 5 two frets higher up the neck.**

67.0

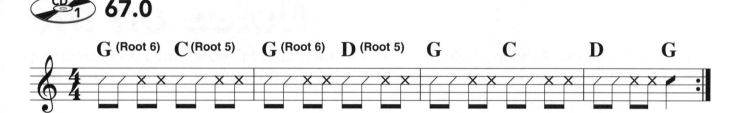

It is also possible to play this progression beginning with a root 5 chord. If **chord $\bar{I}$ is root 5**, then **chord $\bar{IV}$** will be **root 6 two frets lower**, and **chord $\bar{V}$** will be **root 6 at the same fret as chord $\bar{I}$**. This pattern also applies to **all keys**. Listen to the CD to hear the difference between this example and the previous one.

67.1

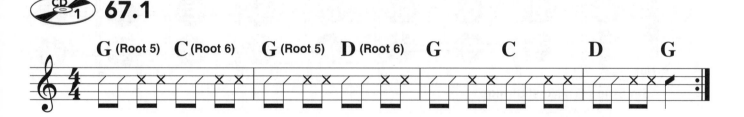

67.2

Here is another example which will give you more practice at changing between root 5 and root 6 bar chords. Notice the use of **staccato** here. As with single notes, staccato with bar chords is achieved by quickly lifting the fingers off the fretboard but not off the strings immediately after strumming the chord.

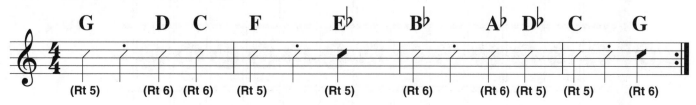

LESSON TWENTY NINE

LEARNING THE WHOLE FRETBOARD

When using moveable chord shapes, it is important to be able to quickly find the correct fret at which to play each chord, and also to be able to play equally well in all keys. The best way to achieve this is to memorize the names of all the notes on the fretboard. This may seem a daunting task, but it can be done and will be well worth it. More advanced guitar playing requires the use of many different chords, which may take their name from **any** of the six strings, so you need to learn them all equally well.

Notes on the

Here is a fretboard diagram of all the notes on the guitar. Play the notes on each string the open note e.g. the open 6th string is an **E** note and the note on the 12th fret of the

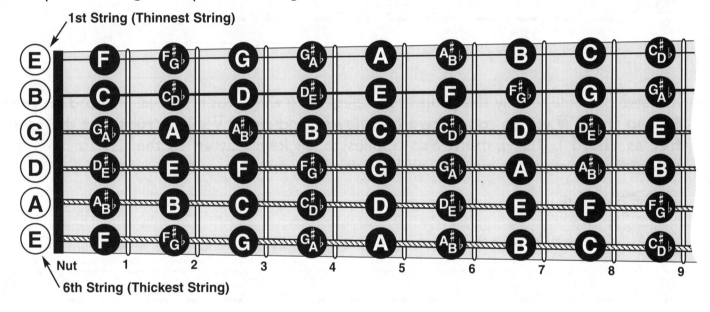

A good way to learn all the notes is to take one string at a time. Call the "in between" notes sharps as you progress up the fretboard and flats as you go back down. The diagram below shows notes on the 4th string only. To practice naming the notes, slide your first finger up one fret at a time and say the name of each note out loud as you go. When you reach the 12th fret where the notes begin to repeat, move back down one fret at a time. You can use any finger to do this exercise, it is the note names that are important, not the fingering.

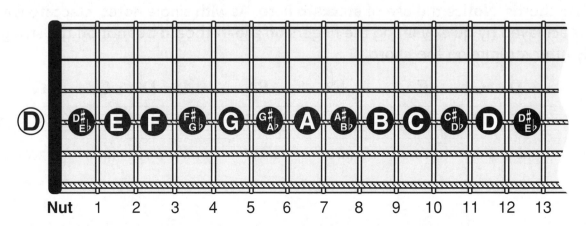

The dots on your guitar are good points of reference. You can use them to help the memorizing process.

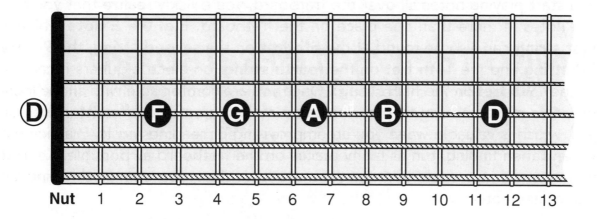

Nut 1 2 3 4 5 6 7 8 9 10 11 12 13

Guitar Fretboard

from the open notes to the 12th fret. The note on the 12th fret is one octave higher than 6th string is also an **E** note, but is one octave higher.

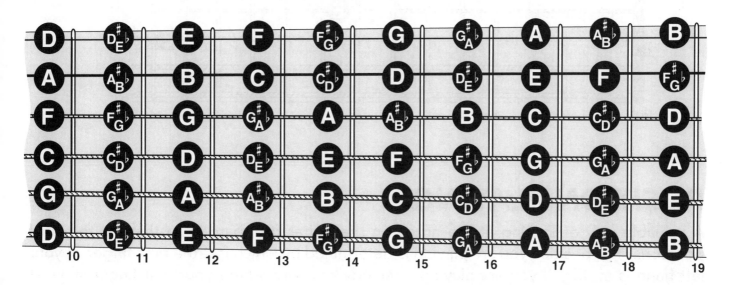

Once you are confident you know the names of the notes along a particular string, pick the name of any note at random and find it on that string as quickly as possible. When this becomes easy, move on to the next string.

Another useful exercise is to find the same note on every string, remembering that a note usually appears twice on each string unless it is at the 11th fret.

Finally, name and play the notes across each fret. Once again use sharps as you go higher in pitch and flats as you go back down.

NOTES IN MORE THAN ONE PLACE

Once you start playing notes all over the fretboard, you quickly realize that you can find the same notes in more than one place on the fretboard. E.g. the **E note** which is the **open first string** can also be found at the **5th fret** on the **second string**, the **9th fret** on the **third string** and the **14th fret** on the **fourth string** (on electric guitars it can also be found at the **19th fret** on the **fifth string**). Once you are comfortable with all the locations of a note, this makes it easy to play the same melody in many different places on the fretboard, which is valuable when you are improvising or reading music. Practice naming any note and then finding it in as many places on the fretboard as possible. Keep doing this for a few minutes each day until you are confident you can quickly find all the locations for any note.

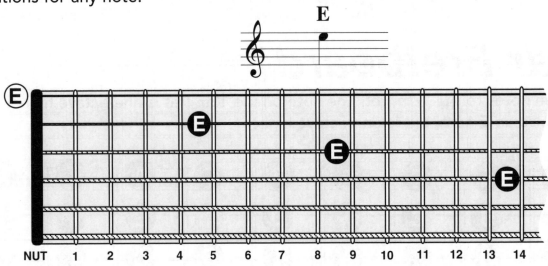

POSITION PLAYING

A valuable way of looking at the notes on the guitar fretboard is to think in terms of **positions**. The position you are playing is determined by which fret the **first finger** of your left hand is at. E.g. if you are playing a melody or chord where your first finger stays at the **first fret**, then you are in the **first position**. If your first finger stays at the **6th fret**, you are in the **6th position**, etc. The example below demonstrates a short phrase in played in several different positions, as shown in the tablature. Experiment and find out how many other positions you can use to play this phrase.

CD 1 68.

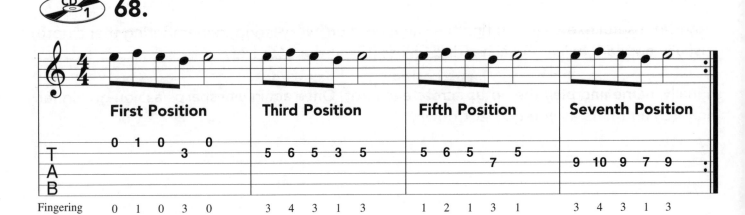

HIGHER AND LOWER OCTAVES OF NOTES

Another valuable exercise for improving your knowledge of the fretboard is to find all possible octaves of any given note. Remember that an **octave** is the distance between any note and its next repeat at a higher or lower pitch.

An example of this would be the note **C#**, which can be found at the **9th and 21st frets** on the **sixth string**, the **4th and 16th frets** on the **fifth string**, the **11th fret** on the **fourth string**, the **6th and 18th frets** on the **third string**, the **2nd and 14th frets** on the **second string**, and the **9th and 21st frets** on the **first string**. These positions are shown in the diagram below. Practice choosing notes at random and finding each one in all possible positions, until you are confident you can instantly find any note in any position.

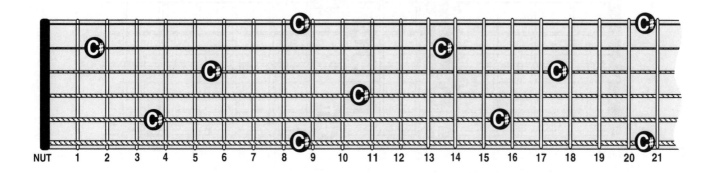

Knowing how to find higher and lower octaves of notes is useful in many ways. You may wish to repeat something you have played but make it sound higher or lower than the first time it was played, or you may play something and think you have the right notes but it sounds too high or too low. Another situation where this is useful is if you are playing call and response with a vocalist or another instrumentalist. You may know which key they are in and what note they are starting on, but you also have to find which octave they are in as well.

The example below shows a phrase played in different positions on the fretboard and also in different octaves.

CD 1 **69.**

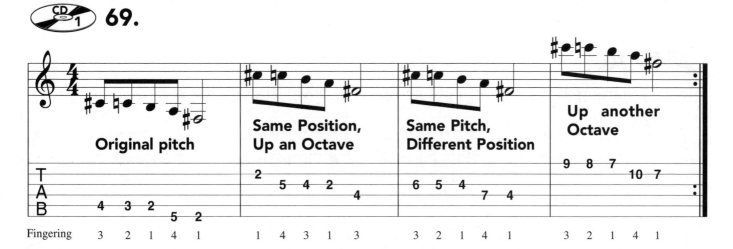

LESSON THIRTY

THE MINOR PENTATONIC SCALE

Just as there are moveable chord shapes, so there are also moveable scales. The most common scale used in lead guitar playing is the **minor pentatonic** scale. Pentatonic means five notes. It's degrees are **1, ♭3, 4, 5** and **♭7**. In the **A minor pentatonic** scale these notes are **A C D E** and **G**. The diagram below shows the A minor pentatonic scale in the 5th position. The notes with a box around them are the root notes (or key notes) In this particular scale, each of them is a different **A** note. This scale formation is often called **pattern 1**.

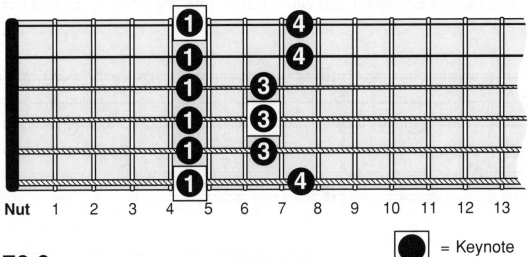

Nut   1   2   3   4   5   6   7   8   9   10   11   12   13

● = Keynote

70.0

Play the scale as indicated here. It may sound familiar to you.

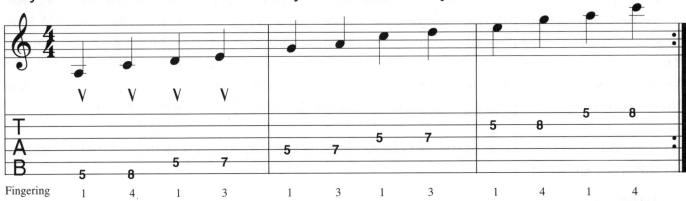

70.1

Now try starting at the highest note and playing down through the scale.

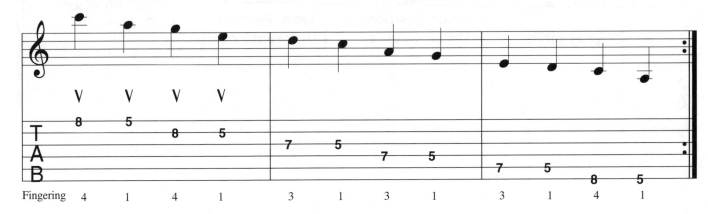

 **71.0**

The next step is to play the scale ascending and descending, as shown here. Try to get a smooth, even sound.

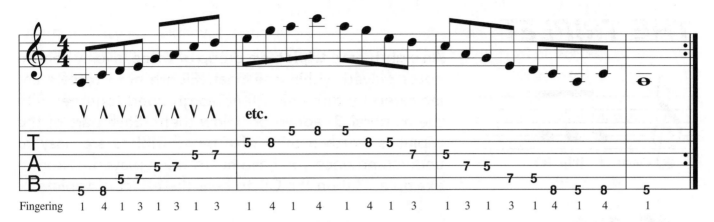

 **71.1**

To help develop your picking it is a good idea to practice playing each note twice.

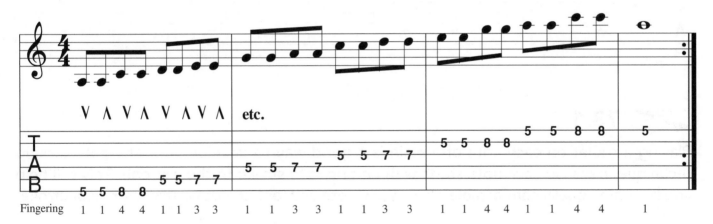

 **72.**

Here is a riff which is derived from the A minor pentatonic scale.

LESSON THIRTY ONE

THE TRIPLET

Count: 1 trip let

An eighth note **triplet** is a group of **three** evenly spaced notes played within one beat. Eighth note triplets are indicated by three eighth notes grouped together with the numeral **3** above or below them. Each part of the triplet is worth a third of a beat. Triplets are easy to understand once you have heard them played. Listen to example 73.0 on the CD to hear the effect of triplets.

73.0

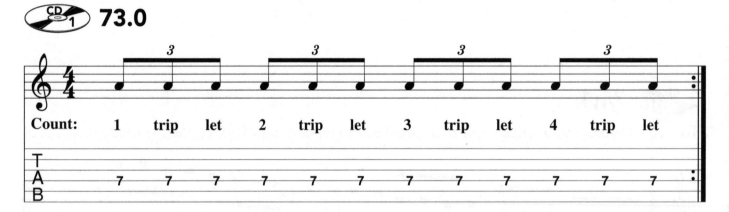

73.1

Playing a triplet on each note of a scale is a good way to develop your alternate picking technique, because each note starts with an opposite stroke to the last one. This will help you become equally comfortable playing any note with either a downstroke or an upstroke.

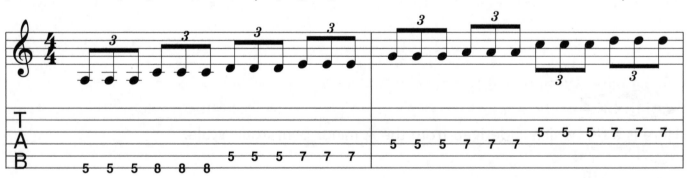

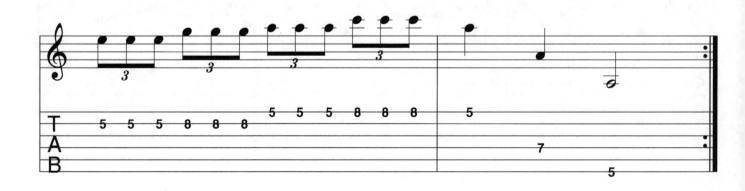

SWING RHYTHMS

A **swing rhythm** can be created by tying the first two notes of the triplet group together.

 **74.0**

 **74.1**

The two eighth note triplets tied together in the example above can be replaced by a quarter note.

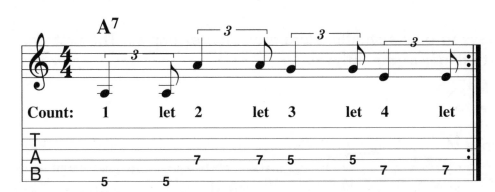

To simplify notation, it is common to replace the  with ♩♪,
and to write at the start of the piece 𝅘𝅥𝅮𝅘𝅥𝅮 = ♩ ♪ as illustrated below.

74.2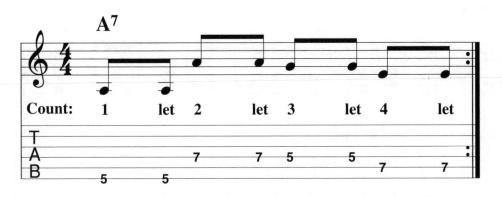

THE SHUFFLE

A **shuffle** is a constant stream of swung eighth notes. It is one of the most common rhythms in Blues and is also used in related styles such as Rock, Jazz, Funk, Gospel and Soul. All the examples on the previous page are shuffles. There is a particular way of playing a shuffle on the guitar which is instantly recognizable. It is played on two adjacent strings like a power chord. The third finger is placed two frets up the neck on the same string as the first finger. The same two strings are played as in the fifth chord. Keep the first finger down even when playing with the third finger. This will result in a smoother, more solid sound. It also helps to use right hand damping with this pattern.

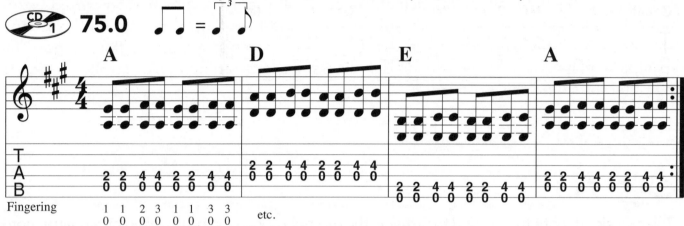

There are many different ways to play a shuffle. Here are some examples. The first one requires the use of the fourth finger at the fifth fret.

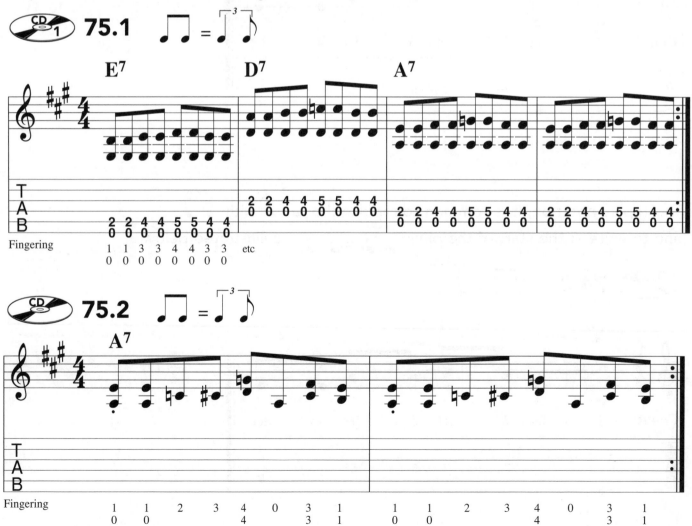

LESSON THIRTY TWO

MORE ABOUT 12 BAR BLUES

In a basic 12 bar Blues, there are usually three different chords. Each of these relates to one basic **Key.** In Blues, the most common chords are those built on notes **1, 4** and **5** of the major scale. So in the key of C, these chords would be **C, F** and **G.** In the Key of A they would be **A, D** and **E.** The example below demonstrates the 12 bar Blues progression played with a **moveable shuffle pattern** in the key of **A.** The first and third fingers remain on the strings, while the fourth finger stretches up two frets on the same string as the third finger. This example is played without right hand damping and uses alternating pick strokes. Listen to the different sound this produces.

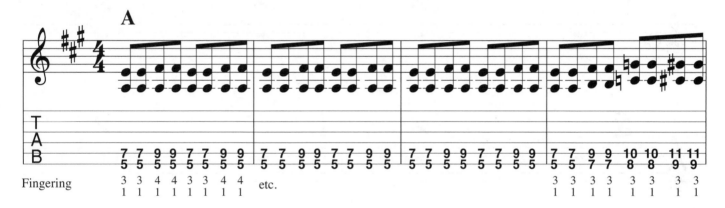

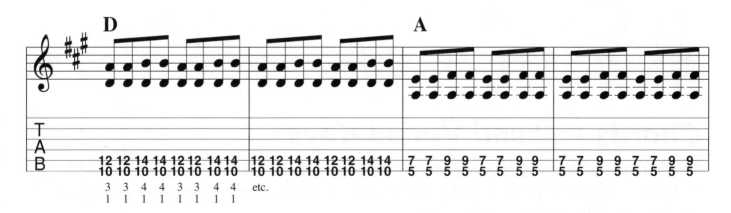

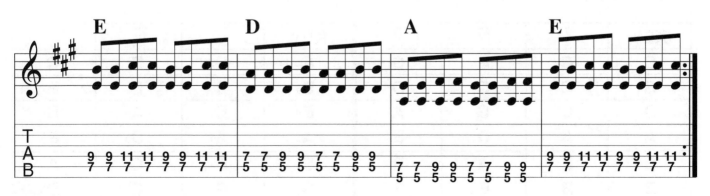

A shuffle pattern can be played in any key simply by moving its root note to the appropriate fret. The following example is in the key of **G** in the **3rd position** (3rd fret).

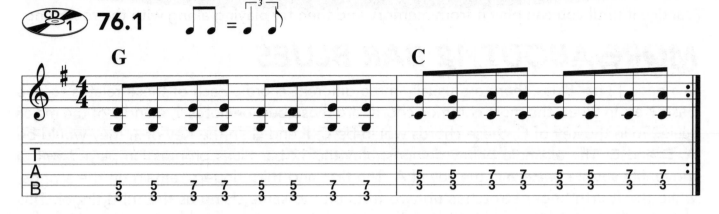

Shown below is the 12 bar Blues progression shown in Roman numerals Ī, IV̄ and V̄ instead of 1, 4 and 5. In this case, the roman numerals refer to chord numbers within a key, rather than positions on the fretboard. The ⅟. symbol is a bar repeat sign (repeat the previous bar).

Chords *Ī* *IV̄* and *V̄* in all Keys

This Table lists chords Ī, IV̄ and V̄ in all twelve keys used in music. By using this table, you can play a 12 bar Blues in any key. Remember that it is common to play all three chords as dominant 7ths when playing Blues.

KEY	Ī	IV̄	V̄	KEY	Ī	IV̄	V̄
C	C	F	G	F	F	B♭	C
G	G	C	D	B♭	B♭	E♭	F
D	D	G	A	E♭	E♭	A♭	B♭
A	A	D	E	A♭	A♭	D♭	E♭
E	E	A	B	D♭	D♭	G♭	A♭
B	B	E	F#	G♭	G♭	C♭	D♭
F#	F#	B	C#				

PENTATONIC BLUES SOLO

Here is a simple 12 bar Blues solo derived from the pattern 1 A minor pentatonic scale. Practice it until you can play it from memory and then try playing along with the recording.

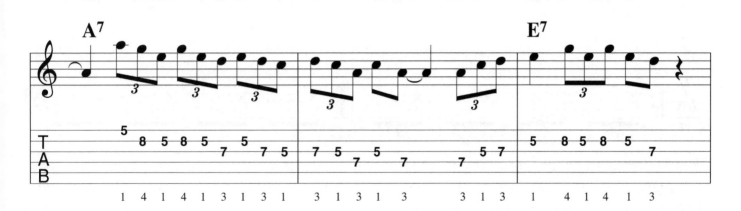

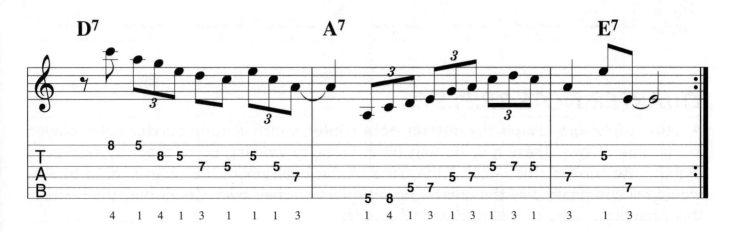

UNDERSTANDING TRIPLET RHYTHMS

In a bar of triplets in $\frac{4}{4}$ time, there are **12** different positions for notes within the bar. The first beat is **1**, the middle note of the first triplet is called the **"trip of one"** and the third note of the first triplet is called the **"let of one"**. The system then continues through the bar - **2**, **trip of 2**, **let of 2**, etc. It is worth practicing playing notes or chords on each of these positions until you can do them at will. Here are some rhythm exercises using triplets. Count them carefully, as there could be either a note or a rest on any part of each triplet. There are three common ways of strumming triplets – all downstrokes, alternate strumming, and playing each new beat with a downstroke (down up down, down up down, etc.). It is important to practice the following exercises with each of these strumming motions.

78.

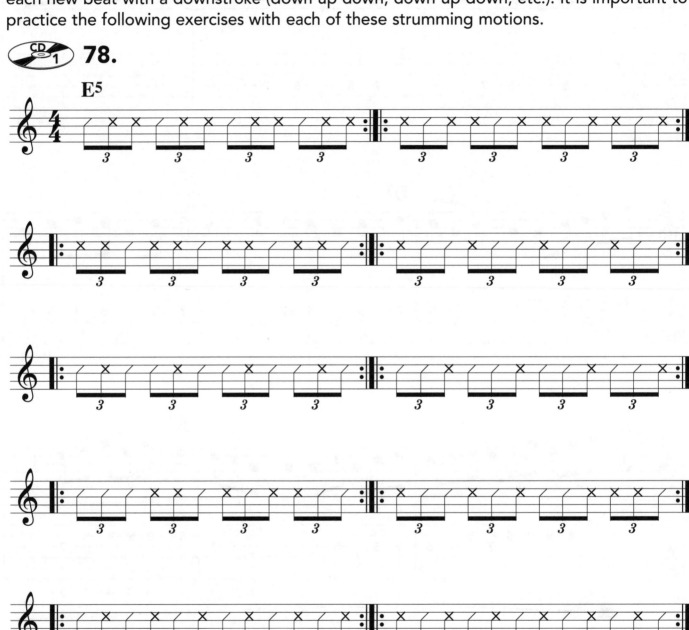

QUARTER NOTE TRIPLETS.

Another triplet grouping is the **quarter note triplet**, which is three quarter notes played in the time of two. These may be difficult at first. Try working up to them by first using eighth note triplets, Then accent the parts of the beat where the quarter note triplets would fall and finally play the quarter note triplets on their own. Count only the beats in this example and try to feel where the notes fall.

79.0

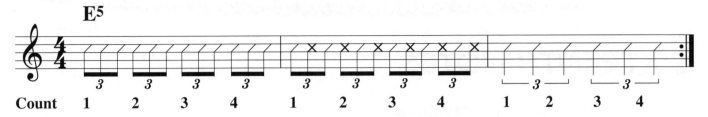

79.1

This example contains both eighth note triplets and quarter note triplets.

80.

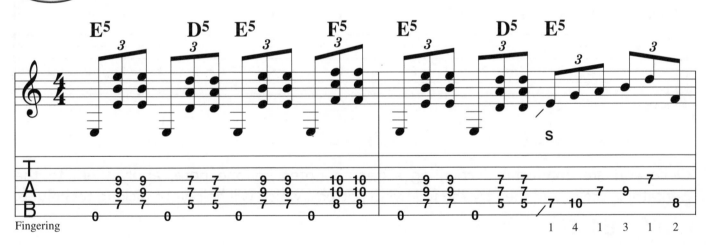

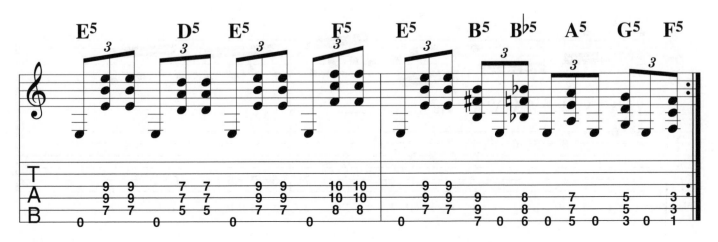

LESSON THIRTY THREE

SIXTEENTH NOTES

This is a **sixteenth note**.
It lasts for **one quarter** of a beat.
There are **four** sixteenth notes in one beat.
There are **16** sixteenth notes in one bar of $\frac{4}{4}$ time.

Two sixteenth notes joined together.

Four sixteenth notes joined together.

Count: 1 e + a
Say: one 'ee' and 'ah'

When counting 16th notes, notice the different sound for each part of the beat – **one ee and ah, two ee and ah**... etc (written **1 e + a, 2 e + a**... etc).

 81.0 **How to Count Sixteenth Notes**

Once you are comfortable counting sixteenth notes on one note, apply them to the pentatonic scale, and then try the following pattern, which will help your picking technique.

 **81.1**

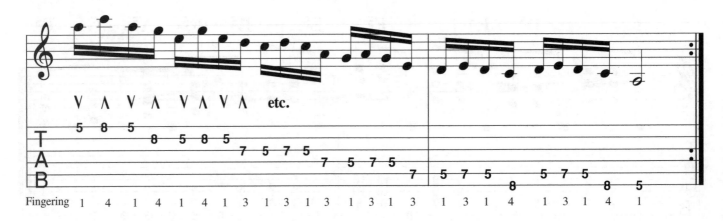

82. Move on Down

Sixteenth notes are often used within a beat in conjunction with eighth notes, as shown in the following example. If you have trouble with the rhythms, practice them on one note until you are confident with them and then try the whole example. All the notes here are within the A minor pentatonic scale. Notice the use of staccato in this example.

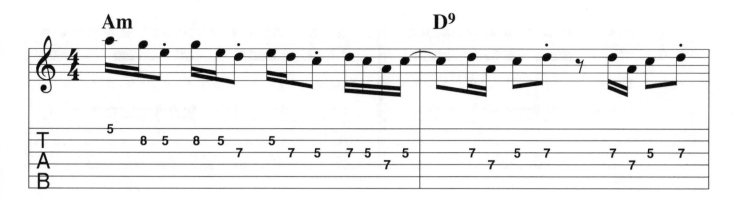

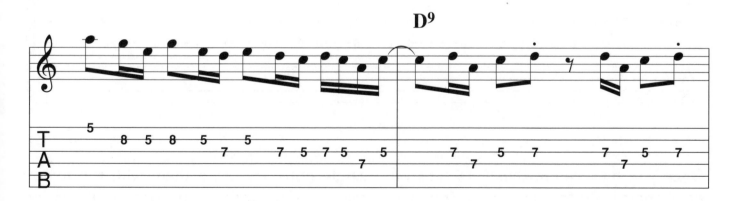

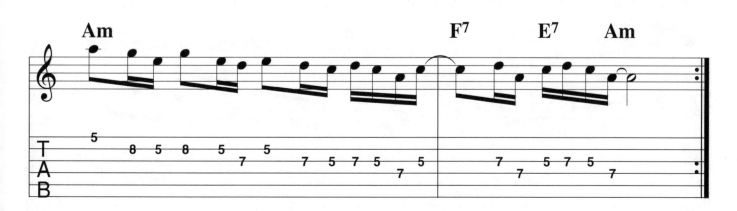

COMMON 16TH NOTE FIGURES

Here are some rhythmic figures which combine sixteenth notes and eighth notes within one beat. These figures are very common in many styles, so you will need to know them well. Practice each one carefully and be sure to tap your foot and count.

83.

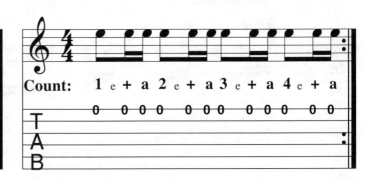

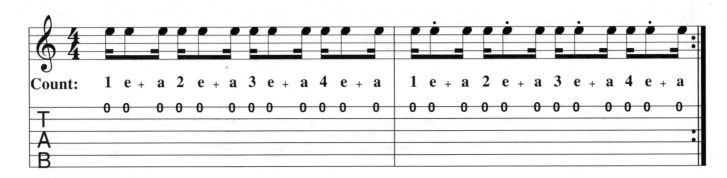

Once you have learnt these rhythms on a single note, try using them with the minor pentatonic scale as shown here. The more familiar you are with these rhythms, the easier you will find it to play melodies containing 16th notes, as well as improvising with them.

84.

As soon as you start to feel comfortable with 16th note rhythms, try using them to create riffs. Here are some examples using the notes of the A minor pentatonic scale.

 **85.0**

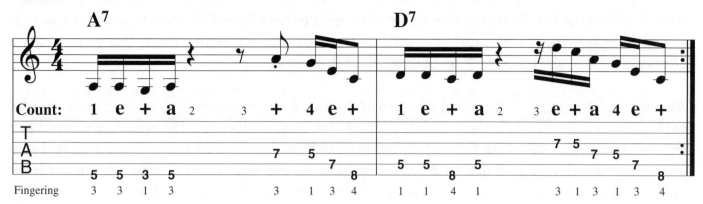

 **85.1**

This one combines three note power chords with 4th intervals.

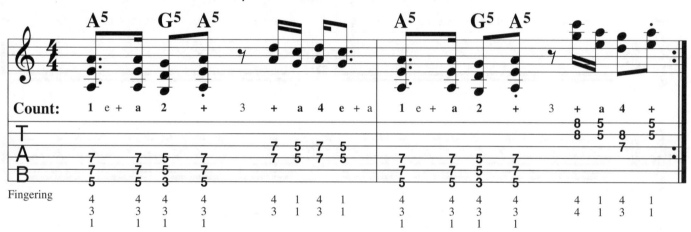

85.2

Here is another on e with a more complex rhythm. Count carefully with this one.

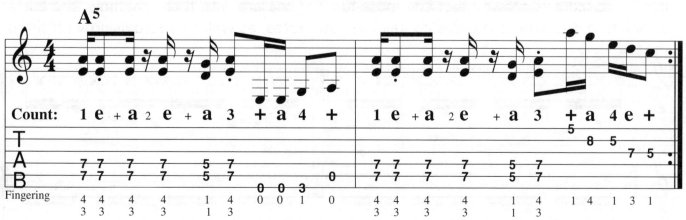

GAINING CONTROL OF SIXTEENTH NOTES

In a bar of sixteenth notes in $\frac{4}{4}$ time, there are **16** different positions for notes within the bar. The first beat is **1**, the second note of the first group of four is called the "**e of one**" the third note of the first group is called the "**and of one**", and the fourth note of the first group is called the "**a of one**". As with other subdivisions of the beat, the system then continues through the bar - **2**, **e of 2**, **and of 2**, **a of 2**, etc.

As with eighth notes, a good way to master the use of 16th notes is to play constant 16ths with the right hand and select which part of the beat will sound by pressing down with the left hand. The other parts of each beat should be sounded as percussive strums. Here are some exercises using this technique. Be sure to use your metronome, count out loud and tap your foot on the beat without any hesitating or extra taps in between beats.

86.

POWER CHORD SIXTEENTH NOTE RHYTHM PARTS

Shown below are some common ways of using sixteenth notes with power chords. Notice the accents on each beat of the bar. Practice each pattern until you can play it easily at a slow tempo, and then try increasing the setting on your metronome two points at a time until you can play them along with the CD.

 **87.**

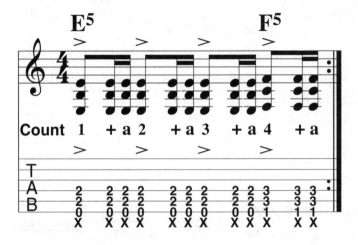

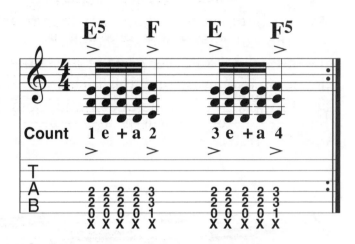

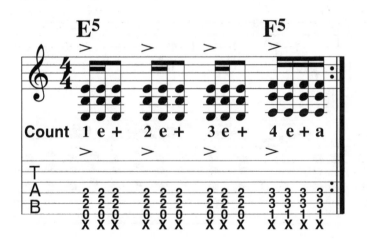

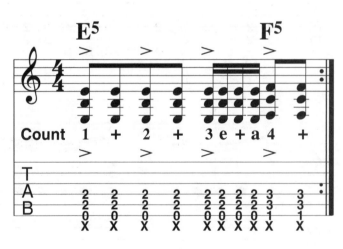

In order to produce a heavier more aggressive sound, try using downstrokes on every strum of a sixteenth note rhythms shown in the following example.

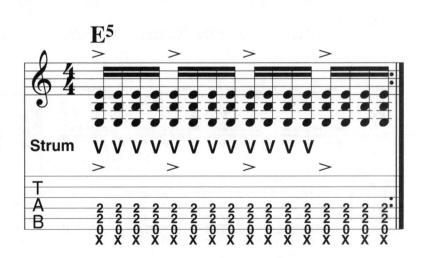

Here are some examples which make use of eighth and sixteenth notes in various combinations. Take each one slowly at first and count out loud until you are confident with the timing.

88. Hammerdrill

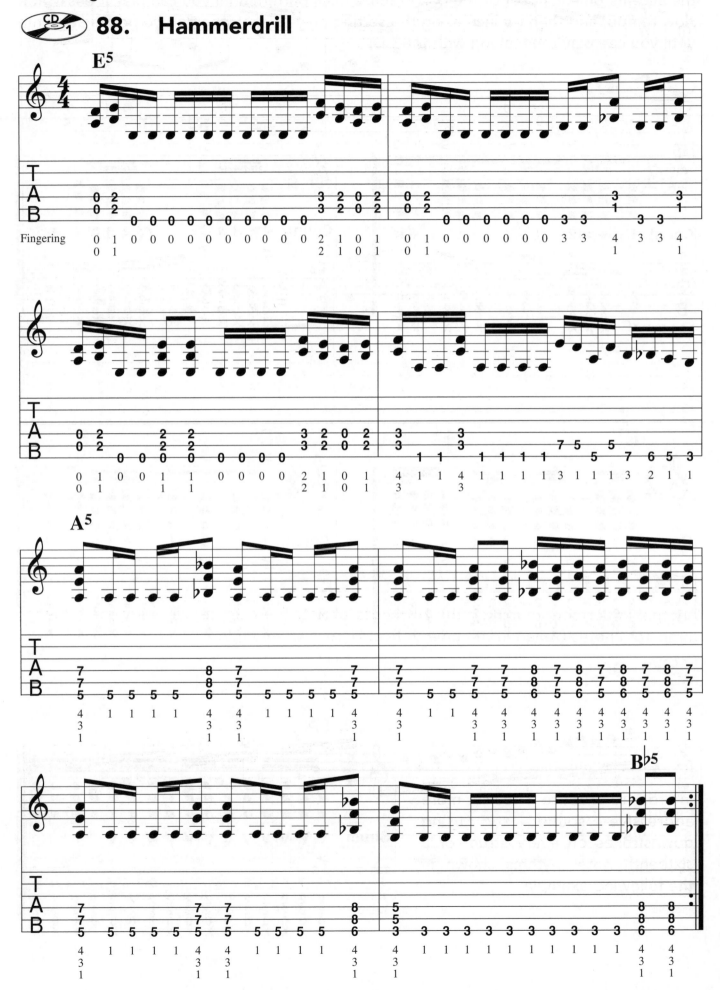

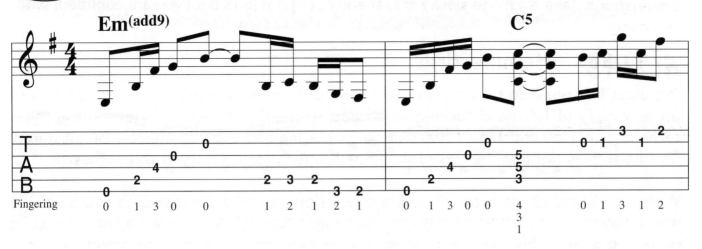

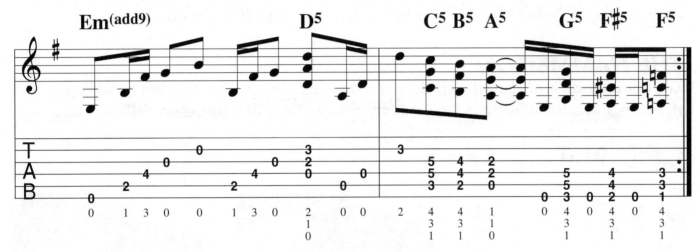

SIXTEENTH NOTE TRIPLETS.

Another important grouping is the **16th note triplet**. These are usually fairly quick, being three 16th notes played in the time of two. Here is an example.

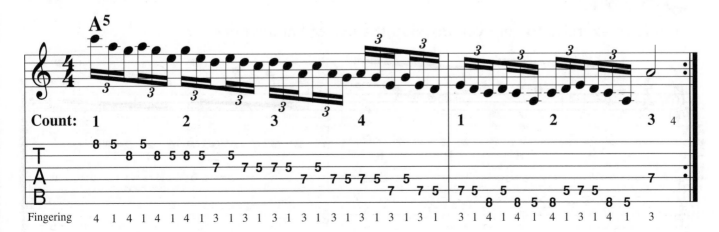

LESSON THIRTY FOUR

SLURS

Although it is possible to make a good sound picking every note, it is more common to use a variety of left hand techniques to add expression to some of the notes. These techniques are essential in all styles of guitar playing and should definitely be mastered. Be sure to play right on the tips of the fingers when practicing these techniques.

When two notes or more are played in succession and only the first note is picked, the notes played by the left hand only are said to be "slurred". A **slur** is a way of connecting notes more smoothly than when articulating every note with the right hand. A **slur** is indicated by a curved line above or below two or more **different** notes.

THE HAMMER-ON

The **hammer-on** is executed by picking a note and then hammering a left hand finger onto the string. The hammer-on is indicated by a curved line and the letter "**H**".

 **91.0**

Begin by playing the note on the 5th fret, fourth string.

Hammer third finger onto 7th fret of fourth string.

 **91.1**

Here is an exercise to help you develop the use of hammer-ons.

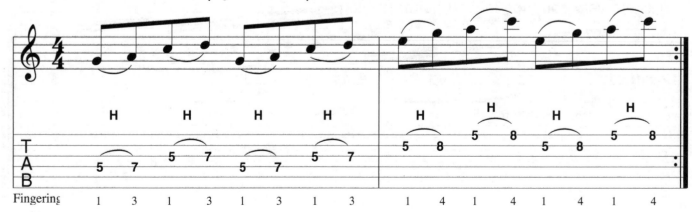

THE PULL-OFF

The pull-off is executed by playing a note and then pulling the left hand finger off the string towards the floor. This causes a new note to sound. The pull-off is indicated by a curved line and the symbol "**P**".

 92.0

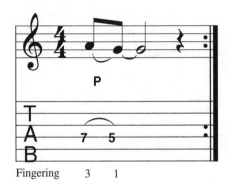

Begin by playing the note on the 7th fret, fourth string.

Pull third finger away to produce note at 5th fret.

 92.1

Here is an exercise for developing control of pull-offs.

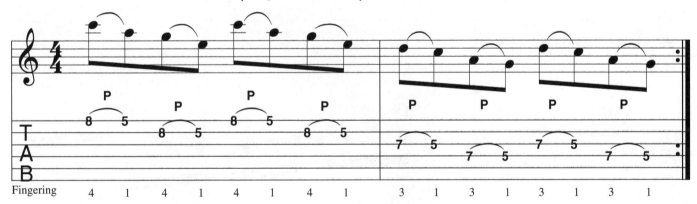

 92.2

The following **lick** (short musical phrase) makes use of both hammer-ons and pull-offs. Licks are very common in lead guitar playing.

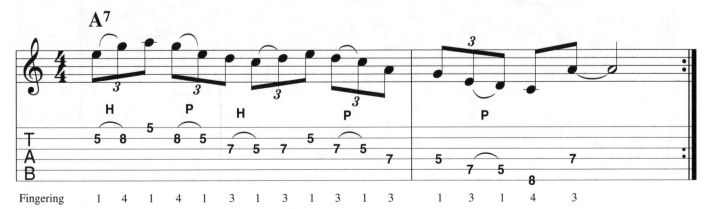

The following example consists of several licks joined together to form a solo. Notice the extensive use of hammer-on's and pull-off's. This solo is played over a chord progression in the key of **A minor**.

 **93. Snappy Fingers**

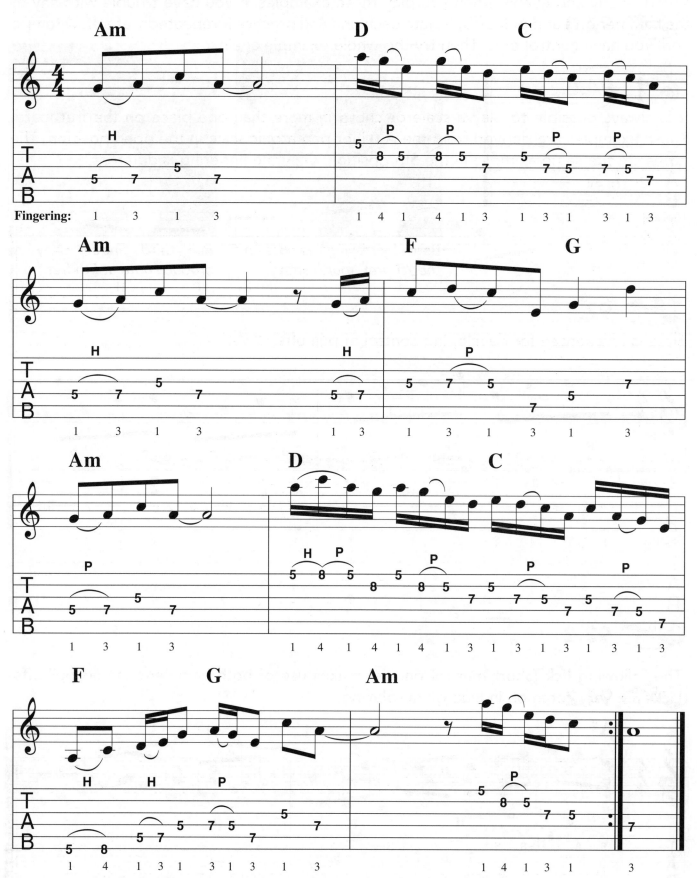

SLURS USING OPEN STRINGS

The examples below demonstrate the use of slurs involving open strings along with other slurs. These examples contain groups of slurred notes where only the first note is picked, while the remaining notes are either hammered-on or pulled-off. Make sure all the notes sound clearly and evenly when you play these examples. If you have trouble with any of the hammer-on's and pull-off's, isolate each one and practice it repeatedly at a slow tempo until you have control of it. Then try the whole example again.

 **94.0**

It is always possible to play a scale or chord in more than one place on the fretboard. These examples are derived from the A minor pentatonic scale in the open position. The notes are the same as those in the 5th position; Only the fingering is different.

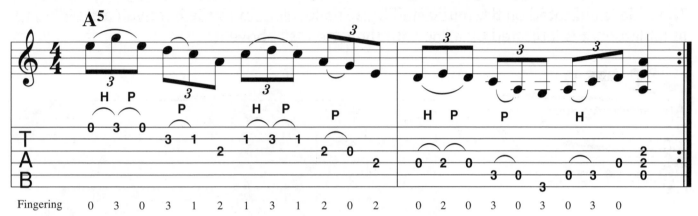

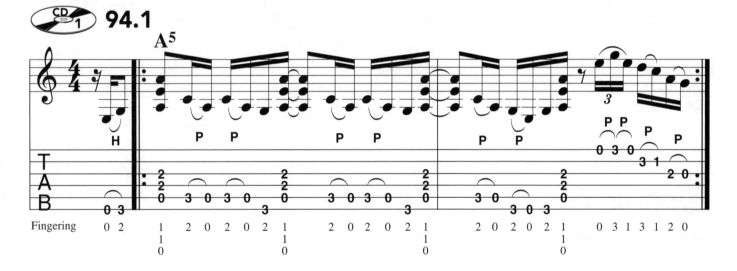

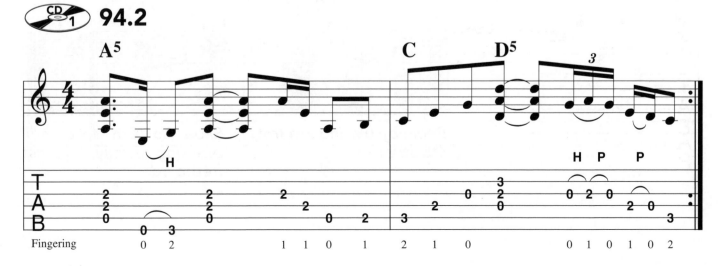

LESSON THIRTY FIVE

THE SLIDE

The **slide** is a left hand technique which involves sliding a finger along the fretboard between two notes on the same string. The finger maintains pressure on the string, so that a continuous sound is produced until the desired note is reached. Only the first note is played by the right hand, the second one is entirely produced by the left hand finger sliding up or down the fretboard. The length of the slide can be one fret or as many frets as you wish. Practice sliding your finger up and down the fretboard. Pick only the first note.

The slide is indicated on the music staff by a line leading up to the note you are sliding to. In tablature, it is indicated by a line with the letter "**s**" above it.

 **95.0**

An ascending slide.

Begin by playing 5th fret, 4th string.

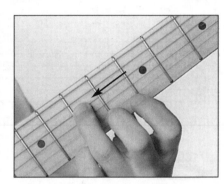

Slide to 7th fret, still pressing firmly against fretboard.

95.1

A descending slide.

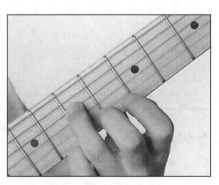

Begin by playing 7th fret, 4th string.

Slide to 5th fret, still pressing firmly against fretboard.

PATTERN 1 EXTENSION

Pattern 1 extension incorporates notes from improvising **pattern 1** with some extra notes on the fretboard. This extended pattern is also commonly used for improvisation. Note the arrows indicating ascending or descending slides.

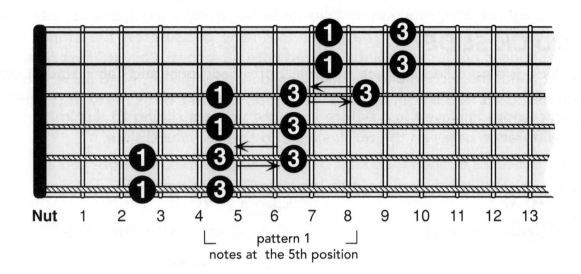

Use the ascending slide on the way up the pattern and use the descending slide on the way down the pattern, as illustrated in the example below.

95.2

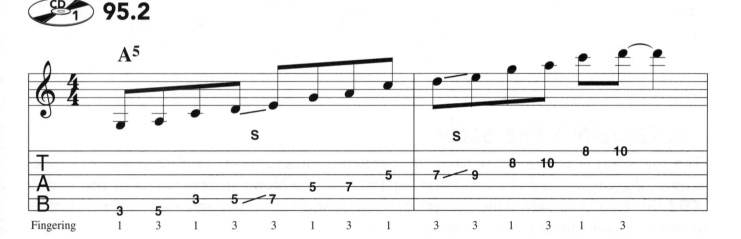

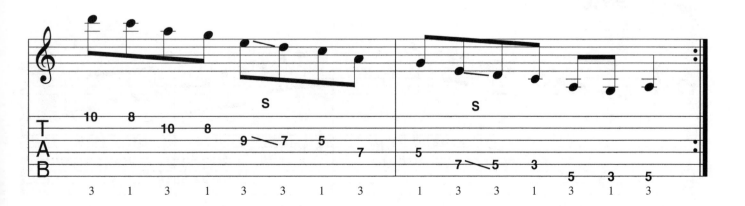

Practice playing pattern 1 extension in different positions on the fretboard and use it to improvise against progressions on the CD. Even though the above example commences on the 3rd fret, the pattern one **starting note** (for determining what position to improvise against a progression) is still the note on the 5th fret of the 6th string, so the pattern is still centred around the 5th position.

THE QUICK SLIDE

A quick slide is also called a **grace note**. In both traditional and Tab notation the quick slide is indicated by a diagonal line leading up to the note, without any fret number before it. The grace note is played just before the note you are sliding to. Listen to the CD to hear the difference between the quick slide and the full valued slide.

96.0

Quick slide (grace note slide).

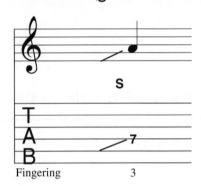

96.1

Full valued slide ("in time" slide).

LICKS USING THE SLIDE

The following licks use notes from the pattern 1 extension at the fifth position. Any of these licks can be used to improvise against the **jam-along progressions** at the end of **CD2**. Be careful to select the correct pattern 1 (and hence pattern 1 extension) starting position to suit the key of each progression.

97.0

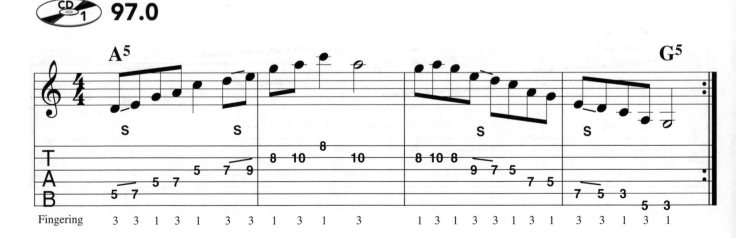

 **97.1**

Once you are familiar with the notes of pattern 1 and pattern 1 extension, it is possible to slide up or down to any note in the pattern. This example demonstrates long slides on the 2nd and 3rd strings. Experiment with other long slides using any notes from these patterns.

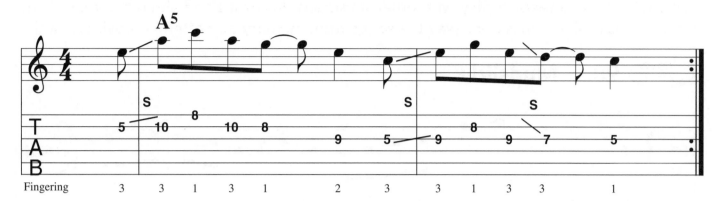

 **97.2**

This lick features the use of quick slides along with triplet rhythms.

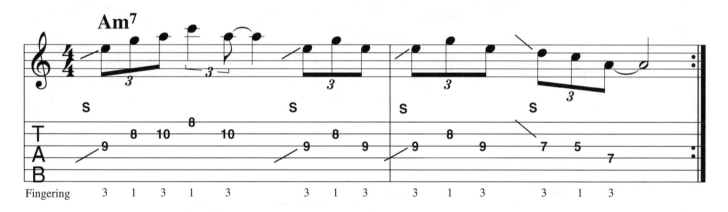

 **97.3**

Here is a lead guitar solo using hammer-ons, pull-offs and slides. All of the slides in this solo are between notes from pattern 1 and pattern 1 extension. However, when sliding to a note it is possible to slide from any fret. The notes in this solo all come from the pentatonic scale, using pattern 1 and pattern 1 extension. Try to memorise the solo and then make up your own licks and solos based on the ideas you find in it. Playing music from memory is important if you intend to play with other musicians. In most band situations there is no written music; all the musicians play the songs from memory and often improvise as well.

98. Mudslide

LESSON THIRTY SIX

BENDING NOTES

The use of bent notes is one of the great sounds of lead guitar playing. Bending between notes originally came from the Blues, where players were imitating the sound of a human voice. The technique is now used in almost every style of guitar playing. A bend is achieved by "pushing" a string with the left hand fingers across the fretboard towards the adjacent strings. This causes the note to rise in pitch. Notes are most commonly bent one tone (2 frets in pitch) or one semitone (1 fret). The examples below use the third finger to bend the notes. You will find bending easier if the second finger also helps "push up" (bend) the string. The bend is indicated in tablature by a **curved arrow** (see **ex. 1** of **CD2** below) and the letter "**B**" above it. In music notation a slur is used to connect the bent notes, so you will need to refer to the letter **B** above the tab.

In the following example, the **C** note on the 5th fret of the 3rd string is bent up a tone to a note equivalent to the **D** note on the **7th fret**. Experience and practice will help you bend to the correct pitch. If you use reasonably light gauge strings on your guitar, bending will be easier.

 1.0   **CD 2 Starts Here**

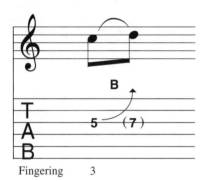

Play note on 5th fret, 3rd string.

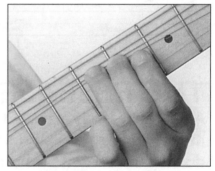

Third finger bends string upwards with help of the second finger.

The common notes to bend within pattern 1 extension are shown in the following example. The example given uses notes from pattern 1 at the 5th position and the diagram also highlights which direction to bend each note. When improvising, you should bend from and to a note in the pattern.

 **1.1**   **(CD2)**

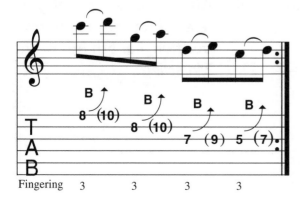

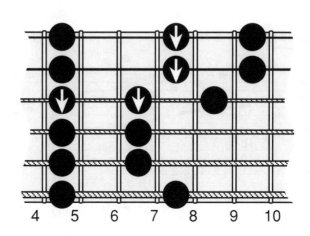

LICKS USING BENDS

CD 2 **1.2**

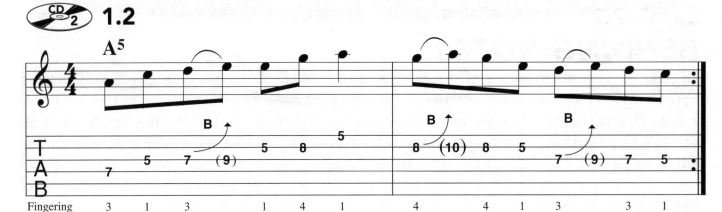

CD 2 **1.3** This lick uses a technique of **barring and rolling** the first finger across the fret. Practice this slowly until you can do it easily.

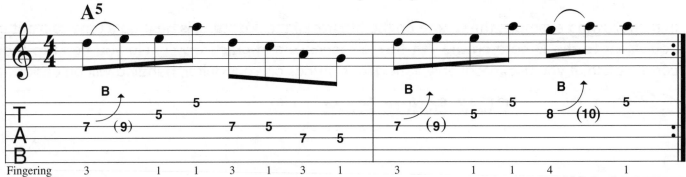

THE RELEASE BEND

A release bend is achieved by bending the string **before** picking the note, then releasing the string back to its original pitch. The letter "**R**" is placed above the tab along with a **downward curved arrow** to indicate a release bend.

CD 2 **2.0**

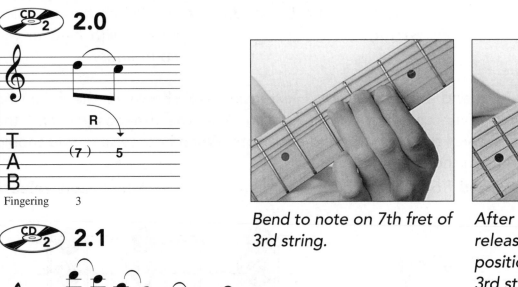

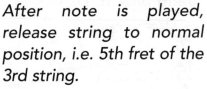

Bend to note on 7th fret of 3rd string.

After note is played, release string to normal position, i.e. 5th fret of the 3rd string.

CD 2 **2.1**

LICKS USING RELEASE BENDS

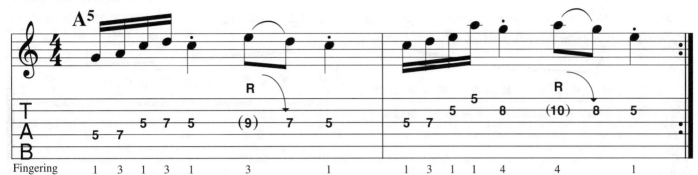

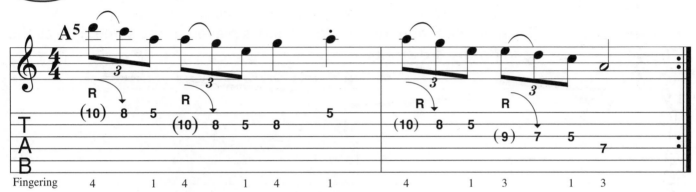

THE QUICK BEND

As with hammer-ons, pull-offs and slides, the bend can also be played as a grace note.

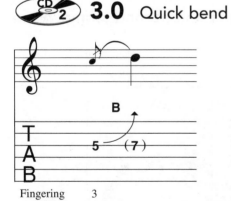

This lick uses a **quick bend** from **D** to **E** on the third string, followed by a **slow release bend** back to **D**.

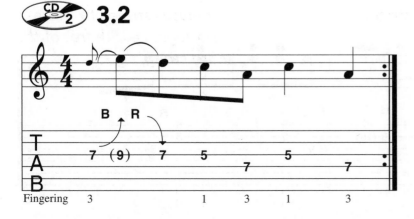

 **4.0**

In this example the bend is held while the second note is played. The example alternates between a bent **E** note on the third string and an **E** note on the second string 5th fret. Both notes are the **same pitch**. The process is then repeated on the second and first strings between two **A** notes of the same pitch.

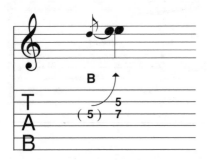 **4.1** This time the E note on the 2nd string is played at the same time as the bend on the 3rd string.

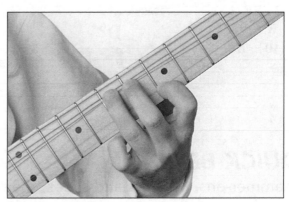

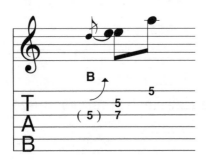 **4.2** In this example the first finger bars the first and second strings while the bend is played.

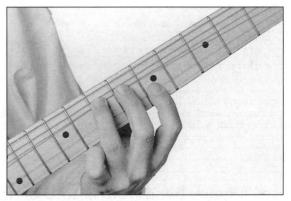

4.3 This lick shows some of the typical sounds created by the use of these techniques.

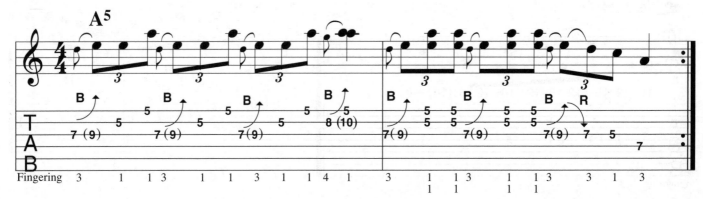

Here is a new lead guitar solo **"Bending the Blues"**, which uses lots of note bending. It also contains hammer-ons, pull-offs and slides, and involves the technique of barring the strings with the first finger. Once again, all the notes come from pattern 1 and pattern 1 extension. The timing of this solo is based on the shuffle rhythm and it contains both eighth note triplets and quarter note triplets.

5. Bending the Blues

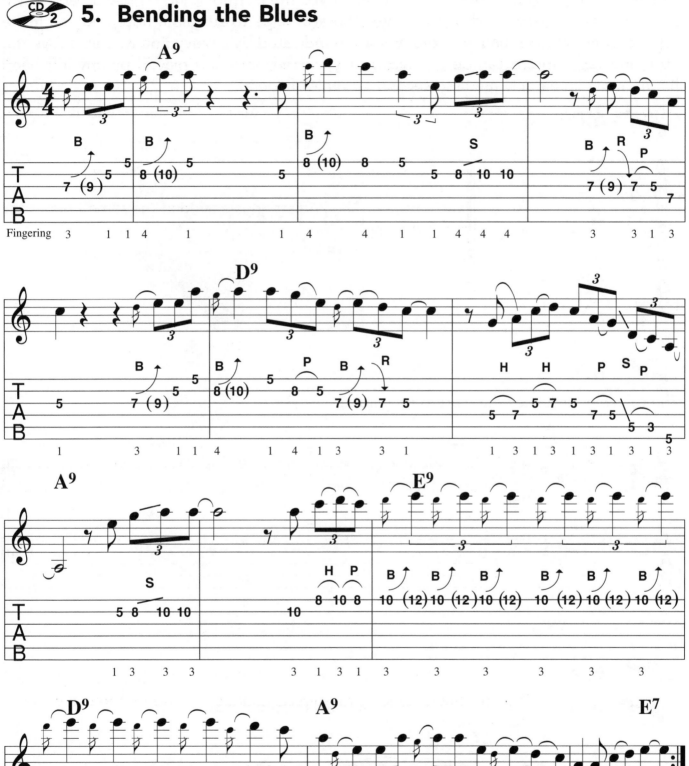

LESSON THIRTY SEVEN

VIBRATO

Vibrato is a technique where the left hand moves the fretted string rapidly up and down small distances towards adjacent strings. Vibrato helps to sustain a note and can make that note more interesting in a solo. Vibrato is indicated by a **wavy line** written above the note and tab. Vibrato can be applied to any fretted note and played by any left hand finger (most commonly the first, second and third fingers).

 **6.0**

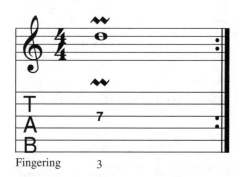

Fingering 3

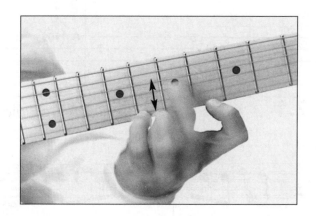

 **6.1**

The following lick uses the vibrato technique.

 **6.2**

This example uses vibrato on bent and standard fretted notes.

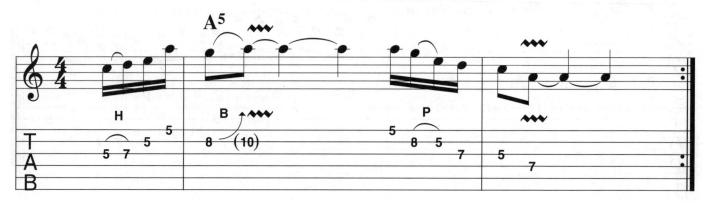

PICK TREMOLO

A **pick tremolo** is played with the pick held in the right hand and involves a rapid playing of a note with continuous alternating down and up strokes of the pick, played as fast as possible. The pick tremolo is indicated by diagonal lines, as shown in the example below. Hold the pick close to the tip and make the rapid movements from the wrist rather than the arm.

7.0

7.1 This lick uses the pick tremolo technique along with hammer-ons.

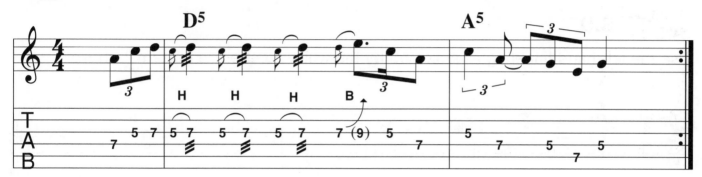

7.2 This one uses pick tremolo on a slowly bent note. Notice also the use of vibrato in this lick.

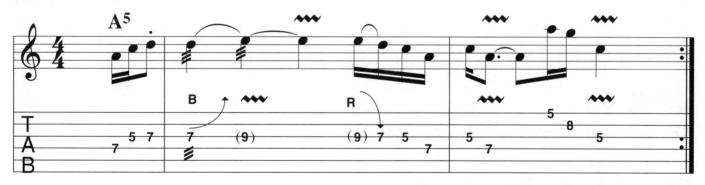

7.3 Here the pick tremolo is used on several consecutive notes.

DOUBLE NOTES

Another technique used by lead guitarists is to play **two notes at a time** (double stops, or double notes). This was commonly used in 1950's Rock 'n' Roll (e.g. Chuck Berry) and is still used today. The most common notes used in pattern 1 are shown in the fretboard diagrams below. Each pair of notes to be played together are surrounded by a box.

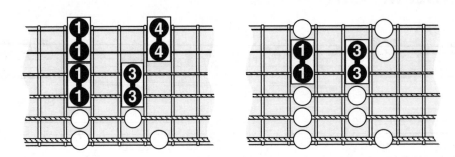

These 6 pairs of double notes are written below in example 65.0 (CD2). They are often used for improvising against a Blues progression.

 **8.0**

Use the left hand fingering as indicated by the white numbers in pattern 1 above.

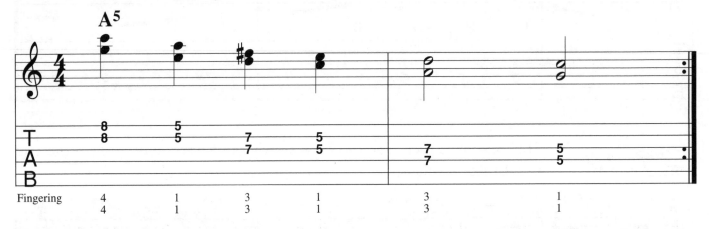

 **8.1**

The following lick also uses double notes.

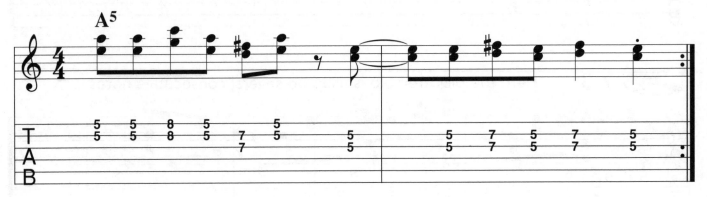

This lead guitar solo uses ideas from the playing of Chuck Berry, Johnny Winter and Jimi Hendrix. It contains all the techniques you have learnt. There are a few notes in the solo which are not in pattern 1. These extra notes come from chords $\underline{I}$, $\underline{IV}$ and $\underline{V}$ in the key of **A**. There are many slides in this solo. As mentioned earlier, it is possible to slide from any fret as long as you end the slide on the correct note.

9. Rockin' Out

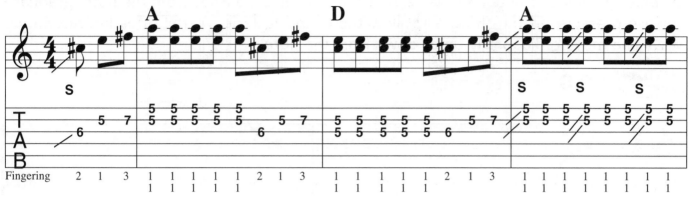

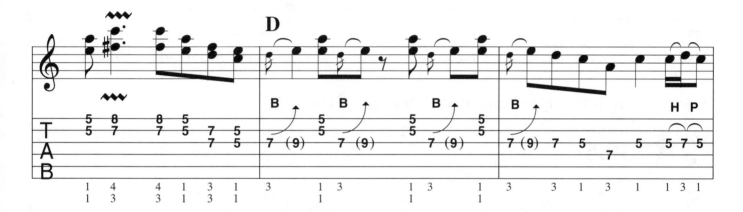

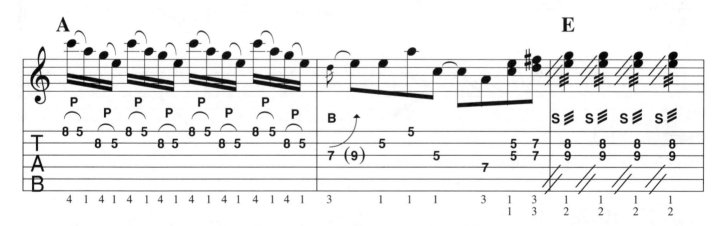

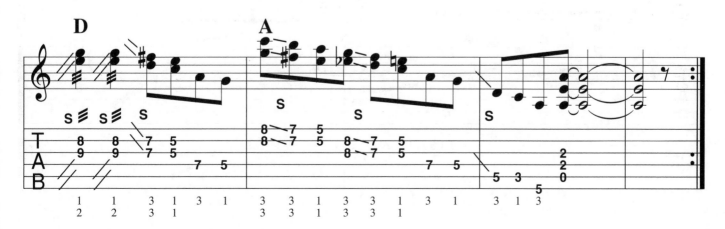

LESSON THIRTY EIGHT

THE TRAIL OFF

The **trail off** is actually another type of slide where instead of sliding **to** a note, you start by playing a specific note and then slide **off** it. As you slide away from the note, gradually release pressure off the string and allow the sound to fade. A trail off is indicated by a wavy line moving diagonally up or down from the note.

CD 2 10.0

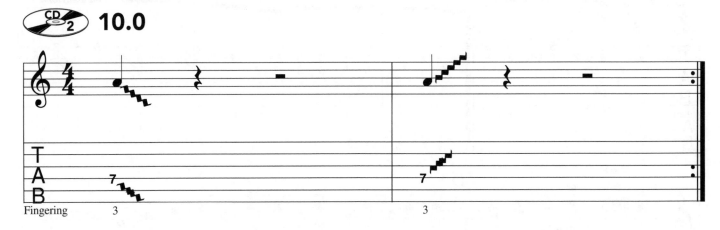

Here are two licks which demonstrate the use of trail offs.

CD 2 10.1

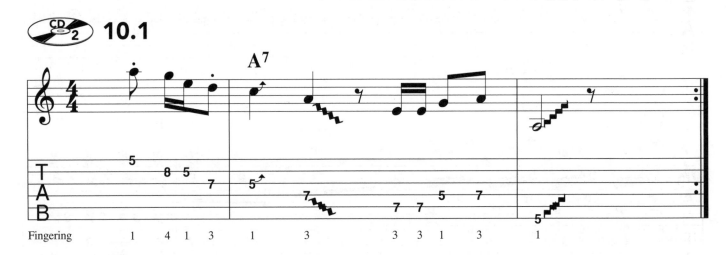

CD 2 10.2

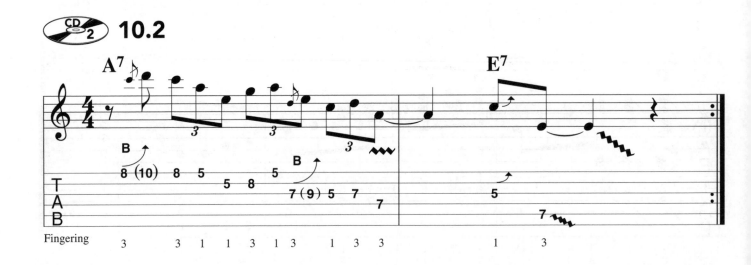

THE TRILL

A **trill** is a rapid succession of hammer-ons and pull-offs, with only the first note being picked. The trill is indicated by the symbol **Tr** above or below the two notes concerned, with the first note being shown as a grace note. Listen to the following example on the CD to hear the effect of the trill.

11.0

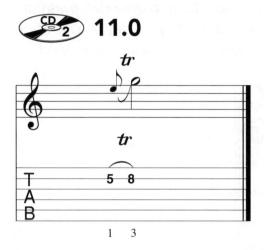

11.1

Here is a lick which makes use of the trill. Experiment with adding trills to some of your own licks.

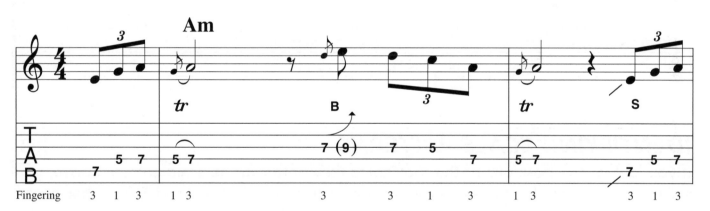

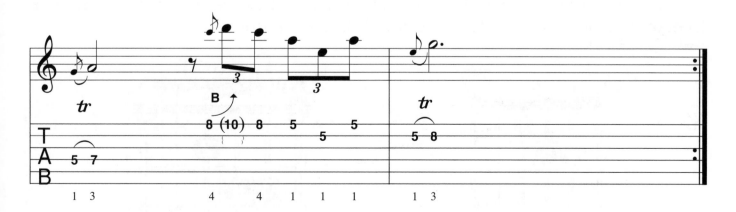

LESSON THIRTY NINE

MOVING TO DIFFERENT KEYS

Just like bar chords, the minor pentatonic scale pattern you learnt in Lesson 30 can be moved up or down the fretboard, enabling you to play in any key. E.g. in the third position (3rd fret) you get a **G** minor pentatonic scale, in the sixth position you get a **B♭** minor pentatonic scale, etc. Here is the fingering pattern for the **C** minor pentatonic scale, which is in the eighth position.

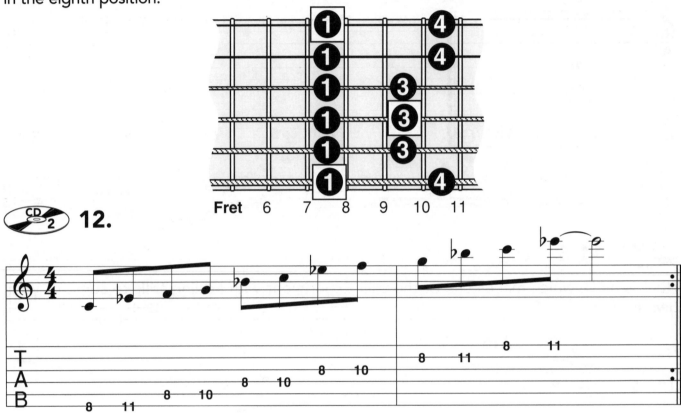

12.

IDENTIFYING SCALE PATTERNS

If you look at the positions of the root notes (key notes) in the scale pattern above, you will notice that they form a triangular pattern. In the basic **E chord** and **E form bar chord** (root 6) below, you can see that the root notes are in the same positions as they are in the scale pattern. Because of this the scale pattern shown above can be described as the **E form** of the scale. This is the form you already know as **pattern 1**.

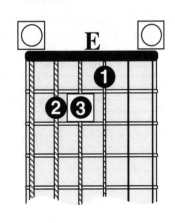

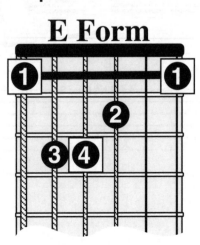

E Form

Here are some licks which use the minor pentatonic scale in different keys. The first one uses the **C** minor pentatonic as shown on the previous page.

13.0

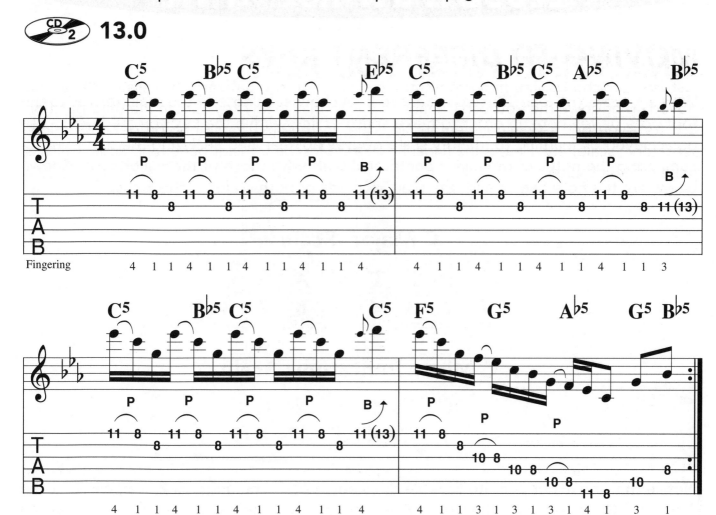

13.1

This one uses the **E** minor pentatonic in the **12th position**.

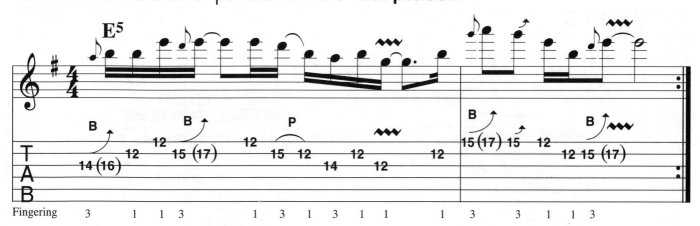

LESSON FORTY

ANALYZING WHAT YOU PLAY

With any scale you learn, it is important to know how each note of the scale relates to the root note or key note, in order to make sense of licks within the key you are in. This can be achieved by learning to identify **scale degrees** by ear, and analyzing them. It is worth comparing the notes of the minor pentatonic scale with those of the major scale. Shown below are the note names and the scale degrees of both scales in the key of **C**.

C Major Scale

C D E F G A B C
1 2 3 4 5 6 7 8 (1)

C Minor Pentatonic Scale

C E♭ F G B♭ C
1 ♭3 4 5 ♭7 8 (1)

Notice that the minor pentatonic scale does not contain the degrees **2** or **6**, and that the **3rd** and **7th** degrees are **flattened**. Play through the C minor pentatonic scale several times, naming the scale degrees as you play each one. When you can do this from memory, transpose it to other keys by moving it up or down the fretboard. Notice that the scale degrees remain the same regardless of what key you are playing in.

Here is a lick created from the **C minor pentatonic scale**. The scale degrees are written above the notes. This is a useful way of analyzing a lick to see what notes were used to create it.

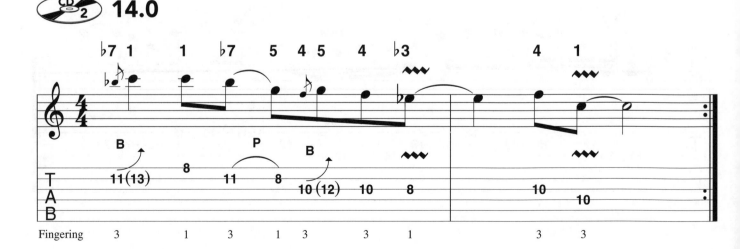

It is a good idea to analyze many licks using a particular scale. This will help you become thoroughly familiar with the sounds available from that scale so you can re-create those sounds at will. Let's look at the example from the previous page. It begins with the ♭7 degree being bent up to the root note (**1**). The root note is then played again, followed by the ♭7. A pull-off is then used to get to the **5th** degree, which is then followed by the **4th** degree being bent up to the **5th** degree. This is followed by the **4th** and ♭**3rd** degrees, and in the last bar the **4th** degree is followed by the root (**1**) an octave lower than at the beginning of the lick.

Analyzing licks in this manner may seem dull at first, but the more you know about exactly what you are playing, the more control you have over what you play, and the more you can interact with other musicians. Stick with it, in time you will instantly know what you or anyone else is playing as soon as you hear it. In fact, to be a good player it is important to be able to hear in your head what you want to play and then produce that sound with your hands. A good way to practice this is to sing a lick and then play what you sang. Below is another example derived from the minor pentatonic scale, this time in the key of **G**. Learn to play it and then analyze it using the method shown above.

 **14.1**

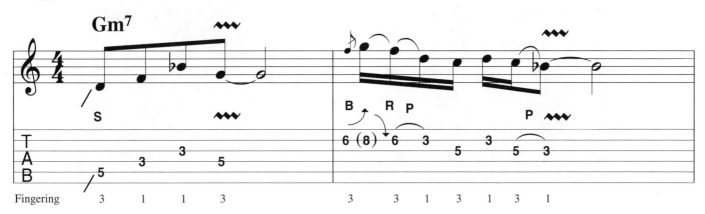

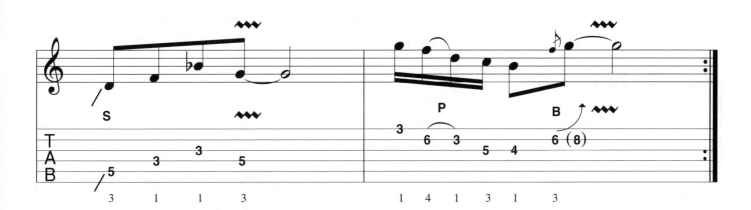

LESSON FORTY ONE

FIVE FORMS OF THE PENTATONIC SCALE

Altogether there are five forms of the minor pentatonic scale. When linked together they cover the whole fretboard. Each form is named by the chord shape it most closely resembles. You have already learned the E form (pattern 1) of the scale. The other four forms are shown in the following pages in the key of **C**, along with the matching chord shape for each one. Practice each form until you know it from memory and then analyze them all in terms of where the scale degrees fall within each fingering. It is especially important to memorize the positions of the **root notes** in each form.

D FORM (PATTERN 2)

In the **D form** of the scale (and D chord form) there is one root note on the 4th string and another one three frets higher on the 2nd string.

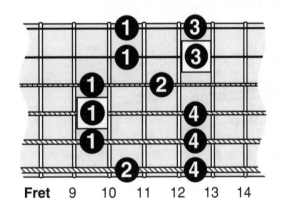

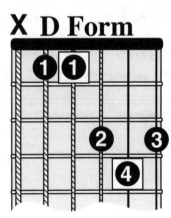

Here is a lick which makes use of the **D form** of the **C minor pentatonic** scale. Analyze it as shown in the previous lesson and try making up some of your own licks using the D form.

 **15.0**

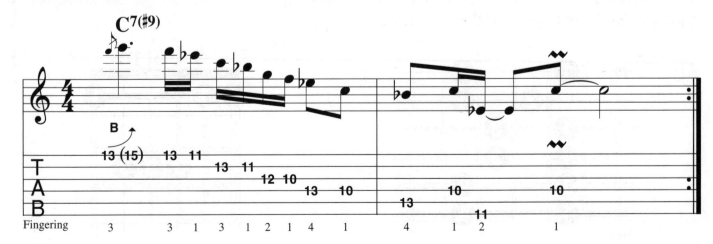

C FORM (PATTERN 3)

In the **C form** of the scale (and C chord form) there is one root note on the 5th string and another two frets lower on the 2nd string.

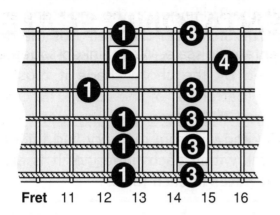

Fret 11 12 13 14 15 16

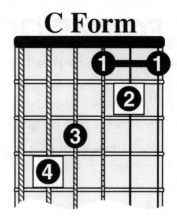

C Form

 **15.1**

This lick is played within the **C form** of the C minor pentatonic scale. As before, analyze it and then try making up some of your own licks from the C form.

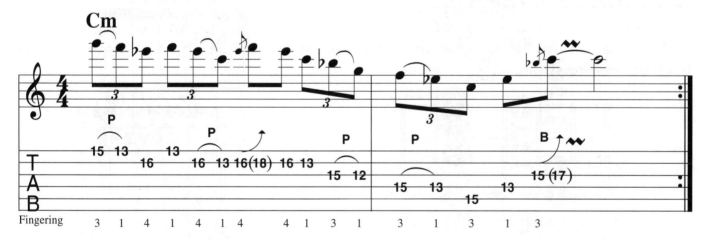

A FORM (PATTERN 4)

In the **A form** of the scale (and A chord form) there is one root note on the 5th string and another two frets higher on the 3rd string.

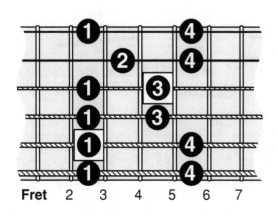

Fret 2 3 4 5 6 7

A Form

 **15.2**

This lick is played within the **A form** of the C minor pentatonic scale, at the 3rd fret. It is also possible to play it up an octave at the 15th fret. Take care with the bends in this lick, especially the second one. The bend is done with the 3rd finger on the 2nd string and then the 4th finger plays the note on the 1st string. The 3rd finger then releases the bend on the 2nd string. Practice this technique separately from the rest of the lick if you need to.

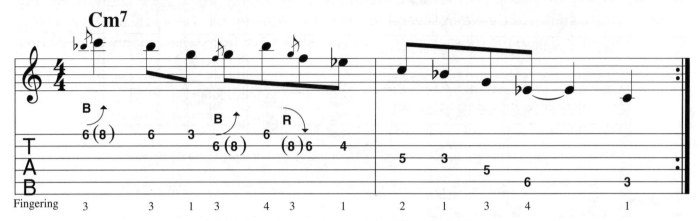

G FORM (PATTERN 5)

In the **G form** of the scale (and G chord form) there is one root note on the 6th string and another on the 1st string at the same fret. In the middle, there is one three frets back on the 3rd string.

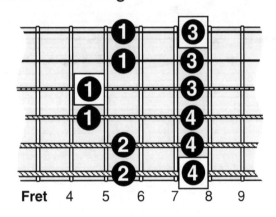

 **15.3**

This lick is played within the **G form** of the C minor pentatonic scale, at the 5th fret. It is also possible to play it up an octave at the 17th fret.

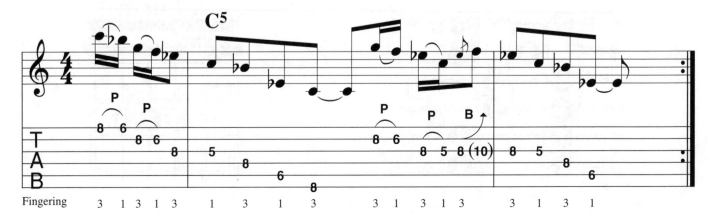

LESSON FORTY TWO

MOVING BETWEEN FORMS

When playing licks or solos, it is common to move between the various forms (patterns) of a scale by sliding from one to the next. Below is a commonly used scale pattern (**sliding pattern 1**) which moves between several forms of the A minor pentatonic scale. The arrows on the diagram indicate the most common notes to slide to or from when changing positions.

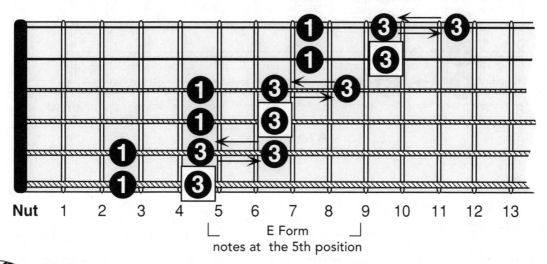

16.0

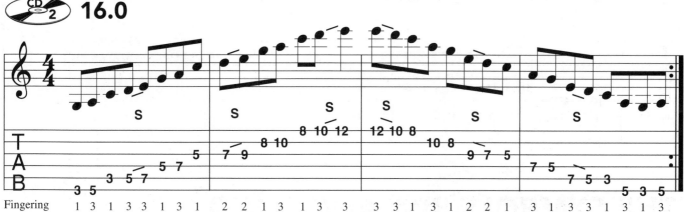

16.1

Here is a lick which makes use of this sliding scale pattern. Once you have the scale memorized, try creating your own licks from it.

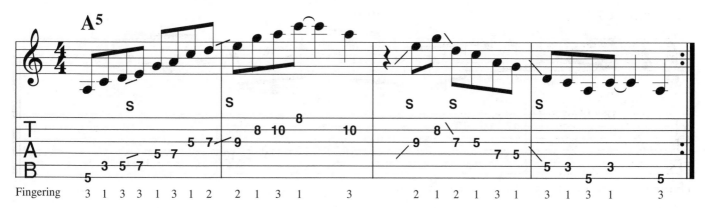

SLIDING PATTERN 2

The diagram below shows another sliding pentatonic scale pattern which is useful for moving between the C, A and G forms of the scale. As with the previous pattern, learn it from memory and then experiment with it to create your own licks.

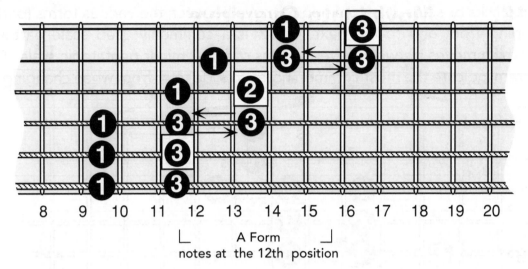

A Form
notes at the 12th position

17.0

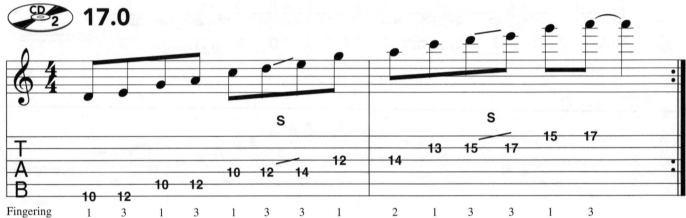

THE SYMBOLS 8VA AND LOCO

The following solo has the symbol **8va** above the music. This means it is played an octave higher than written. This symbol is often used for very high notes, as it makes them easier to read. When the notation returns to its normal pitch, the word **loco** is written above the music.

17.1

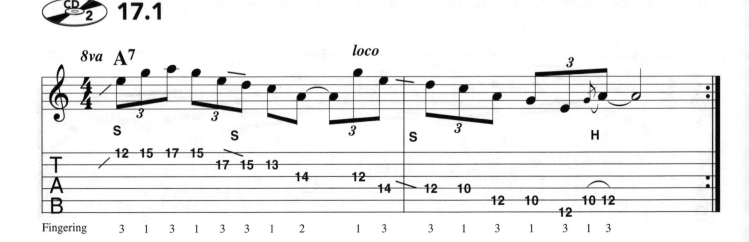

Here is a solo in the key of **B minor** which moves freely between the different forms of the minor pentatonic scale. You can slide or bend from any note of the scale to any other note of the scale to get from one form to the next. As well as this, you can use a rest to move to a totally different place on the fretboard if you wish to. Learn this solo and then experiment with moving around between the forms as you improvise.

18. Movin' Into Overdrive

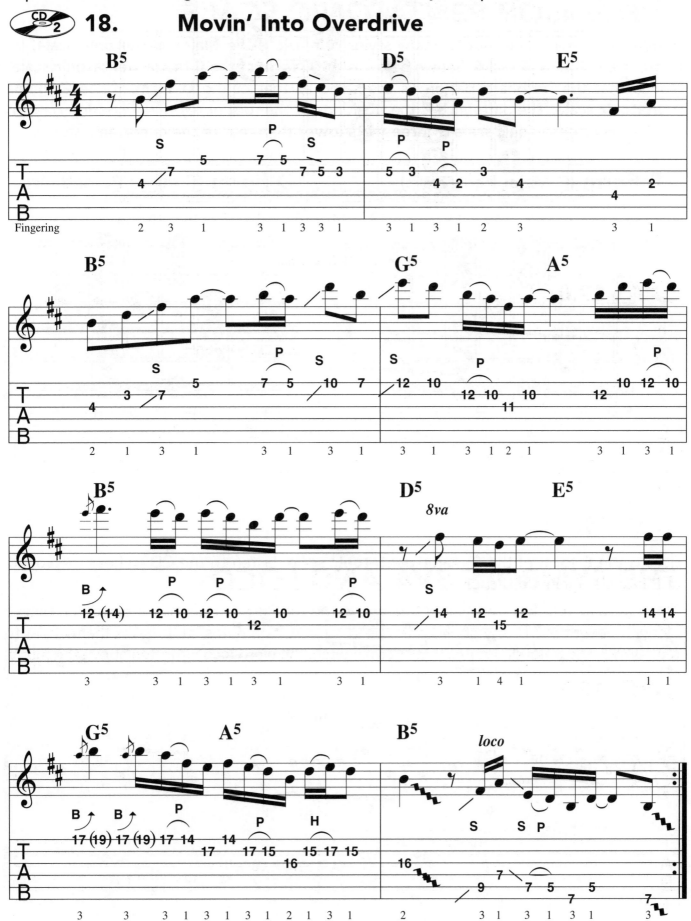

LESSON FORTY THREE

THE MAJOR PENTATONIC SCALE

Another common scale used in many styles of music is the **Major pentatonic scale**. Its degrees are **1**, **2**, **3**, **5** and **6**. Shown below is the **E form** of the **C major pentatonic** scale. Notice that the fretboard pattern is the same as that of the **D form** of the **C minor pentatonic** scale. The difference is the positions of the root notes. The fingering pattern for the major pentatonic scale is **three frets lower** than that of the minor pentatonic.

E Form (C Major Pentatonic)

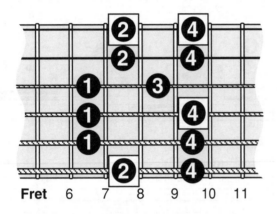

D Form (C Minor Pentatonic)

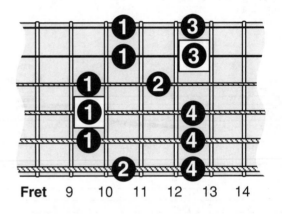

19.

Here is the **E form** of the **C major pentatonic** scale. Listen to the CD to hear the sound of this scale against a **C** chord.

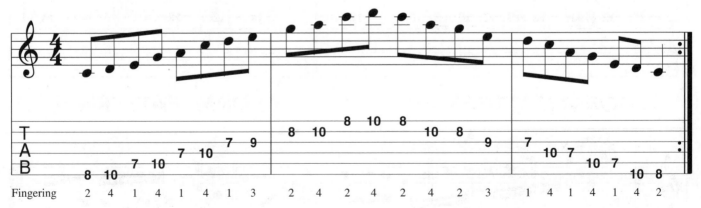

  **20.**

Here is a lick which is derived from the E form of the C major pentatonic scale. The fingering used here is different from the scale itself. Once you have learned a scale pattern it is often necessary to change the fingering depending on the type of lick you are playing. Experiment with fingerings for any lick you know until you find the one which suits you best.

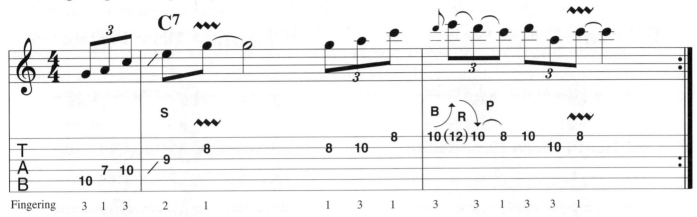

Shown below are the other four forms of the C major pentatonic scale. Because these patterns closely resemble those of the minor pentatonic scale, it is important to memorize the scale degrees and particularly the positions of the root notes.

D FORM (PATTERN 2)

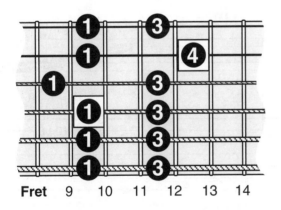

C FORM (PATTERN 3)

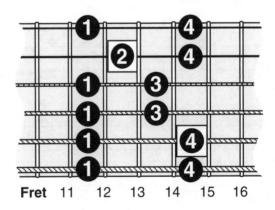

A FORM (PATTERN 4)

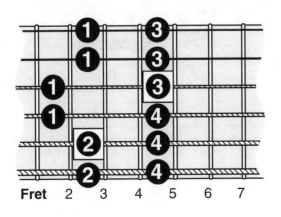

G FORM (PATTERN 5)

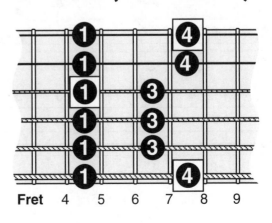

RELATIVE MAJOR AND MINOR PENTATONICS

Because there are relative major and minor keys for every key signature, it is possible to use the same pentatonic scale in a major key and it's relative minor. If you look at the diagrams below, you will see that the G form of the C major pentatonic scale is identical to the E form of the A minor pentatonic. The fingering remains exactly the same, only the positions of the root notes change. This applies to all the fingering patterns. Experiment!

G Form (C Major Pentatonic)

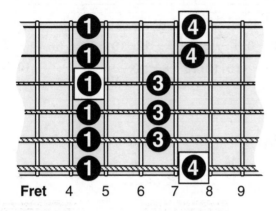

E Form (A Minor Pentatonic)

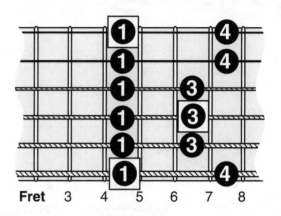

The following example demonstrates the use of the C major/A minor pentatonic scale played against the chords of **C** and **Am**. Because these are relative keys, the scale sounds good over both chords.

 **21.**

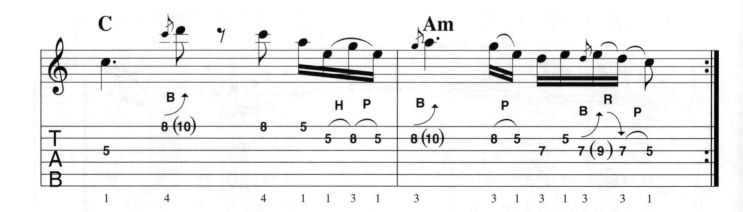

22. No Time to Cry

The following lead guitar solo moves between all of the five patterns. Notice how the notes work equally well against all of the chords. This is because both the chords and scales belong to the keys of both **C major** and **A minor** which are relative keys.

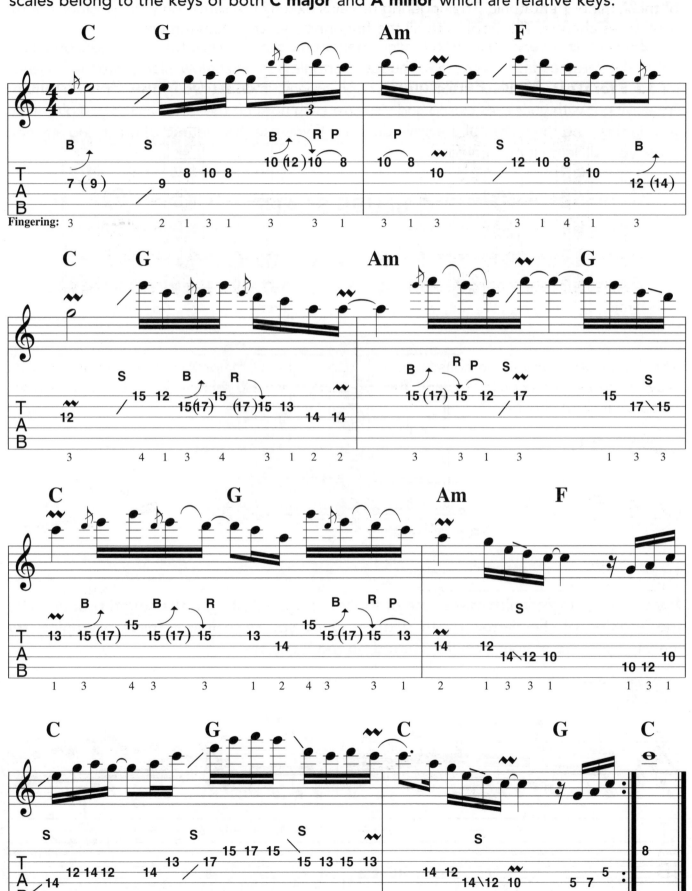

LESSON FORTY FOUR

THE BLUES SCALE

The **Blues scale** is very similar to the minor pentatonic scale, except that it contains one extra note – the flattened fifth degree (♭**5**). The scale formula is shown below, along with the fingering for the **E form** of the **C Blues scale**. Play through it many times until you have it in your memory. Try playing it with your eyes closed and visualize each note on the fretboard as you play it. As you do this, sing the names of the scale degrees. If you use this method of practicing any new scale, you will learn it much quicker.

C BLUES SCALE

C E♭ F G♭ G B♭ C
1 ♭3 4 ♭5 5 ♭7 8 (1)

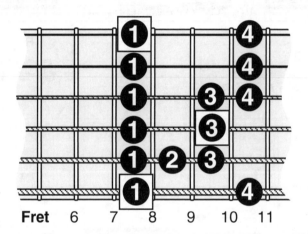

Here is an example which makes use of the Blues scale. Listen to the sound produced by the addition of the flattened 5th degree. Once you have learnt these examples, try making up some of your own licks based on the Blues scale.

 **23.**

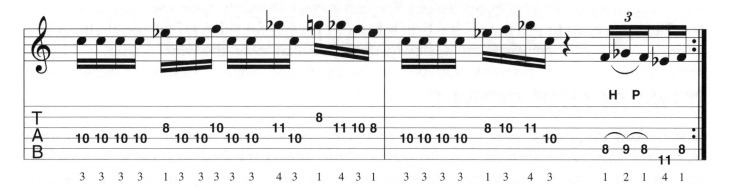

FIVE FORMS OF THE BLUES SCALE

Like the minor pentatonic scale, there are five different forms of the Blues scale which cover the whole fretboard. In fact, this principle of five fingering patterns applies to **all** scales. The diagrams below demonstrate the fingering patterns for the **D form**, **C form**, **A form** and **G form**. Memorize the fingerings and then transpose them to other keys by moving them up or down the fretboard. Remember that there is only one note added to the minor pentatonic, so you already know the forms, you just need to add the ♭5 degree.

D FORM (PATTERN 2)

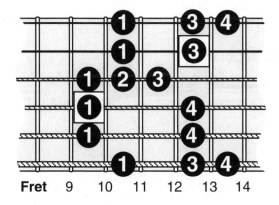

C FORM (PATTERN 3)

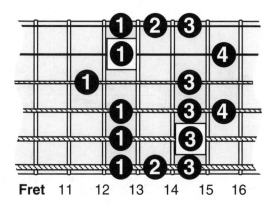

A FORM (PATTERN 4)

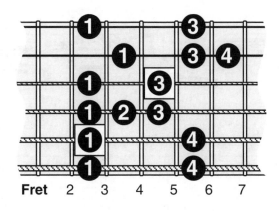

G FORM (PATTERN 5)

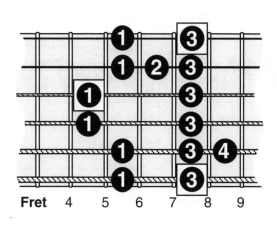

Here is a funky Blues solo in the key of **E** which moves through various different forms of the Blues scale. Listen to the CD several times to become familiar with all the rhythms and expressions and then work on it slowly until you can play the whole solo with your metronome or drum machine. Once you are confident with it, gradually increase the tempo until you can play it along with the CD.

Just before the high **E** note at the end of bar 8, you will notice the word *Rake* written above the tab. This indicates that the pick is raked across the 2nd and 3rd strings before striking the E note on the 1st string. This technique is common in Blues and is also frequently used by Rock players like Jeff Beck and Mark Knopfler. For an in-depth study of Blues playing, see *Progressive Complete Learn to Play Blues Guitar Manual*.

24. Talkin' Trash

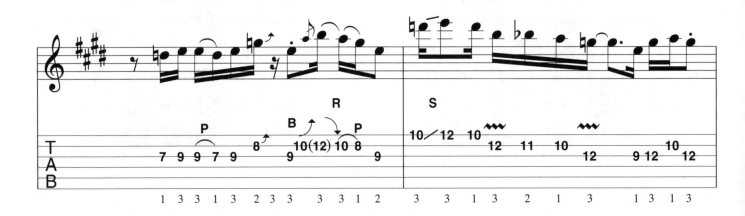

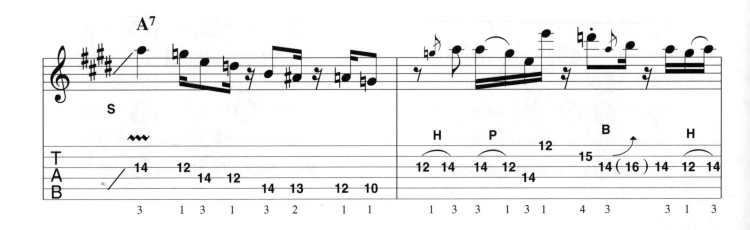

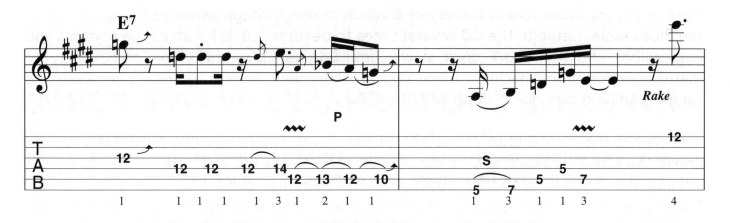

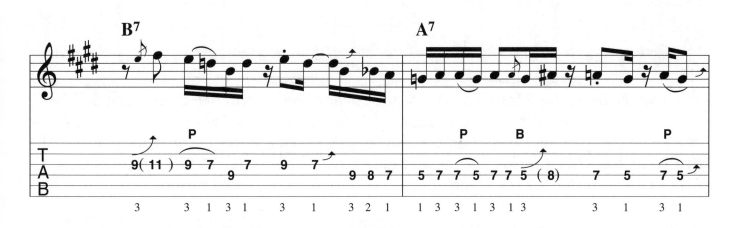

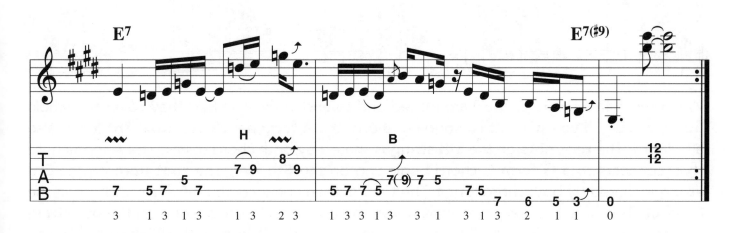

LESSON FORTY FIVE

MOVEABLE CHORD SHAPES IN FIVE FORMS

To become a good guitar player, it is important to have a system for identifying moveable chord shapes all over the fretboard in any key. Most moveable chord formations are closely related to the **five basic major chord shapes** shown below.

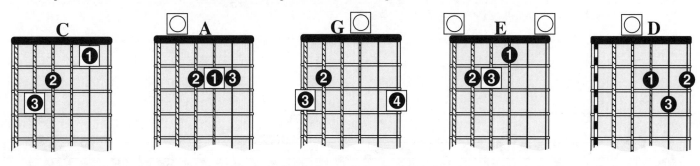

You already know the E form bar chord (root 6) and the A form bar chord (root 5). The C, G and D chords can also be used as the basis for bar chords. There are also many other moveable chord shapes based on these 5 shapes which are useful for Blues playing. The **five basic bar chord forms** are shown below. Notice the order of these forms - **C**, **A**, **G**, **E** and **D**. This order is easy to memorize if you think of the word **caged**.

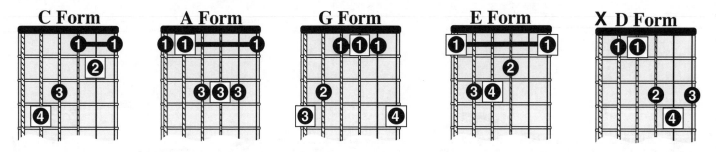

When these five forms (shapes) are placed end to end in the one key, they cover the whole fretboard. E.g. if you start with an **open C chord**, the **A form** bar chord at the **3rd fret** is also a C chord. The **root note** on the **5th string** is shared by both chord forms. The A form chord then connects to a **G form** C chord beginning on the **5th fret**. The **root note** on the **3rd string** is shared by both chord forms. The G form then connects to an **E form** C chord at the **8th fret**. This time there are **two root notes** shared by both forms – one on the **6th string** and one on the **1st string**. The E form then connects to the **D form** at the **10th fret**, this time the shared **root note** is on the **4th string**. To complete the pattern, the D form connects back to the **C form** at the **12th fret**. The shared **root note** between these two forms is on the **2nd string**. This C form is **one octave higher** than the open C form. After this, the whole pattern repeats. The example below demonstrates **all five forms being played as C chords.**

25.

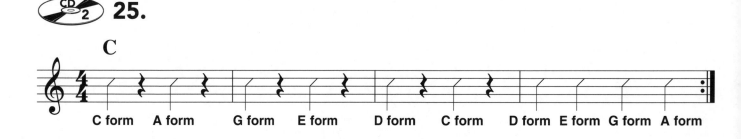

THREE NOTE CHORD VOICINGS

Some of these chord forms are difficult to play, particularly the G form. The most important thing is to be able to **visualize** these shapes, especially the positions of the root notes. Remember that major and minor chords are made up of three different notes. Any more notes in a chord shape are just doublings of those notes. This means it is possible to play just **three notes** from any of these chord forms instead of using the whole shape. Some common examples of **three note voicings** on the top three strings are shown below, along with an example which makes use of them. Once you have learnt them, try transposing them to other keys.

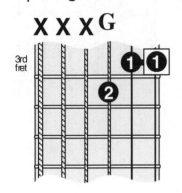
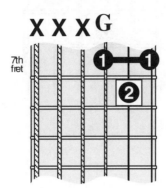
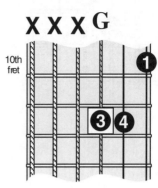

 **26.0**

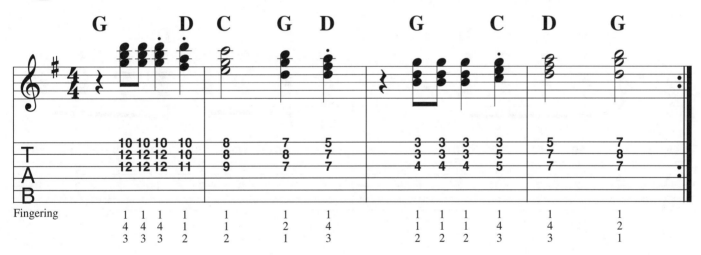

 **26.1**

You should also practice using your chord shapes as arpeggios, as shown here.

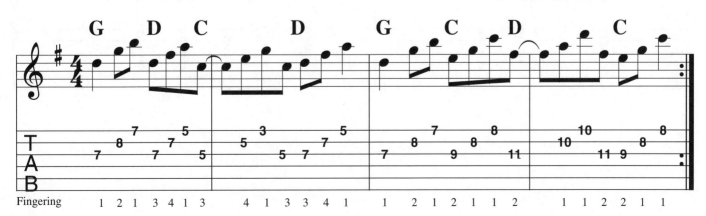

FOUR NOTE CHORD VOICINGS

Here are some useful **four note voicings** of major chords. Memorize the shapes and then transpose them to other keys. This is easy once you know the positions of the root notes.

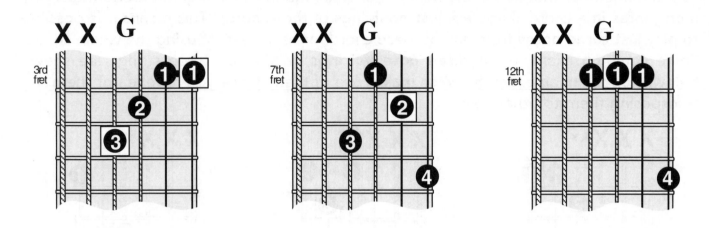

 **27.**

This example makes use of two of the above four note voicings. Experiment with these chords to come up with your own ideas.

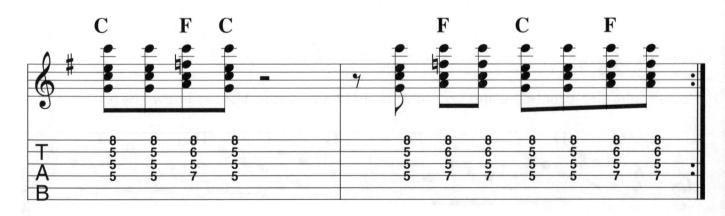

ROOT 4 AND ROOT 3 CHORDS

Just as there are root 6 and root 5 chords, there are also moveable chords which have their root notes on the 4th, 3rd or 2nd strings. Shown below is a D form **root 4** major chord shape, and a progression which uses this shape for all three chords by moving it along the fretboard. This shape is difficult to play at first, so be patient with it.

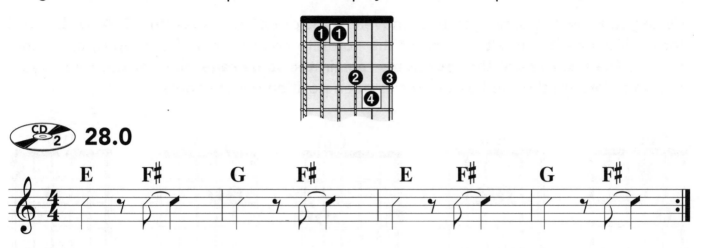

 **28.0**

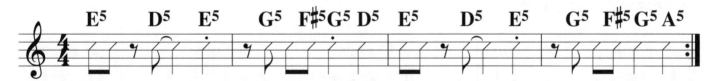

 **28.1**

A power chord can easily be created from the above shape by leaving out the note on the first string. The chord can then be played with two or three notes. Here is an example.

The most common **root 3** chord is a 3 note chord played with either the first finger or the 3rd finger and covering the 2nd, 3rd and 4th strings. Practice alternating between the first and third finger bar as demonstrated in this example.

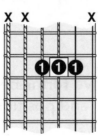

 **29.**

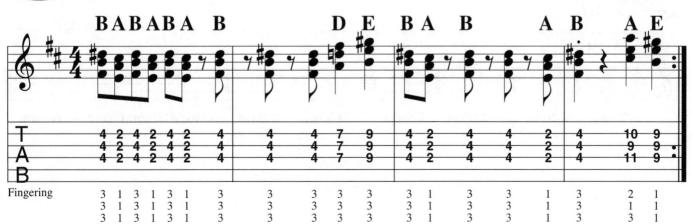

LESSON FORTY SIX

MOVEABLE MINOR CHORD SHAPES

Once you know the basic system of moveable major chord shapes (the **C**, **A**, **G**, **E** and **D** forms) it is possible to alter some of the notes to create other chord types, e.g. minor chords. **The positions of the root notes remain the same regardless of the chord type.** Shown below are the five basic forms as open position minor chords.

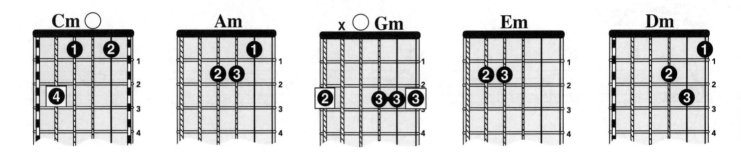

Like major chords, these minor forms can be joined end to end in the same order (CAGED) to cover the whole fretboard. The diagrams below show the five basic forms of moveable minor chords.

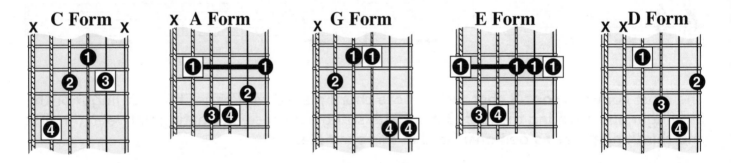

The example below demonstrates **all five forms** being played as **C minor chords**. Practice them slowly and memorize the shapes and positions of the root notes. When you can do this easily, transpose them to other keys.

CD 2 **30.**

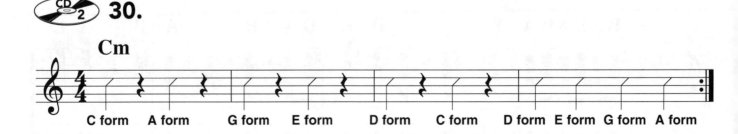

The following example uses an **F minor** chord shape which requires the use of a **half bar** across three strings. The term "half bar" means the first finger is barring some strings, but not all six. Practice playing it both as a full chord and an arpeggio until you can sound all the notes clearly and then play the whole example.

THREE AND FOUR NOTE MINOR CHORD VOICINGS

Shown below are some useful three and four note voicings for minor chords and some examples using them along with the major chord shapes you learnt in the previous lesson. The shapes are all shown as G minor chords, but once you know them from memory, transpose them to all other possible root notes. Try taking each one around the key cycle.

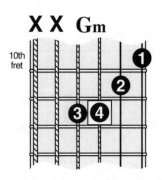
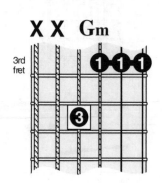
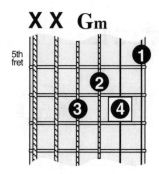

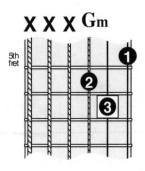
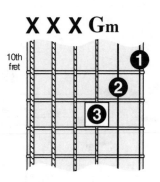

 **32.**

This example uses the four note voicings shown at the top of the page.

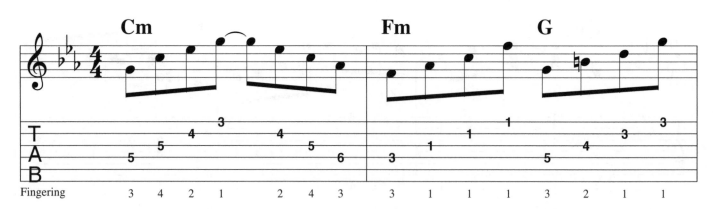

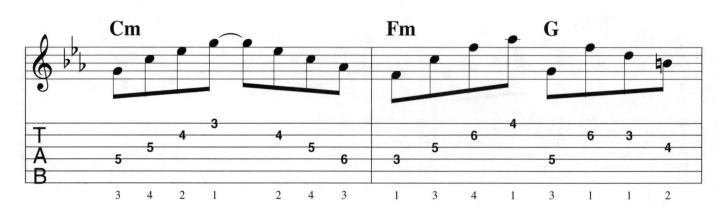

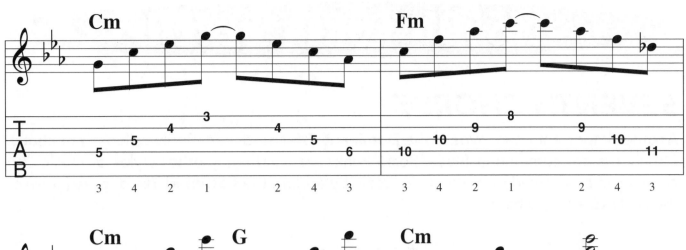

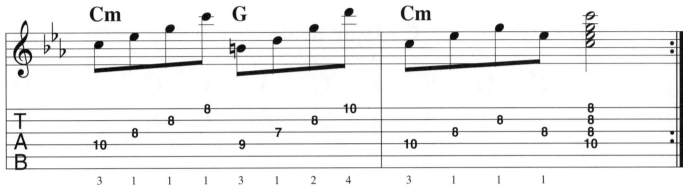

 **33.**

This one moves frequently between minor and major chords.

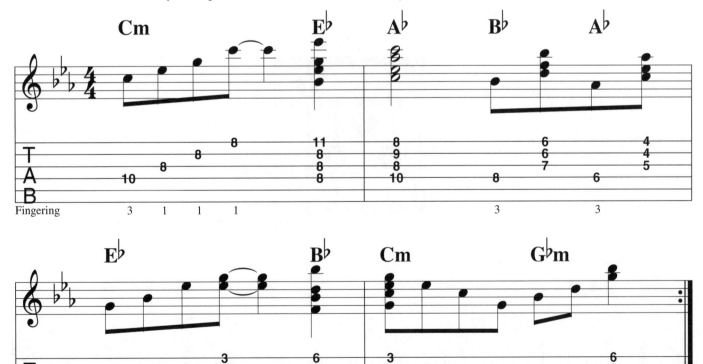

LESSON FORTY SEVEN

SEVENTH CHORDS

Another important chord type is the **Dominant 7th** chord, commonly called a **7th chord**. 7th chords are common in Blues, Rock, Funk, Jazz and many other styles of music. 7th chords can be derived from the major scale by adding the **flattened 7th** degree (note) of the scale to a major chord.

C Major Scale

C	D	E	F	G	A	B	C
1	2	3	4	5	6	7	8

C Chord

C	E	G
1	3	5

C7 Chord

C	E	G	B♭
1	3	5	♭7

Here is a common fingering for a **C7** chord. Practice changing between **F, B♭** and **C7** as shown in the following example.

Like major chords, most moveable 7th chord shapes also follow the **five basic open chord forms**, i.e. **C7**, **A7**, **G7**, **E7** and **D7**. Here are the most common shapes for these chords.

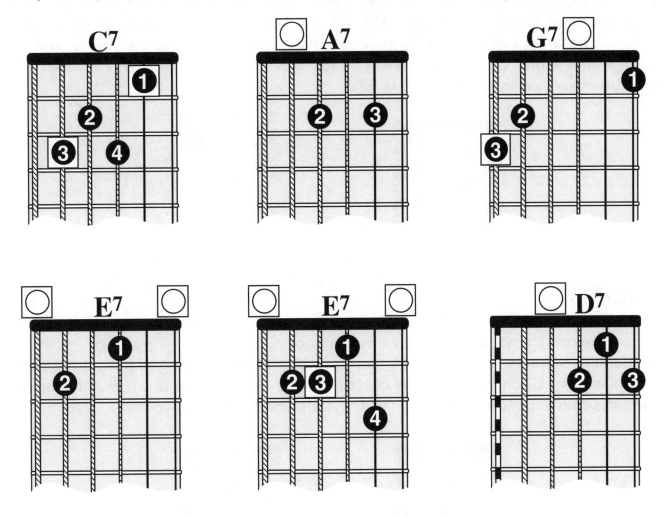

Notice that there are two shapes here for the **E7** chord. It is also possible to find alternative fingerings for the other chords. Once you know which notes make up a particular chord, it is possible to arrange these notes in any order as long as the fingering is practical. The following example should help you become familiar with these basic 7th chord shapes.

34.1

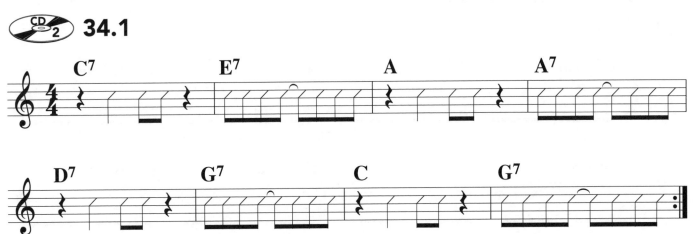

MOVEABLE 7TH CHORD FORMS

Most moveable 7th chord shapes also follow the five basic forms found in chords containing open strings, i.e. **C7**, **A7**, **G7**, **E7** and **D7**. The first position **C7** chord shown below can be described as a **C7 form**. If you damp out the 1st and 6th strings, this form becomes moveable, e.g. if you move it to the **6th fret**, it becomes an **F7** chord which would be described as a **C form** of an **F7**.

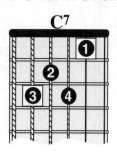
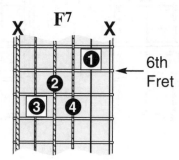

6th Fret

VOICINGS

As with all chords, there is more than one fingering on the guitar for a C7 chord. The diagram below shows an alternative voicing for C7. The term "**voicing**" means the arrangement of notes in a particular fingering, with the notes arranged from the lowest to the highest. The C7 chord will always contain C (1), E (3), G (5) and B♭ (♭7), but it is possible to arrange these notes in any order. The fingering shown below is voiced 3, ♭7, 1, 5.

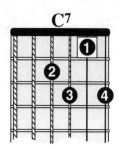
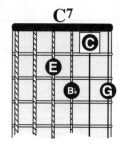

Like the previous C7 shape, this chord is also moveable. The **root note (C)** in this voicing is on the **2nd string**, so when moving the chord along the fretboard, whichever note is under your first finger will be the name of the chord. The following example moves between the chords **C7**, **F7** and **G7**.

 **35.**

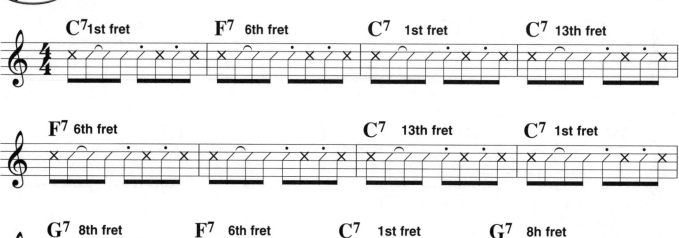

Below are six new moveable 7th chord shapes to go with the two C7 shapes you have already learnt. All these shapes are used in many styles, so be sure to memorize them well.

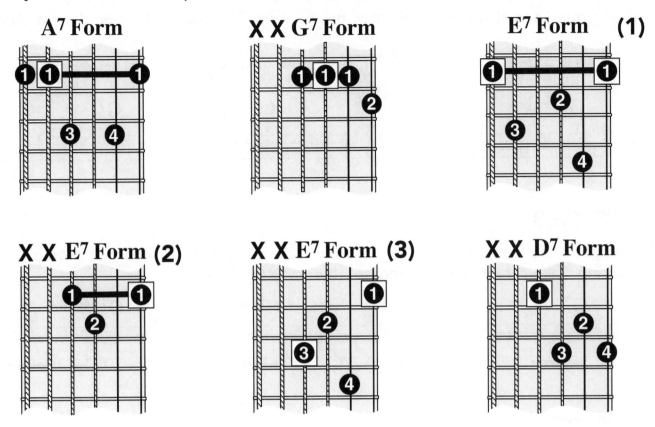

A⁷ Form　　**X X G⁷ Form**　　**E⁷ Form (1)**

X X E⁷ Form (2)　　**X X E⁷ Form (3)**　　**X X D⁷ Form**

Notice that there are three shapes here for the **E7** chord. It is also possible to find alternative fingerings for the other chords shown here. Once you know which notes make up a particular chord, it is possible to arrange the notes in any order as long as the fingering is practical.

Here are some exercises to help you get comfortable with these 7th chord shapes. The first one uses the **A7 form** moved to a different position on the fretboard for each chord. The **root note** on the **5th string** will tell you which fret to move to for each chord.

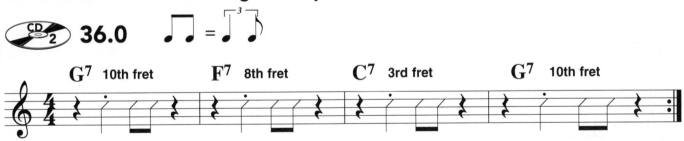

36.0

G⁷ 10th fret　　F⁷ 8th fret　　C⁷ 3rd fret　　G⁷ 10th fret

36.1

This one uses a **G7 form** moved between the same chords as the previous example. This time the **root note** is on the **3rd string**.

G⁷ 12th fret　　F⁷ 10th fret　　C⁷ 5th fret　　G⁷ 12th fret

36.2

This example uses all three variations of the **E7 form**. The **root note** is on the **1st string**.

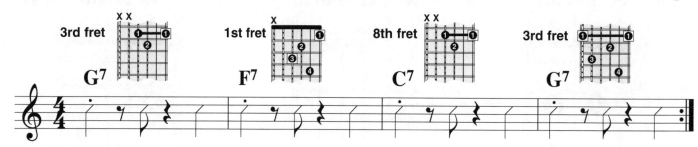

36.3

To complete the five forms, here is one which uses the **D7 form**. The **root note** is on the **4th string**. Take care with the change of rhythm in the final bar.

37.

After learning each of the 7th chord forms, try joining them all up in the one key. This example uses all the moveable 7th chord shapes you have learnt so far. Each of the shapes is played here as a **C7** chord.

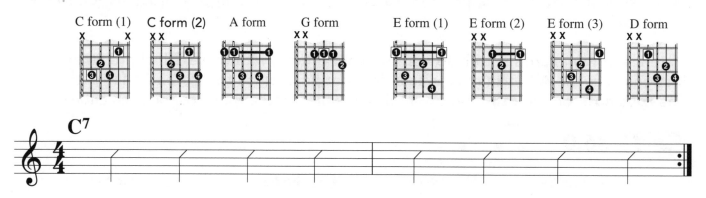

38.

Don't forget to experiment with playing 7th chords as arpeggios, as shown here.

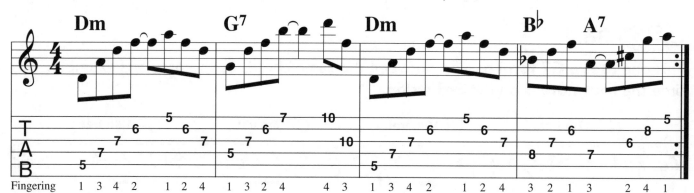

SWAMP SOUNDS

Another popular sound is the use of hammer-ons with 7th chords. It is particularly common in Southern R+B styles often referred to as **Swamp Music**. Here is the basic sound. Practice it slowly at first to be sure all the notes are sounding clearly.

 **39.0**

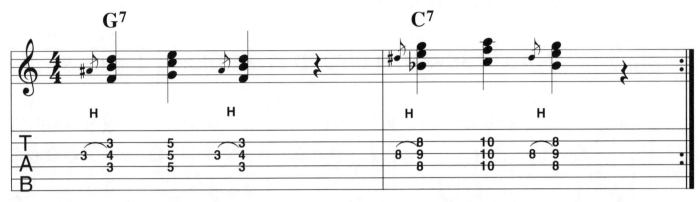

 **39.1**

Here is the basic pattern again, this time with single note riffs added to it.

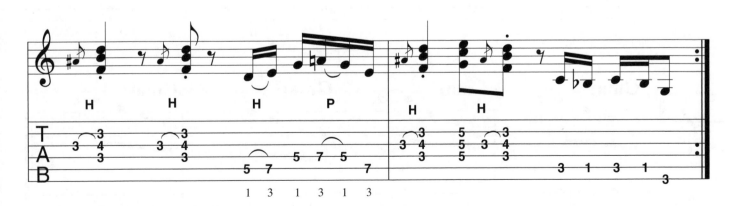

LESSON FORTY EIGHT

MAJOR 7TH CHORDS

Another important chord type is the **major 7th**. Some common voicings are shown below. These shapes follow the five basic forms.

Chord Symbol   *Chord Formula*

| Maj7 | **MAJOR SEVENTH CHORD FORMULA** | 1 3 5 7 |

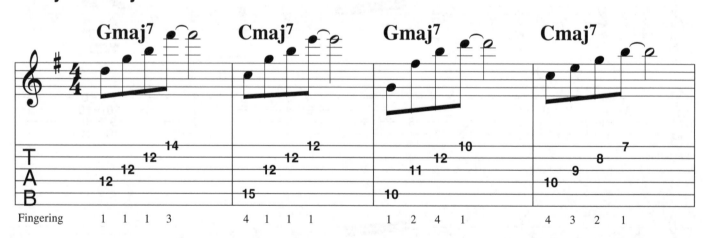

40.

In this example, the major 7th chords shown above are played as arpeggios as either **Gmaj7** or **Cmaj7**.

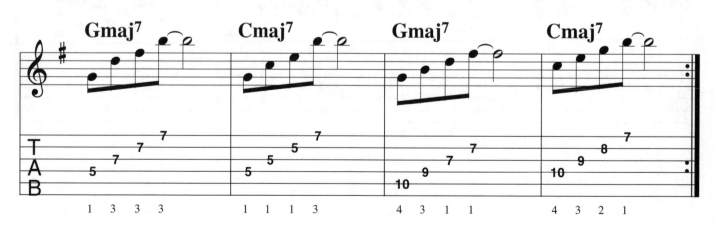

MINOR 7TH CHORDS

Minor 7th chords are also commonly used in Rock and all its related styles. The diagrams below show some commonly used minor 7th shapes. You can determine the forms by the positions of the root notes.

Chord Symbol

| m7 | **MINOR SEVENTH CHORD FORMULA** | 1 ♭3 5 ♭7 |

Chord Formula

The following example is a 12 bar Blues which makes use of minor 7th chords. Try playing these chords as arpeggios, as well as experimenting with combinations of these and other chords you know.

41.

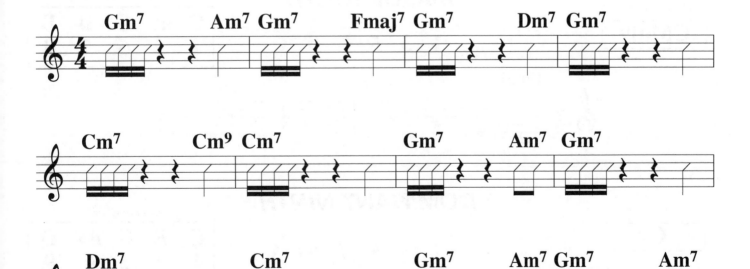

LESSON FORTY NINE

EXTENDED CHORDS

When you play Fusion, Funk, Jazz, Blues, Hip-Hop or Modern R&B, you will often find chords which extend past the 7th, notably the various types of 9th, 11th and 13th chords. These higher numbers come about by repeating the scale from which they are derived over two octaves. Thus, in the higher octave the 2nd becomes the 9th, the 4th becomes the 11th and the 6th becomes the 13th as shown below in the key of C.

C	D	E	F	G	A	B	C	D	E	F	G	A	B	C
1	2	3	4	5	6	7	8	9	10	11	12	13	14	15

As mentioned previously, most chords are made up of various 3rd intervals stacked one on top of the other. This means that by going through a scale in thirds (i.e. skipping every second note) it is easy to create chords up to a 13th. A **major triad** contains the degrees **1**, **3** and **5** of the major scale. A **major 7th** chord is created by adding the **7th** degree on top of the major triad. This 7th degree is a 3rd above the 5th of the chord. By adding another 3rd on top of the major 7th chord, a **major 9th** chord is created. By adding another 3rd on top of the major 9th chord, a **major 11th chord** is created. If you add another 3rd on top of the major 11th chord, a **major 13th** chord is created. The 13th is as high as the chord can go, because if you add a 3rd on top of the major 13th chord, you end up with the tonic of the chord again.

Depending on the nature of the 3rd and 7th degrees of the chord, 9ths 11ths and 13ths may be either major, minor or dominant in quality. E.g. if you add a **9th degree** on top of a **dominant 7th** chord, you end up with a **dominant 9th** chord (usually just called a 9th chord). If you add a 9th degree on top of a **minor 7th** chord, you end up with **a minor 9th** chord, etc. Written below are the formulas for some typical 9th, 11th and 13th chords.

Chord Symbol

CMaj9

MAJOR NINTH

1 3 5 7 9

Notes in Chord

C	E	G	B	D
1	3	5	7	9

Cmaj⁹

Chord Symbol

C9

DOMINANT NINTH

1 3 5 ♭7 9

Notes in Chord

C	E	G	B♭	D
1	3	5	♭7	9

C⁹

MINOR NINTH

Chord Symbol

Cm9

1 ♭3 5 ♭7 9

Notes in Chord

C	E♭	G	B♭	D
1	♭3	5	♭7	9

ELEVENTH CHORDS

By adding another 3rd interval on top of a 9th chord, it is possible to create an 11th chord. Depending on the 3rd and 7th of the chord, you can create major, minor and dominant 11th chords. The chord shown below is a C minor 11th (**Cm11**). By raising the 3rd of the chord from E♭ to E♮ it could be changed to a dominant 11th chord (**C11**). By raising the 3rd and the 7th it could be changed to a major 11th (**CMaj11**).

MINOR ELEVENTH

Chord Symbol

Cm11

1 ♭3 5 ♭7 9 11

Notes in Chord

C	E♭	G	B♭	D	F
1	♭3	5	♭7	9	11

THIRTEENTH CHORDS

By adding another 3rd interval on top of an 11th chord, various types of 13th chords can be created. Once again depending on the 3rd and 7th of the chord, you can create major, minor and dominant 13th chords. The chord shown below is a C dominant 13th (**C13**). By flattening the 3rd of the chord it could be changed to a minor 13th chord (**Cm13**). By raising the 7th it could be changed to a major 13th (**CMaj13**).

THIRTEENTH

Chord Symbol

C13

1 3 5 ♭7 9 11 13

Notes in Chord

C	E	G	B♭	D	F	A
1	3	5	♭7	9	11	13

MEMORIZING SCALE AND CHORD DEGREES

Since most chords are formed from notes of the major scale of the key, you need to know the notes of all 12 major scales from memory in order to be able to create any chord in any key. The following chart shows all existing major scales up to the 13th for reference in constructing chords. Try memorizing one scale per week until you know them all. You should also make a habit of choosing any starting note and building all chord types up to the 13th on that note.

Note's Position in Scale → / Scale ↓	1	2	3	4	5	6	7	8	9	10	11	12	13
A	A	B	C#	D	E	F#	G#	A	B	C#	D	E	F#
A♭	A♭	B♭	C	D♭	E♭	F	G	A♭	B♭	C	D♭	E♭	F
B	B	C#	D#	E	F#	G#	A#	B	C#	D#	E	F#	G#
B♭	B♭	C	D	E♭	F	G	A	B♭	C	D	E♭	F	G
C	C	D	E	F	G	A	B	C	D	E	F	G	A
C#	C#	D#	E#	F#	G#	A#	B#	C#	D#	E#	F#	G#	A#
D	D	E	F#	G	A	B	C#	D	E	F#	G	A	B
D♭	D♭	E♭	F	G♭	A♭	B♭	C	D♭	E♭	F	G♭	A♭	B♭
E	E	F#	G#	A	B	C#	D#	E	F#	G#	A	B	C#
E♭	E♭	F	G	A♭	B♭	C	D	E♭	F	G	A♭	B♭	C
F	F	G	A	B♭	C	D	E	F	G	A	B♭	C	D
F#	F#	G#	A#	B	C#	D#	E#	F#	G#	A#	B	C#	D#
G	G	A	B	C	D	E	F#	G	A	B	C	D	E
G♭	G♭	A♭	B♭	C♭	D♭	E♭	F	G♭	A♭	B♭	C♭	D♭	E♭

OMITTING NOTES FROM CHORDS

The more notes you add to chords, the more difficult they are to play and the more muddy they can sound. For this reason it is common to omit notes from extended chords, keeping only the notes which most clearly indicate the quality (sound) of the chord. The most frequently omitted note is the **5th**, although sometimes the 3rd or the root can be omitted. Usually the bass will be playing the root note anyway. With a dominant 7th chord, as long as the ♭7 degree is in the chord you still get the effect of a 7th chord. With a dominant 9th chord, as long as you have the 3rd, ♭7th and 9th, you have the effect of a 9th chord, etc. Shown below are some common voicings of various 9th, 11th and 13th chords, along with some examples demonstrating their use. The first two are **Major** and **Minor 9ths**.

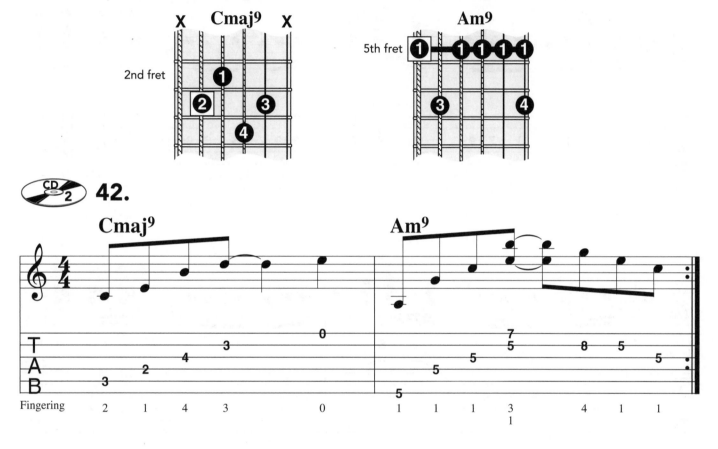

Here are some commonly used **dominant 9th** chord (usually just called 9th chords) shapes and an example making use of them.

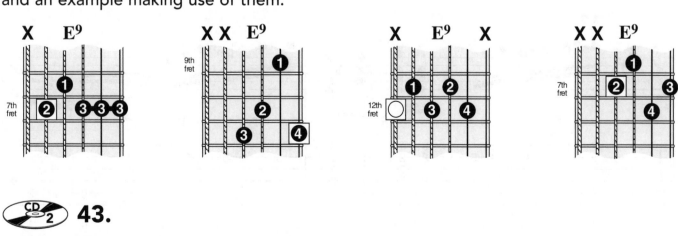

SLIDING CHORDS

Sliding chords from one fret to another is a technique often used in rhythm guitar playing. The slide is indicated by a line between the chords accompanied by the letter **S**. The following solo makes use of this technique with the top three notes of a 9th chord. Notice also the alternation between single note riffs and chords. Take it slowly and work on it with a metronome or drum machine until you can play the whole thing without losing your timing. Then gradually increase the tempo until you can play it along with the CD.

 44. Funky Freddy

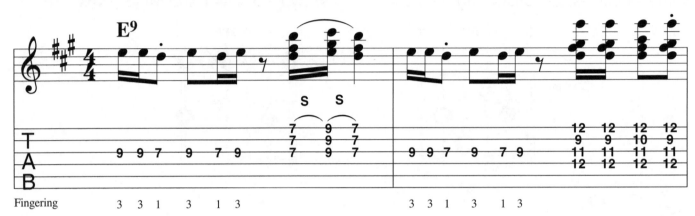

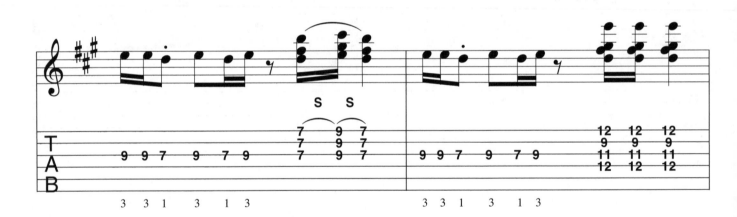

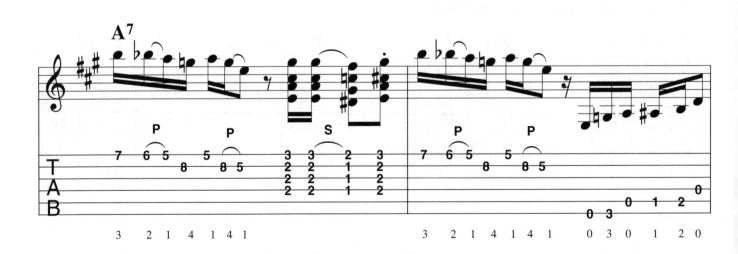

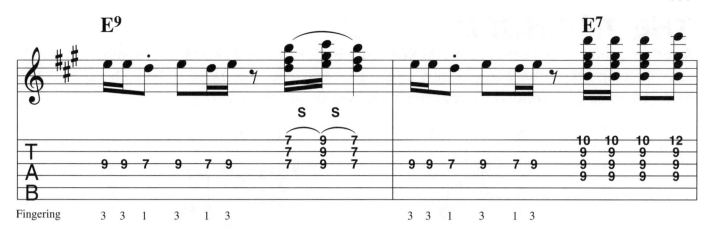

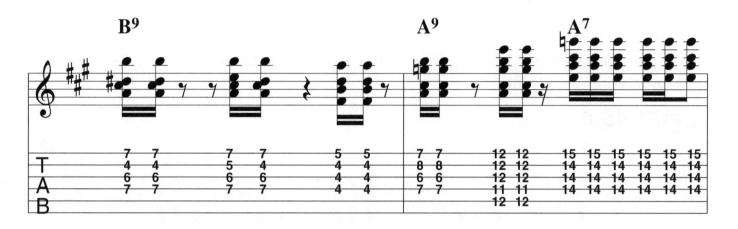

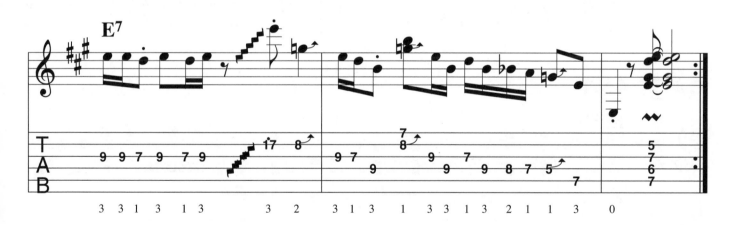

THE 7#9 CHORD

Another useful chord often found in R&B and Funk is the **7#9 chord**. It is similar to a ninth chord except that the actual ninth degree of the chord is raised. This chord is often referred to as the **Hendrix chord**. Here are two common fingerings.

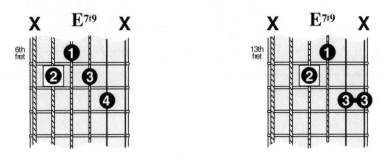

Here are two examples showing how these chords may be used. In the first one, the sixteenth notes are swung.

45.0

45.1

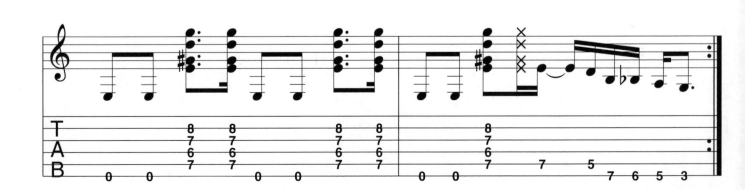

LESSON FIFTY

PLAYING WITH A BAND

After you've worked on all the chords, scales, techniques and rhythms, the most important thing is knowing where and when to use them. This will usually depend on what the other instruments are playing. If you are not sure what to play, you can always get ideas from what the bass and drums are doing. When you are playing with other musicians, the most important thing is to listen to each other and try to respond to each other.

THE BASS

The bass helps to keep solid time and provide the basic feel and drive along with the drummer. The bass and bass drum parts are often closely linked. The bass also spells out the chords and lays the foundation for the harmony of the song. Together, the bass and drums are called the **rhythm section**. While a singer or horn player has time to breathe between phrases and a guitarist or keyboard player leaves space between lines or chords, the drummer and bass player have to play consistently to keep the groove going and feeling good. It is the job of the rhythm guitarist to "lock in" with the rhythm section to keep the feel tight and drive the song forward.

Most electric basses have four strings which correspond to the bottom four strings of the guitar (**E**, **A**, **D** and **G**). The difference is that they are tuned one octave lower than the guitar. The strings are much thicker than guitar strings and the lower frets are wider apart. Like the electric guitar, the bass has pickups (usually two) and is played through an amplifier. The bass is usually played with the index and middle fingers of the right hand, or "slap" style with the thumb and index finger, but it can also be played with a pick. The photo below shows a typical electric bass.

BASS MUSIC NOTATION

Bass music is written on the lines and spaces of the **bass staff**, which is similar to the treble staff, except that it uses a **bass clef** (shown below).

THE BASS CLEF

There is a bass clef at the beginning of every line of bass music.

THE BASS STAFF

A staff with a bass clef written on it is called a **bass staff**.

Notes on the bass staff are lower than those on the treble staff and the notes appear in different places. Every note is **one line or space down** from where it would be on the treble staff. The notes on the lines and spaces of the bass staff are shown below.

NOTES ON THE BASS STAFF

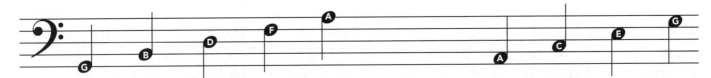

To remember the notes on the lines of the bass staff, say:
Good **B**oys **D**eserve **F**ruit **A**lways.

To remember the notes in the spaces of the bass staff, say:
All **C**ows **E**at **G**rass.

The following example demonstrates a riff played by the guitar and bass together (an octave apart). Listen to the recording to hear the effect this produces. The fingering is the same on both instruments as shown in the tablature.

 **46.   Guitar and Bass Together**

THE DRUMS

The drums set up and keep the basic feel of a song. They also drive the rhythm forward and provide endless rhythmic ideas for the other instruments through the use of accents, fills, and rhythmic patterns. The great thing about listening to the drummer is that you have three or four different parts that you can play around or lock in with. Many musicians (especially guitarists) rely on the drummer to keep time for them, but in a good band everybody has a strong sense of time and no-one relies on anyone else. If you are not confident keeping time for yourself, work with a metronome or drum machine every day until you are confident. The photo below shows all the basic parts of a drumkit.

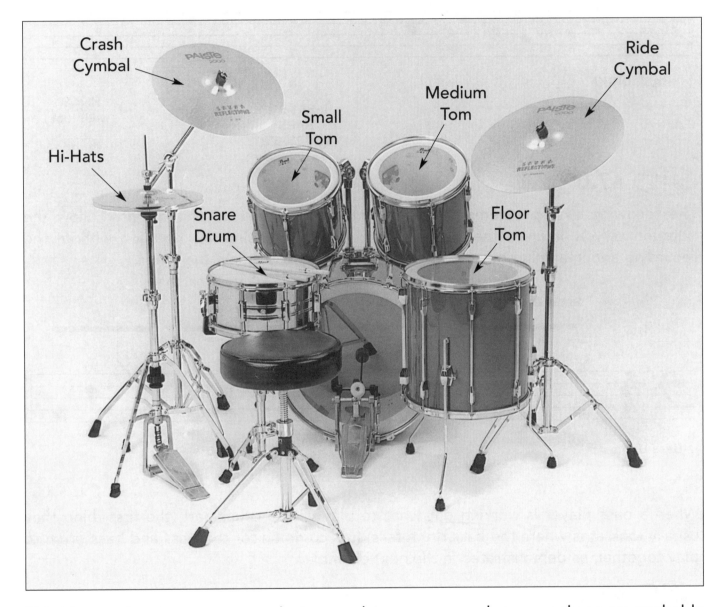

This kit contains three tom toms, but many drummers use only two, as these are probably the least necessary part of the kit. In fact, most drum parts can be played using only the snare drum, the bass drum and the hi hat cymbals. The **bass drum** is played with the right foot and produces what is often called the "bottom end" sound of the drums. The **snare drum** is usually played with the left hand, but the right hand is also used for certain beats as well as playing fills. The **hi-hat and ride cymbals** are generally played with the right hand, but once again the left hand may be used in certain situations. The **crash cymbal** is played with either hand, depending on which one is most practical for each musical situation. The **tom toms** (toms for short) can also be played by either hand. **The hi-hat cymbals** can also be played by the left foot and the most common sounds using the open hi hats are achieved by using a combination of the right hand and the left foot.

DRUM NOTATION

Drum music is usually written in the spaces of the **bass staff**, including the space above the staff; to represent different parts of the drum kit. The most commonly used system is shown below. Notice that cymbals are notated with an **X** instead of a notehead.

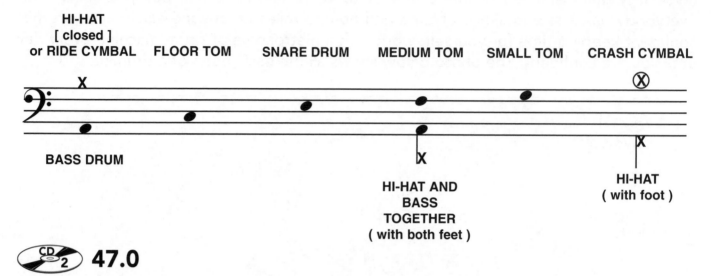

🔘47.0

The following example demonstrates a simple Rock beat on the drums. Follow the notation as you listen to the recording and then try reading the notation without the recording and imagining the sounds of the drums as you follow the notes.

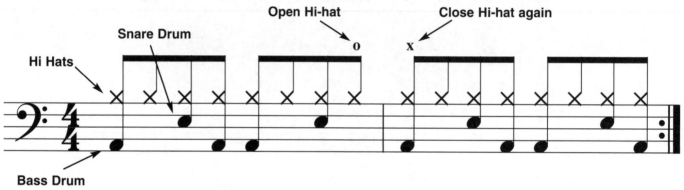

When a bass player is working out what to play with a drum part, the first thing they usually look at is where the bass drum falls. It is common for the bass and bass drum to play together, as demonstrated in the next example.

🔘47.1

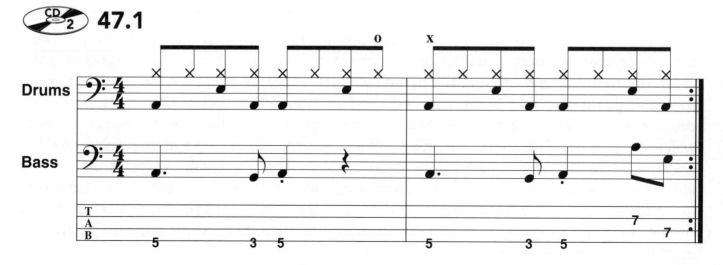

LESSON FIFTY ONE

PLAYING WITH A RHYTHM SECTION

If you were going to add a guitar part to the bass and drum parts shown in the previous example, there are several things you could do. The first thing is to play a constant eighth note rhythm along with the hi-hat part as demonstrated in the following example. When playing this type of part, listen carefully to the drums and make sure your playing is exactly in time with them. Because the hi-hats create a short, crisp sound, it is a good idea to use right hand damping when playing along with them. This helps the band to sound tight.

47.2

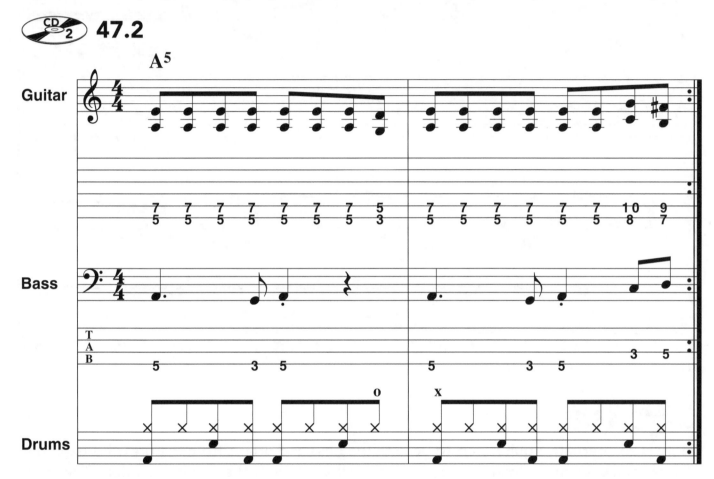

47.3

Another approach is to play with some parts of the bass line and some part of the drum part, but leave space in between for the other instruments to be heard. This is demonstrated in the following example which uses exactly the same bass and drum parts as the previous example.

The following pages contain examples of guitar, bass and drums working together. Analyze them and notice where notes are played together and where one instrument leaves space for the others. A good general principle to use is: if one part is busy, it is best to have something simple played with it, rather than all the parts being busy. Interplay, communication and "locking in" together are the most important aspects of playing as a band. Always learn your own part well enough that you can listen to what everyone is playing rather than just hearing yourself.

CD 2 48.0

CD 2 48.1

Here is an alternative guitar part to go with the bass and drums from the previous example. There is always more than one part which will work with the rhythm section. The most suitable part for any instrument depends on the style of music. The best way to broaden your knowledge of what to play is to listen to a lot of different music and pay attention to how the instruments work together. Ask your teacher or guitar-playing staff in a music store to recommend some albums in different styles until you know what to listen for.

The next two examples are shuffles, as indicated by the swing symbol next to the CD number. Use the ideas presented here to create some parts of your own.

49.

50.

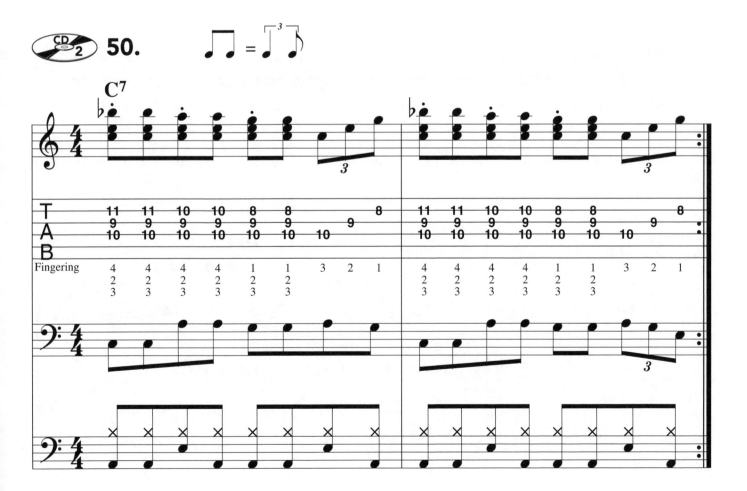

TWELVE EIGHT TIME ($\frac{12}{8}$)

Another useful time signature, particularly in Blues and related styles is **twelve eight time** ($\frac{12}{8}$). This means there are **twelve eighth note beats** in each bar. A bar of eighth notes in twelve eight time sounds the same as a bar of triplets in four four time. Although there are twelve individual beats which can be counted, twelve eight time is usually still counted in four as demonstrated in the following example.

51.0

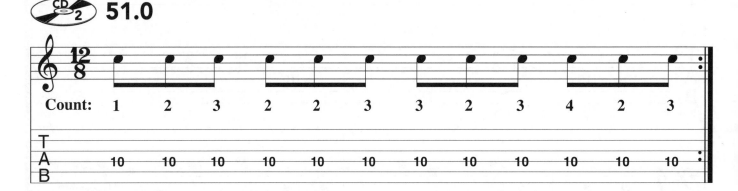

One of the main reasons for using the twelve eight time signature instead of $\frac{4}{4}$ is that it becomes easier to count when the eighth notes are subdivided. Since there is a number on each eighth note, sixteenth notes can be counted as **+** (**and**) as demonstrated in the following example. These sixteenth notes may be played straight or swung. On the recording, they are played straight the first time through and swung the second time through. This counting example is followed by a lick which makes use of 16th notes in $\frac{12}{8}$ time.

51.1

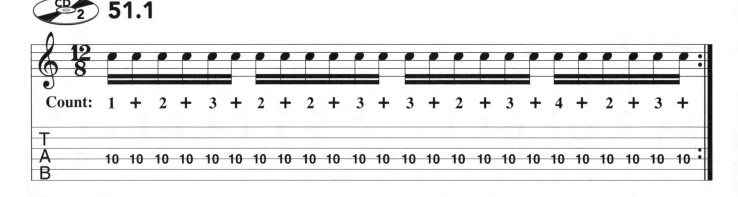

52.

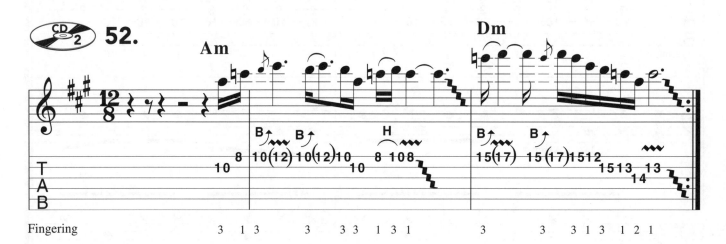

Here are two examples of guitar and rhythm section parts in $\frac{12}{8}$ time. The sixteenth notes are swung in both these parts. As with previous examples, experiment with the ideas shown here to create some of your own parts.

 **53.**

 **54.**

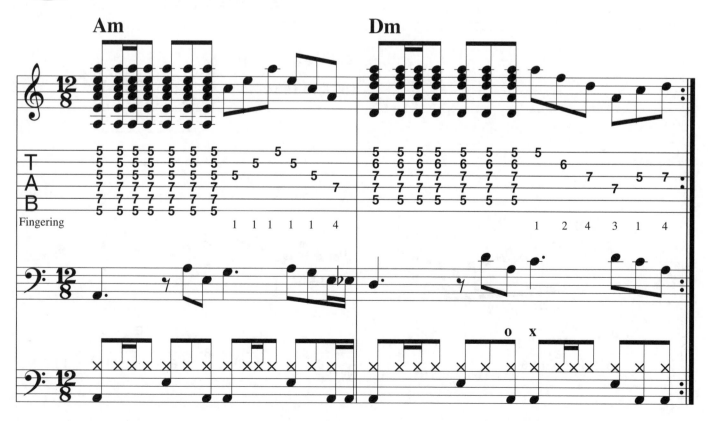

THIRTY SECOND NOTES

Another thing you may encounter in ¹²⁄₈ time (and other time signatures) is thirty second notes. One sixteenth note divides into two thirty second notes. The example below is shown in ⁶⁄₈ time, which is equivalent to half a bar of ¹²⁄₈ time. The thirty second notes are counted **1e+a 2e+a 3e+a, 2e+a 2e+a 3e+a,** etc, but are probably best felt rather than counted.

55.

To finish this lesson, here is a 12 bar Blues solo in ¹²⁄₈ time using ideas from the playing of Blues players Otis Rush, Albert King and Stevie Ray Vaughan. Although it is derived totally from the Blues scale, this one is a real challenge. Some of the rhythms here are particularly tricky, so take your time with it and listen to the CD over and over until you get it. Also listen to how the instrumental parts work together on the recording.

56. The Blues Never Die

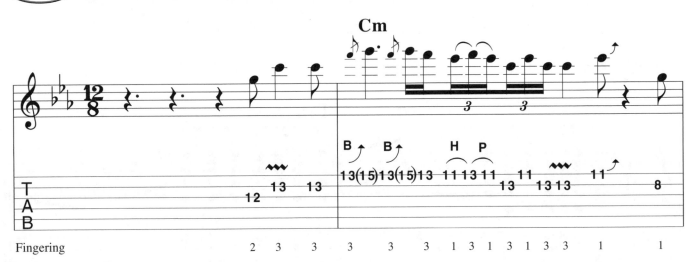

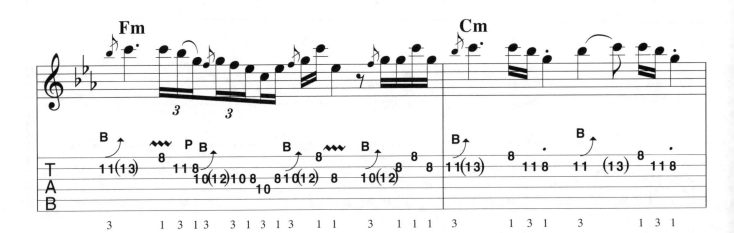

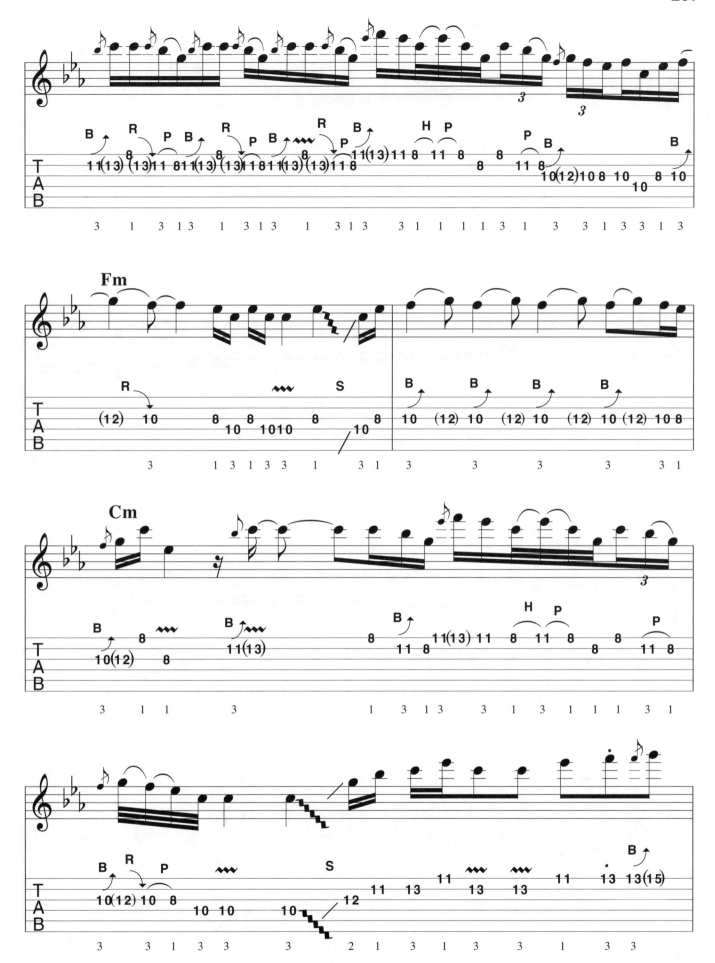

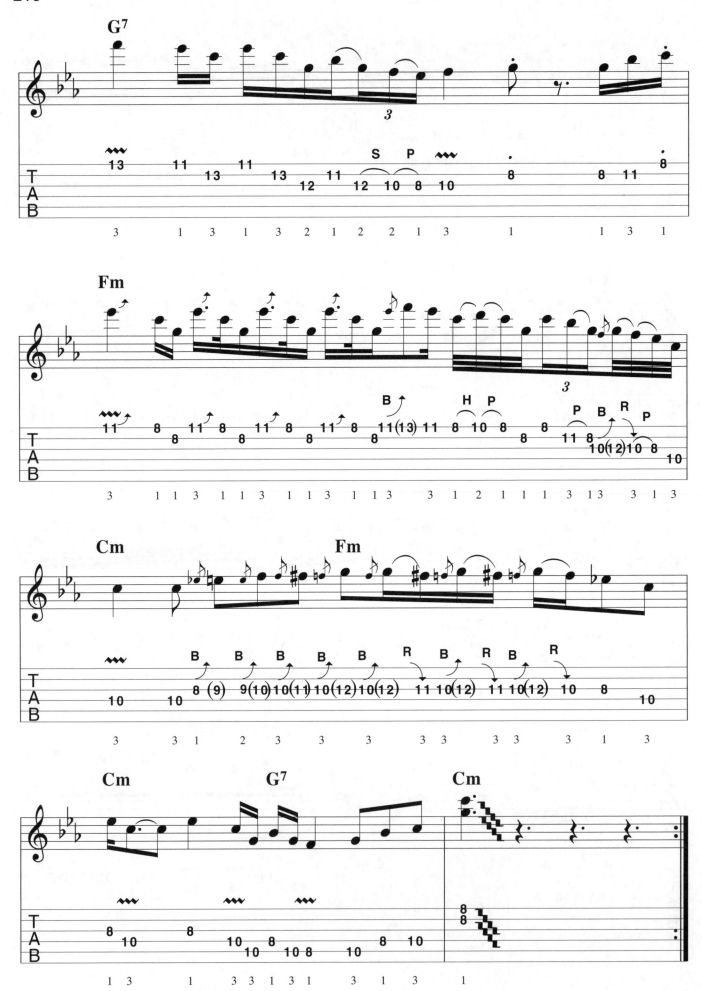

LESSON FIFTY TWO

MOVEABLE MAJOR SCALES

Like the pentatonic and Blues scales, there are five basic moveable fingerings for the major scale. These are shown below in the **key of C** (C Major Scale). Memorize each one, especially the positions of the **root notes** and then learn the sequences and examples shown on the following pages and experiment with them to create your own ideas.

C FORM

A FORM

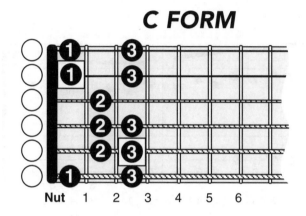

G FORM

E FORM

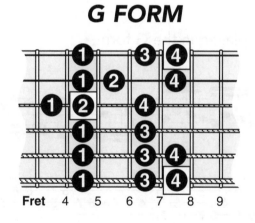
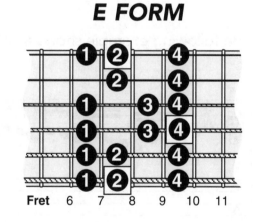

D FORM

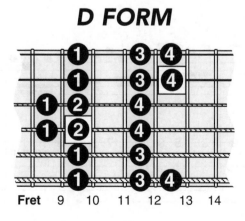

Once you know the fingering for each scale form, practice each one using various sequence patterns as shown in the following examples. This helps you learn the scale more thoroughly as well as being good for your technique. This first one uses the A form.

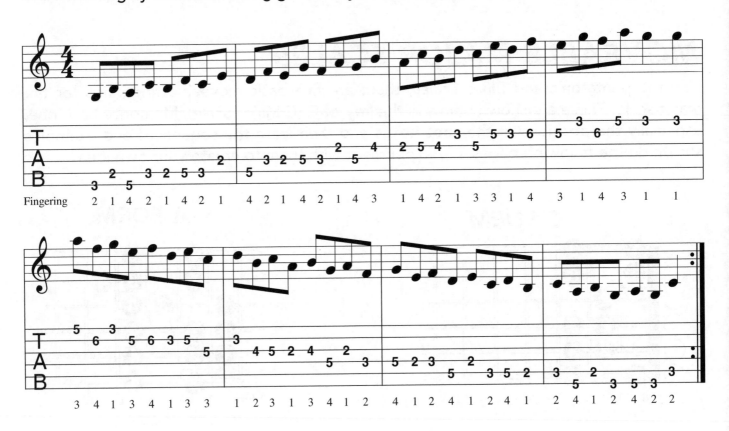

The following example shows a 16th note sequence played in the G form.

CD2 **57.**

This example shows a triplet run using hammer-ons and pull-offs played in the D form.

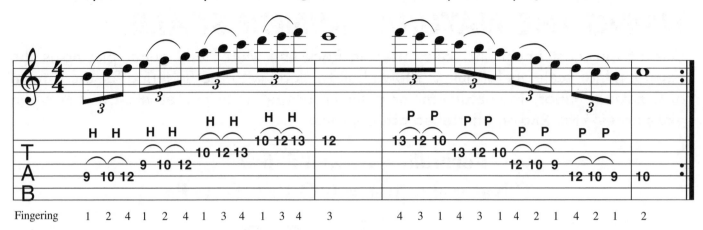

It is important to remember that scales are just the raw material for making music and are not an end in themselves. The purpose of learning all the forms and practicing sequence patterns is to become comfortable with them in order to make melodic statements. Once you are confident with the scale forms, experiment with various techniques (e.g. bends, hammer-ons, slides, etc) and create some of your own licks and solos from them. The following example shows a lick derived from the G form. Try out your own ideas from the major scale with the C Major/A minor Jam-Along track on the CD (CD2 ex 87 – page 236).

CD2 **58.**

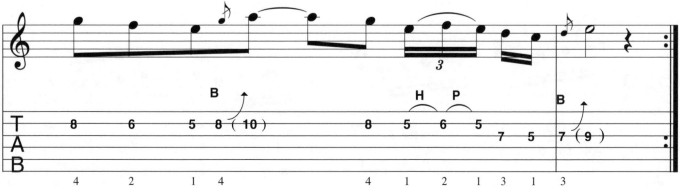

LESSON FIFTY THREE

USING THE NATURAL MINOR SCALE

One of the most important scales used in Rock and Metal lead guitar playing is the **natural minor** scale. Its formula is shown below, along with the fingering for the **E form** of **C natural minor**. The natural minor is similar to the minor pentatonic, but it has two extra notes – the **2nd** and flattened **6th** degrees.

$$\text{Formula} - 1 \ 2 \ \flat 3 \ 4 \ 5 \ \flat 6 \ \flat 7$$

$$\text{C Natural minor} = C \ D \ E\flat \ F \ G \ A\flat \ B\flat$$

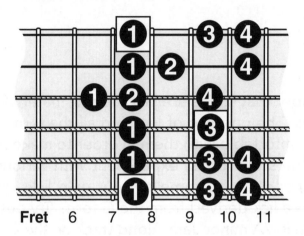

59.

60.

Here is a lick derived from the natural minor scale. Once you can play it, move it up and down the fretboard to several other keys.

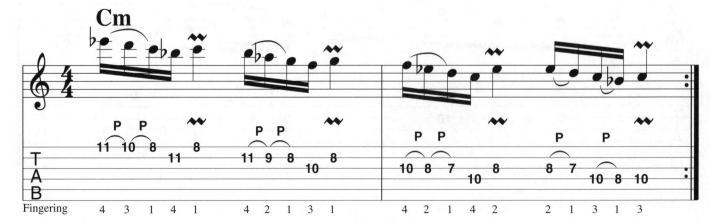

Here are some more natural minor licks in different keys. The first is in **A minor** and the second is in **E minor**. Try using the ideas presented here to create some of your own licks.

61.

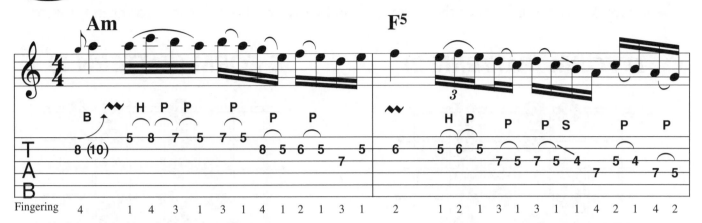

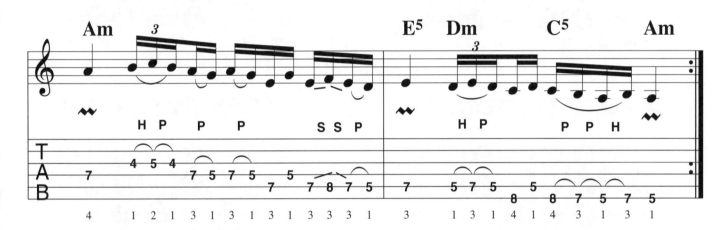

62.

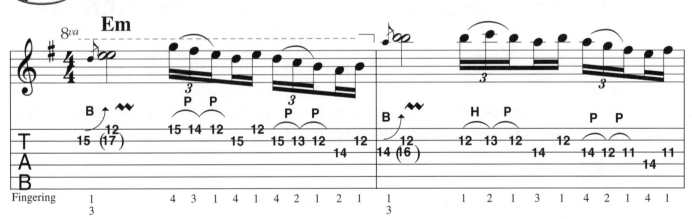

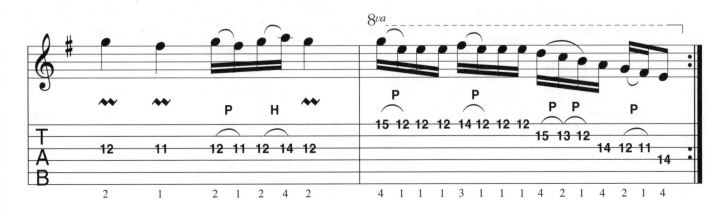

5 FORMS OF THE NATURAL MINOR

As with most scales, there are five basic forms of the natural minor which cover the whole fretboard. The fingerings are similar to those of the minor pentatonic, but have two extra notes. You already know the E form of the scale. Shown below are the other four forms in **C minor**.

D FORM (PATTERN 2)

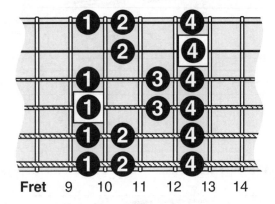

C FORM (PATTERN 3)

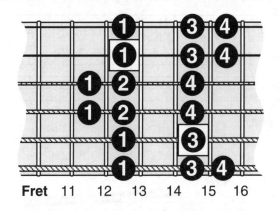

A FORM (PATTERN 4)

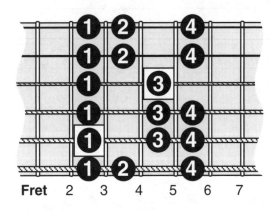

G FORM (PATTERN 5)

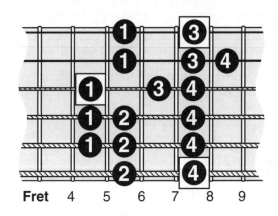

Once you are comfortable with the fingerings for these forms, try making up some licks from them. Here's one derived from the **G form** in **C minor**.

 **63.**

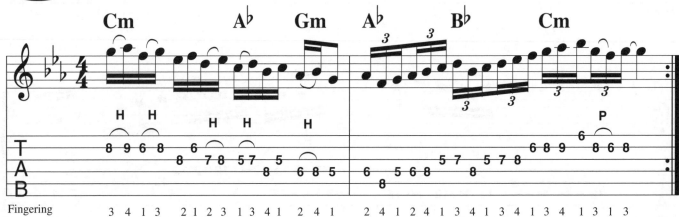

RELATIVE MAJOR AND MINOR FINGERINGS

Like the pentatonic scales, it is possible to use the same fingerings for major and natural minor scales. If you look at the diagrams below, you will see that the G form of the C major scale is identical to the E form of the A natural minor scale. Once again, the fingering remains exactly the same, only the positions of the root notes change. This applies to all the fingering patterns.

C MAJOR - G FORM

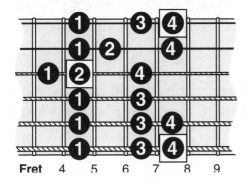

A MINOR - E FORM

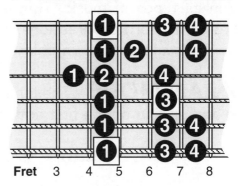

Shown below are the remaining four forms of the natural minor scale, along with the pattern of identical fingerings between major and relative minor scales. This pattern remains the same regardless of whether the scales are major and natural minor, or pentatonic.

C form major	=	A form minor
A form major	=	G form minor
G form major	=	E form minor
E form major	=	D form minor
D form major	=	C form minor

A MINOR - D FORM

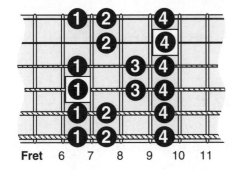

A MINOR - C FORM

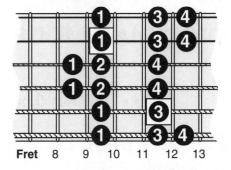

A MINOR - A FORM

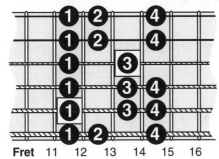

A MINOR - G FORM

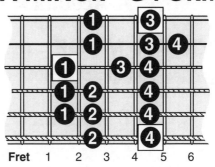

LESSON FIFTY FOUR

MODES

The term **mode** is another name for a scale. There are seven different modes which can be derived from the major scale by starting on each of the seven notes of the major scale. These modes were first used in ancient Greece and have been widely used throughout history in all types of music. They are particularly useful for improvising or composing melodies over chord progressions. The names of the seven modes and their relationship to the major scale are shown below.

1. IONIAN MODE – The Ionian mode is another name for the major scale itself. By starting and ending on the first note of the major scale (C) you can play the Ionian mode.

$$C \ Ionian = C \ D \ E \ F \ G \ A \ B \ C$$

2. DORIAN MODE – The Dorian mode starts and ends on the second note of the major scale (in this case D).

$$D \ Dorian = D \ E \ F \ G \ A \ B \ C \ D$$

3. PHRYGIAN MODE – The Phrygian mode starts and ends on the third note of the major scale (in this case E).

$$E \ Phrygian = E \ F \ G \ A \ B \ C \ D \ E$$

4. LYDIAN MODE – The Lydian mode starts and ends on the fourth note of the major scale (in this case F).

$$F \ Lydian = F \ G \ A \ B \ C \ D \ E \ F$$

5. MIXOLYDIAN MODE – The Mixolydian mode starts and ends on the fifth note of the major scale (in this case G).

$$G \ Mixolydian = G \ A \ B \ C \ D \ E \ F \ G$$

6. AEOLIAN MODE – The Aeolian mode starts and ends on the sixth note of the major scale (in this case A).

$$A \ Aeolian = A \ B \ C \ D \ E \ F \ G \ A$$

7. LOCRIAN MODE – The Locrian mode starts and ends on the seventh note of the major scale (in this case B).

$$B \ Locrian = B \ C \ D \ E \ F \ G \ A \ B$$

 **64.**

Here is an exercise containing all of the modes derived from the major scale. Listen to the sound of each mode against the chords indicated above the music.

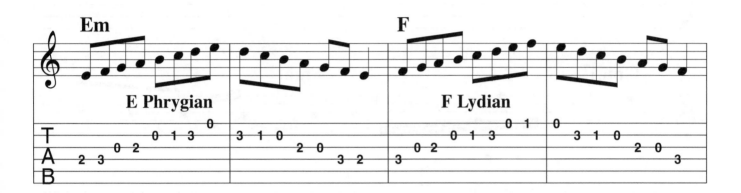

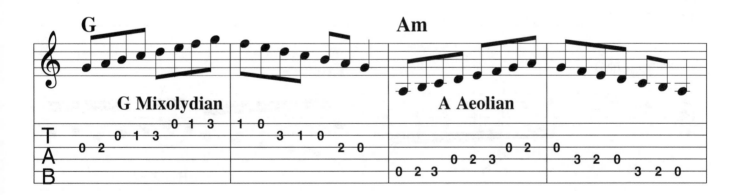

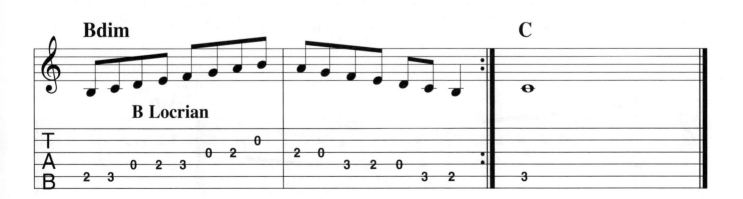

65. So Long Ago

Here is a simple solo which uses all of the natural notes contained in the various modes derived from the C major scale and is played over a chord progression which fits all seven of the modes. Try this approach any time you are soloing over a progression in a major key or one which alternates between a major key and its relative minor. You can practice this with the C Major/A minor Jam-Along progression at the end of the book (CD2 ex 87).

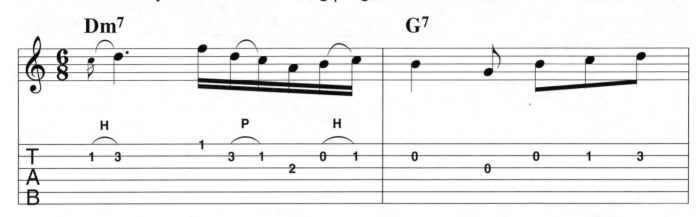

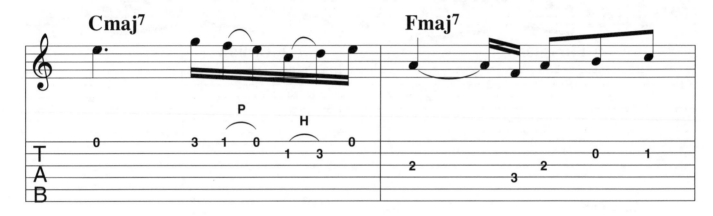

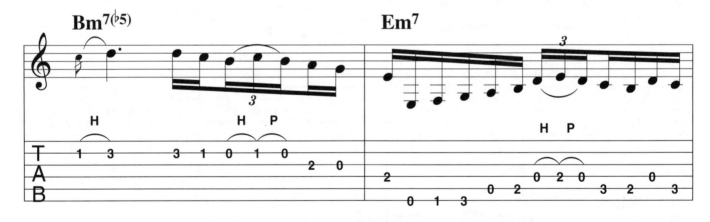

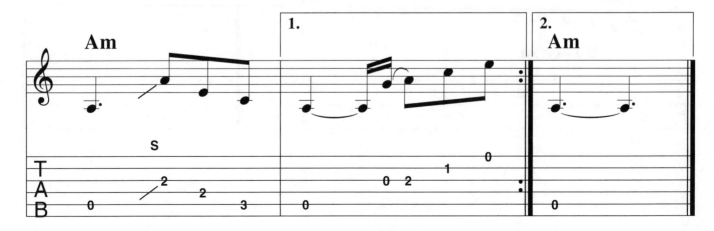

MODE FORMULAS

All of the modes derived from the major scale can be played in many different positions on the fretboard and can be played in any key. Just as there are twelve major keys, there are also twelve possible starting notes for each of the modes. Any note of the chromatic scale can be used as a starting note for any mode. This requires a knowledge of the formula for each mode. The scale degrees of each mode are listed below.

Ionian =	1 2 3 4 5 6 7
Dorian =	1 2 ♭3 4 5 6 ♭7
Phrygian =	1 ♭2 ♭3 4 5 ♭6 ♭7
Lydian =	1 2 3 ♯4 5 6 7
Mixolydian =	1 2 3 4 5 6 ♭7
Aeolian =	1 2 ♭3 4 5 ♭6 ♭7
Locrian =	1 ♭2 ♭3 4 ♭5 ♭6 ♭7

If you are serious about using modes in your playing it will be necessary to memorise the formula for each of these modes. Don't try to memorise them all at once, take one mode at a time and learn the formula as it relates to the **sound** of the mode. Learn the fingerings for the mode and experiment with it. Learn the licks which are given at the end of each group of fingerings and then listen to your favourite recordings and try learning some solos which use each mode. In this book all of the scales and modes are written with C as the starting note, as this makes it easy to compare the modes. However, it is important to eventually learn all modes in all keys. All you need to work out a mode in any key is the starting note and the formula. Here is the Dorian mode shown in four different keys.

C Dorian =	C	D	E♭	F	G	A	B♭
	1	2	♭3	4	5	6	♭7

F Dorian =	F	G	A♭	B♭	C	D	E♭
	1	2	♭3	4	5	6	♭7

A Dorian =	A	B	C	D	E	F♯	G
	1	2	♭3	4	5	6	♭7

B Dorian =	B	C♯	D	E	F♯	G♯	A
	1	2	♭3	4	5	6	♭7

MODAL TONALITIES

Although it is possible to change modes within a key along with the chord changes, it is common in Rock, Jazz and Fusion to treat one mode as the basic tonality. A typical example of this is Carlos Santana, who often uses the Dorian mode as the basis for a song.

Shown below is the **E form** of the **C dorian** mode. The notes are identical to those found in the **D form** of **B♭ Major** (Ionian mode). The crucial difference is the positions of the root notes. This is what determines the tonality. Run through the scale ascending and descending, pausing on each root note as you come to it. Notice that the tonality sounds minor rather than major. This is because if you start on C as the root note, the mode contains a flattened 3rd degree. Practice using it to improvise over the Dorian Tonality Jam-Along Progression on CD2 (ex 91).

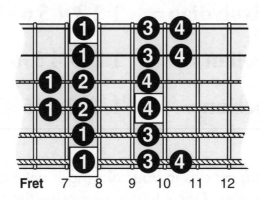

C Dorian = C D E♭ F G A B♭

1 2 ♭3 4 5 6 ♭7

 **66.**

Once you are comfortable with the sound of the mode, try the following lick which is derived from it.

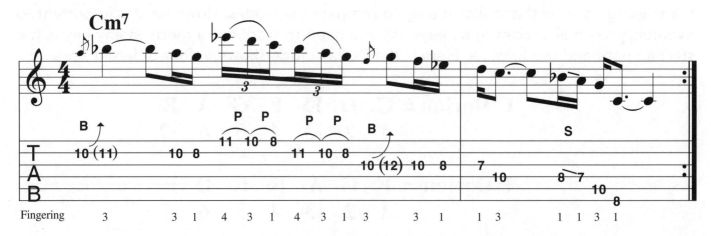

Like the major scales from which they are derived, each mode can be played in five basic forms which cover the fretboard. Use your knowledge of the forms to work out the fingerings for each of the modes, remembering that they are the same as those of the major scale, but the positions of the root notes are different for each mode. For an in–depth study of modes, see *Progressive Scales and Modes for Guitar, Progressive Complete Learn to Play Lead Guitar Manual* or *Progressive Complete Learn to Play Jazz Guitar Manual.*

LESSON FIFTY FIVE

USING THE HARMONIC MINOR SCALE

Another important scale used in Hard Rock and Metal guitar playing is the **harmonic minor** scale. Its formula is shown below, along with the fingering for the **E form** of **C harmonic minor**. The only difference between this and the natural minor is that the **seventh** degree is **raised** by a semitone.

Formula – 1 2 ♭3 4 5 ♭6 7

C Harmonic minor = C D E♭ F G A♭ B

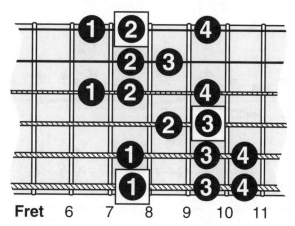

Fret 6 7 8 9 10 11

CD 2 67.

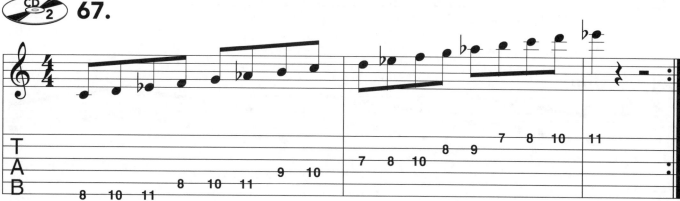

CD 2 68.

Once you know the basic fingering, try this lick which is derived from the harmonic minor scale.

As with all scales, it is important to play licks from the harmonic minor up and down the fretboard in all keys. Here is an example in **B minor** to learn and transpose.

69.

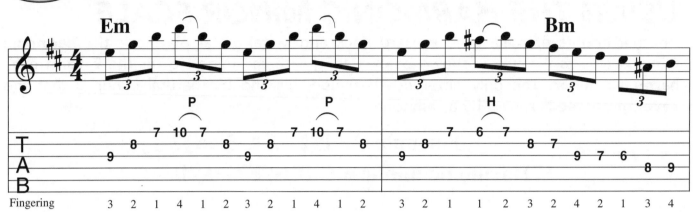

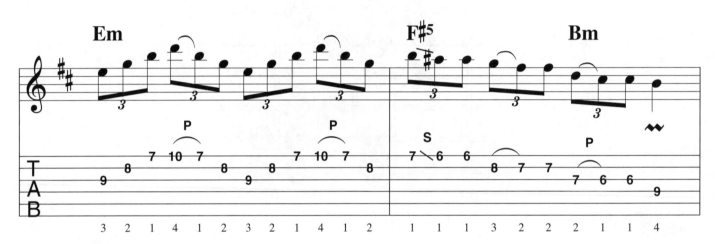

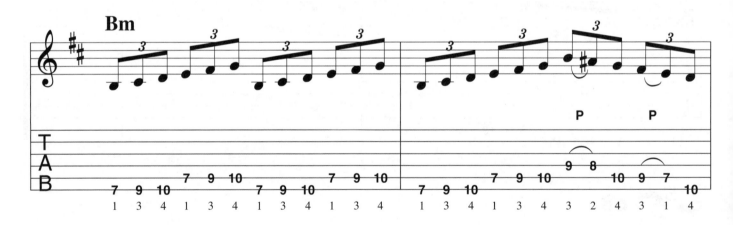

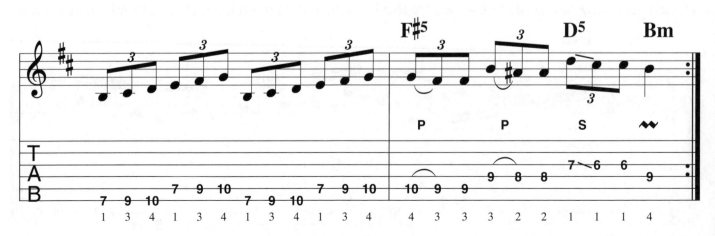

5 FORMS OF THE HARMONIC MINOR

You already know the E form of the harmonic minor scale. Shown below are the other four forms.

D FORM (PATTERN 2)

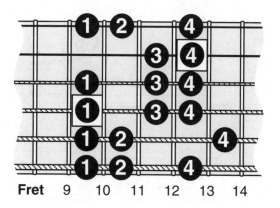

C FORM (PATTERN 3)

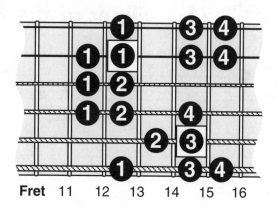

A FORM (PATTERN 4)

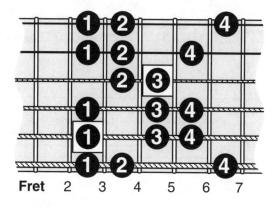

G FORM (PATTERN 5)

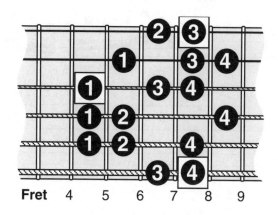

Once you are comfortable with the fingerings for these forms, try making up some licks from them. Here's one derived from the **C form** in **C minor**. This one has a Classical flavor to it. Many metal players (e.g. Yngwie Malmsteen and both guitarists from Metallica) are influenced by Classical composers, particularly Bach and Paginini.

 **70.**

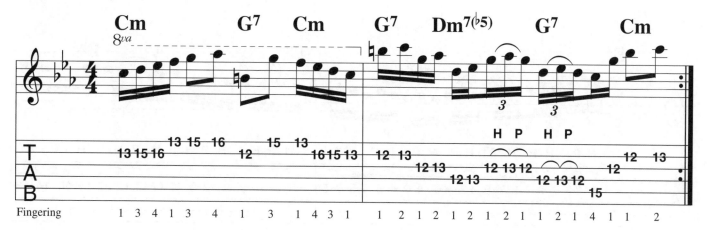

Here is a solo which makes use of all the scales and techniques you have learnt up to this point. Take it slowly at first and be sure to get all the techniques such as vibrato, bends, slides, slurring and pick tremolo. Listen to the CD many times until you know the sound of the solo, as this will make it easier to learn. When you can play the whole solo, work on it with your metronome until you can play it at a reasonable tempo and then try playing it along with the CD.

71. Flight of the Raven

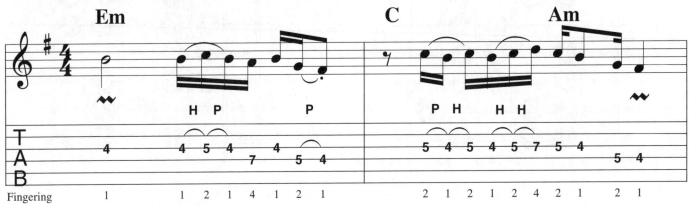

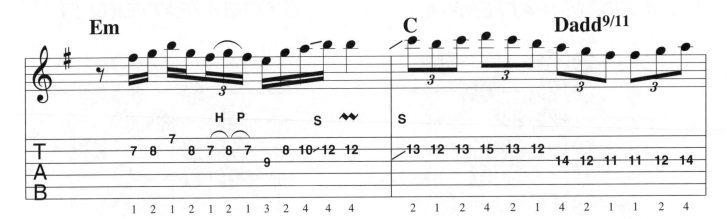

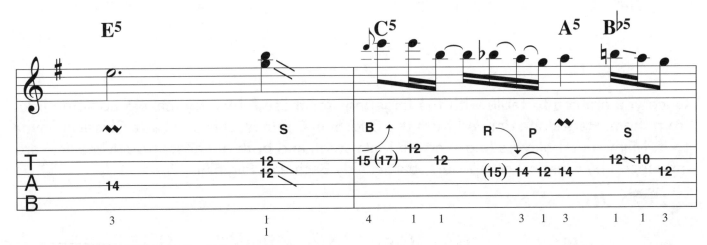

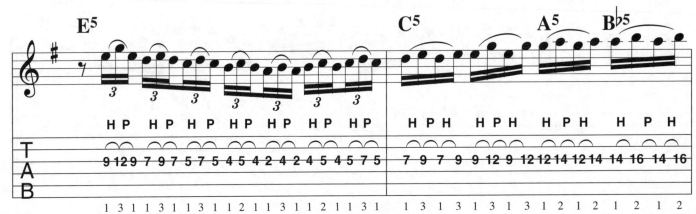

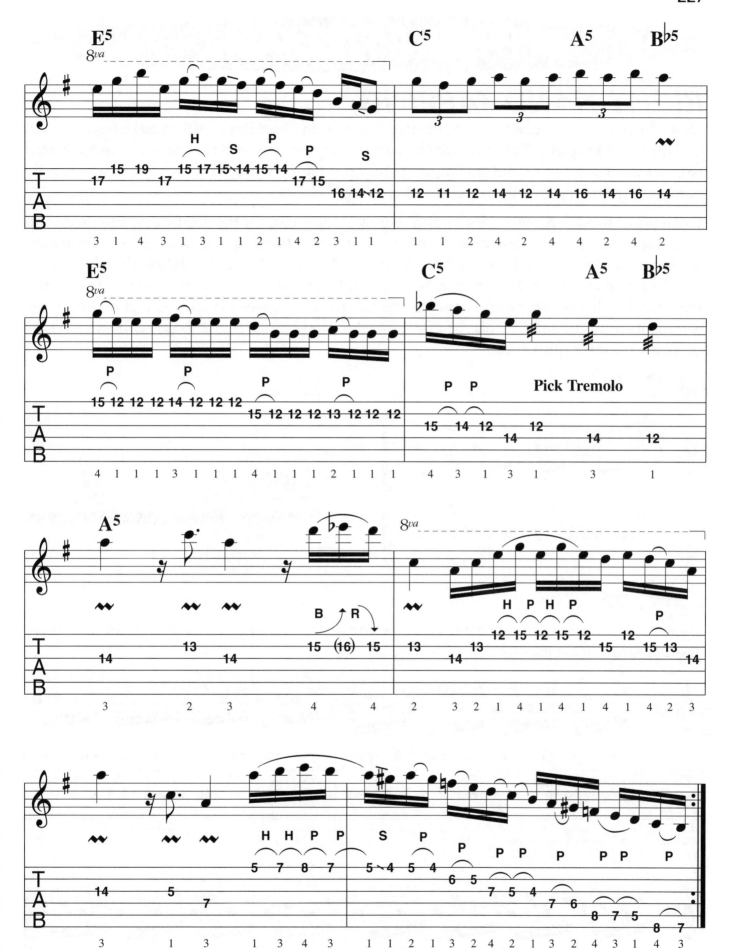

LESSON FIFTY SIX

RIGHT HAND TAPPING

One of the most popular techniques associated with Hard Rock and Metal guitar playing is right hand **tapping**. This involves the use of hammer-ons and pull-offs on the fretboard with either the index or middle finger of the right hand. To begin with, try a **single tap** by hammering-on to the 12th fret of the 3rd string.

Once you can sound notes clearly and evenly by tapping on the fretboard, the next step is to tap a note and then pull-off immediately after tapping the note. In the following example, the left hand holds a B note at the 4th fret, 3rd string while the right hand middle finger taps the 12th fret (a G note) and then pulls off immediately to sound the note held with the left hand. Listen to the CD to hear the effect of this technique. A tap is indicated by the letter **T** above the tablature. Remember that the pull-offs here are all played with the right hand.

72

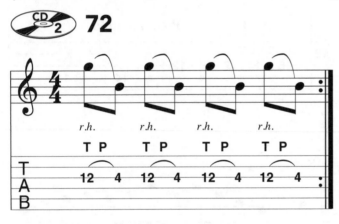

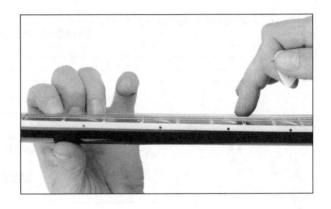

73.

When you can easily play the previous example, try this one which moves up and down the 3rd string a bit more.

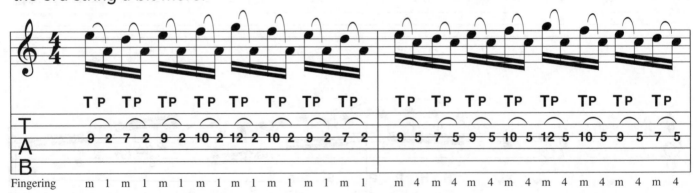

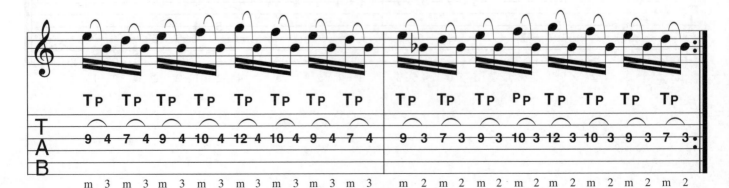

ADDING LEFT HAND SLURS

Another common technique is to use a left hand hammer-on immediately after the right hand tap and pull-off. Here is an example. Take it slowly at first and make sure all the notes sound clearly and evenly. Learn it in two bar sections and then put the whole thing together.

74.

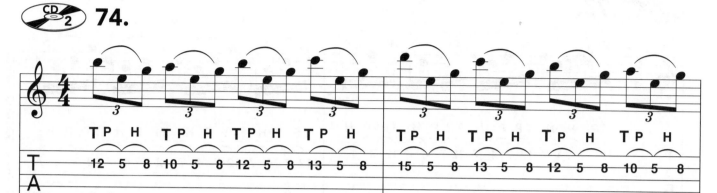

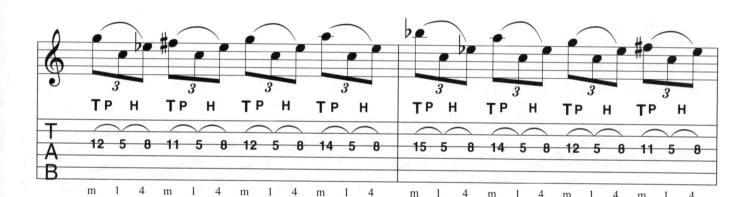

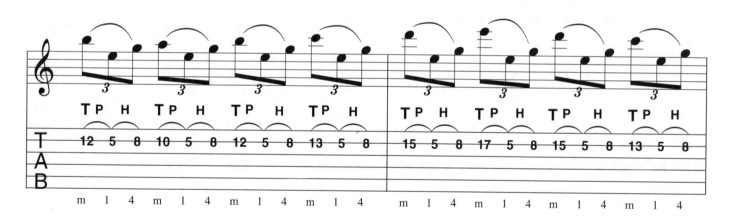

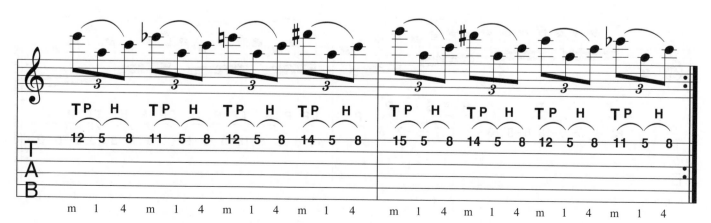

Here are a couple more tapping licks which make use of left hand slurs. These ones include both hammer-ons and pull-offs along with the right hand taps and pull-offs. As with previous examples, play them slowly with your metronome until you have control of all the notes and then gradually increase the tempo.

75.

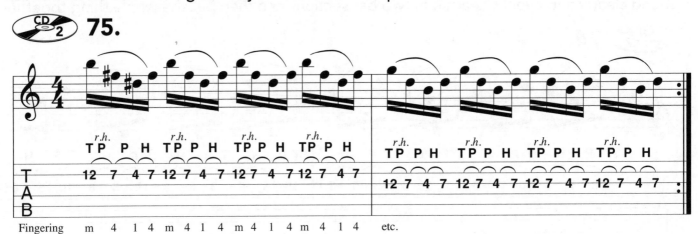

Fingering   m   4   1   4   m   4   1   4   m   4   1   4   m   4   1   4   etc.

76.

This one includes the use of open strings. Play it carefully and make sure there are no unwanted extra strings ringing.

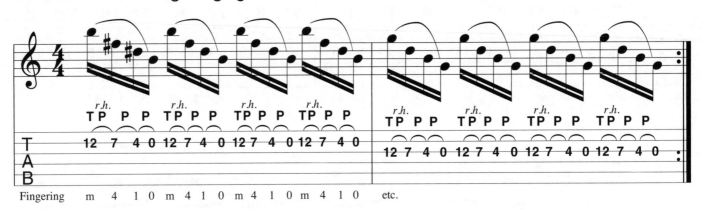

Fingering   m   4   1   0   m   4   1   0   m   4   1   0   m   4   1   0   etc.

The following lick combines the tapping technique with normal fretted notes.

77.

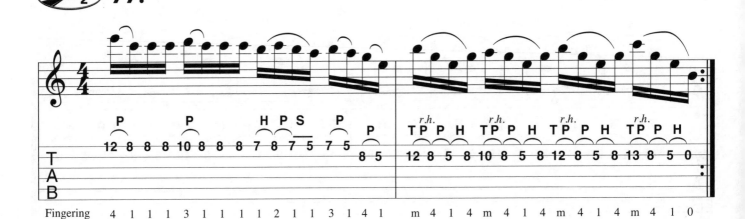

Fingering   4   1   1   1   3   1   1   1   1   2   1   1   3   1   4   1   m   4   1   4   m   4   1   4   m   4   1   4   m   4   1   0

LESSON FIFTY SEVEN

HARMONICS

Another interesting technique is the use of **harmonics**. A harmonic is a bell-like sound that is produced by lightly touching the string directly above the fretwire, then picking the string. The string is not pressed against the fretboard.

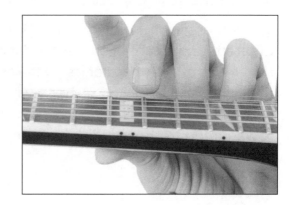

The easiest harmonics to play are **natural harmonics**, found at the 5th, 7th and 12th frets. Listen carefully to the recording to hear the correct effect for this technique. Harmonics are notated on the tab with a dot and the wording *har....* above the tab.

78.

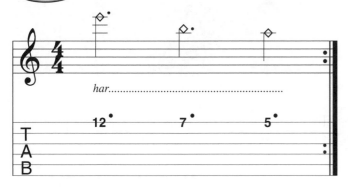

79.

Here is an example which makes use of natural harmonics.

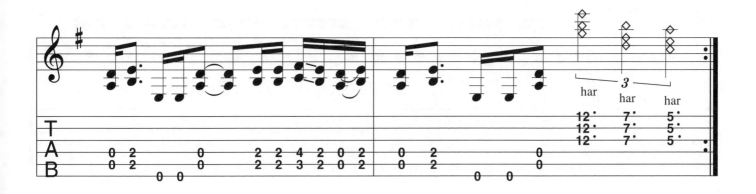

PICK HARMONICS

Another important technique is the **pick harmonic**. It is produced by holding the pick very close to the tip. The string is struck with the pick but the thumb is so close to the string that it touches the vibrating string a fraction of a second after it has sounded, almost muting the string. If executed correctly a sharp, piercing harmonic is produced.

Experiment with holding the pick in different positions and striking the string at slightly different angles until you are producing a clear sounding harmonic. Listen to the CD to hear the effect of pick harmonics. Different harmonic pitches can be obtained by simply moving the right hand closer or further away from the bridge. In the following example the same pick harmonic is played four times, but the right hand moves along the string from the bridge towards the fretboard. Pick harmonics are notated in the tablature with a dot and *p.har.......*

CD 2 80.

Here are some licks which make use of pick harmonics.

CD 2 81.

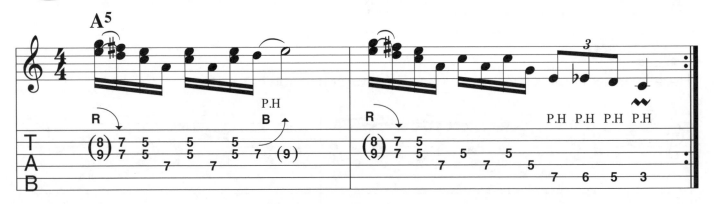

CD 2 82.

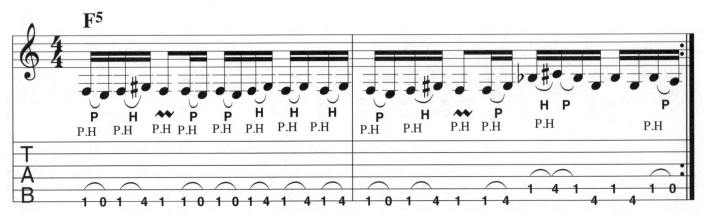

TOUCH HARMONICS

One more type of harmonic used in Rock guitar playing is the **touch harmonic**. These harmonics are produced by lightly touching the string above the fret with a right hand finger after a lower note has been picked on the same string. In the following example the note A on the 2nd string, 2nd fret is played. As the string is sounding the middle finger of the right hand reaches across and lightly touches the 3rd string above the 7th fretwire. Touch harmonics are notated in the tablature with a dot and *t.har.......*

83.

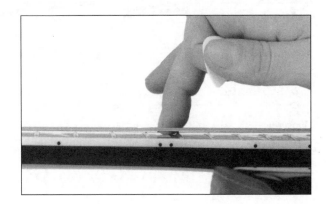

84.

Here is an example which features the use of touch harmonics.

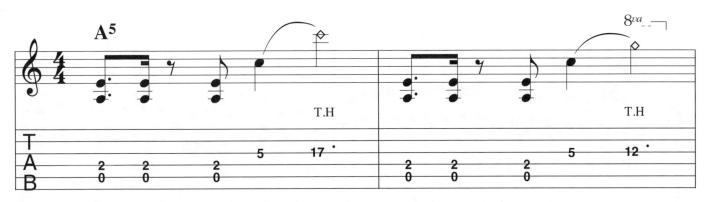

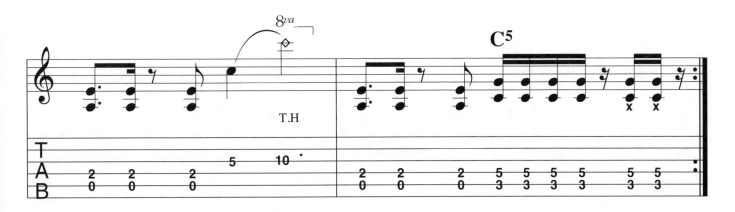

85. Hit and Run

Here is a solo which contains all the new techniques you have learnt in the last two lessons. This one is a real challenge, so be patient with it and you will reap the rewards.

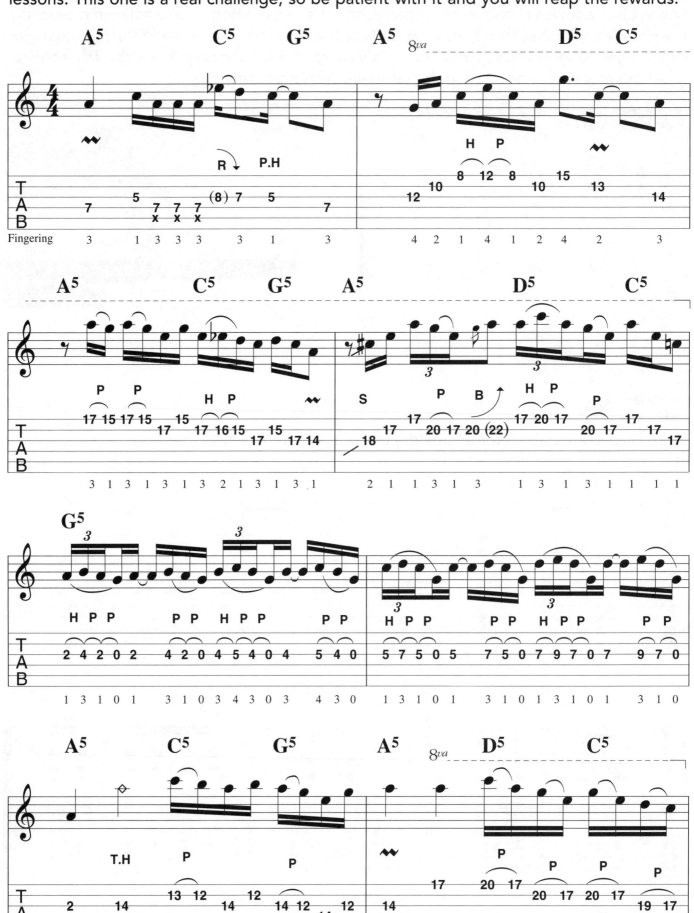

JAM ALONG PROGRESSIONS

Congratulations on finishing the book! By now you should be sounding very good and be getting a lot of pleasure from your guitar. To add to that pleasure, and help you practice everything you have learned, there are some extra tracks which have been recorded on the CD for you to jam along with. Try out any of the licks in the book with these progressions, and make a habit of improvising your own licks and solos. As well as this, you should play with other musicians as much as possible, as this will help to develop your playing and also put your licks in a musical context. Keep practicing, keep playing, and good luck.

 **86.** **Medium Tempo Rock Progression in A**

 **87.** **Rock Ballad in C Major/A minor (CD2 ex22)**

 **88.** **Blues Shuffle in G**

 **89.** **Slow Heavy Blues in E (with stops)**

 **90.** **Flight of the Raven (Key of E minor - CD2 ex71)**

 **91.** **Santana Style Dorian Tonality (C Dorian)**

LISTENING

It is important to listen to different styles of music. Even though you may have a favorite style, the best players in any style have influences which come from other styles. Don't just listen to current players. Go back and listen to the earlier players who invented and developed the sounds and techniques of the electric guitar, particularly Blues players such as BB King, Otis Rush, Buddy Guy, Gatemouth Brown, Magic Sam, Lightnin' Hopkins, T-Bone Walker, Albert Collins, Debbie Davies, Peter Green, Stevie Ray Vaughan, Ronnie Earl and Robben Ford.

Some Rock players and bands to listen to are Jimi Hendrix (a major innovator), Eric Clapton, Lynyrd Skynyrd (featuring three guitars skillfully arranged), Jimmy Page (Led Zeppelin) Angus and Malcolm Young of ACDC, David Gilmour (Pink Floyd), Tony Iommi (Black Sabbath) Nancy Wilson of Heart, Eddie Van Halen, Brian May (Queen), Mark Knopfler, Gary Moore, Lita Ford, Jennifer Batten, Steve Vai and Joe Satriani, and also James Hetfield and Kirk Hammett of Metallica.

For great rhythm ideas, listen to Funk players such as Prince, Leo Nocentelli (the Meters) Nile Rogers (Chic) and the various guitarists who have played with James Brown and Parliament/Funkadelic. For skillful use of effects, listen to Andy Summers of the Police and Edge from U2. For more complex playing listen to Jazz/Rock Fusion players like John Scofield, Frank Gambale, Larry Carlton and Scott Henderson. You could also go right back through the history of Jazz and find a wealth of great players, from Charlie Christian to Wes Montgomery.

When you are listening to albums, try to sing along with the solos and visualize which strings and frets you would play and the techniques you would use to achieve the sounds you are hearing. This helps you absorb the music and before long, it starts to come out in your own playing. It is also valuable to play along with albums, sometimes imitating what you are hearing and other times improvising. This is very good ear training and is also a lot of fun.

CHORD FORMULA CHART

The following chart gives a comprehensive list of chord formulas, together with an example based on the **C Scale**:

CHORD NAME	CHORD FORMULA	EXAMPLE	
Major	1 3 5	C:	C E G
Suspended	1 4 5	Csus:	C F G
Major add Ninth	1 3 5 9	Cadd9:	C E G D
Minor	1 ♭3 5	Cm:	C E♭ G
Augmented	1 3 ♯5	Caug:	C E G♯
Major Sixth	1 3 5 6	C6:	C E G A
Major Sixth add Ninth	1 3 5 6 9	C6/9:	C E G A D
Minor Sixth	1 ♭3 5 6	Cm6:	C E♭ G A
Minor Sixth add Ninth	1 ♭3 5 6 9	Cm6/9:	C E♭ G A D
Seventh	1 3 5 ♭7	C7:	C E G B♭
Seventh Suspended	1 4 5 ♭7	C7sus:	C F G B♭
Minor Seventh	1 ♭3 5 ♭7	Cm7:	C E♭ G B♭
Diminished Seventh	1 ♭3 ♭5 ♭♭7	Cdim:	C E♭ G♭ B♭♭ (A)
Major Seventh	1 3 5 7	Cmaj7:	C E G B
Minor Major Seventh	1 ♭3 5 7	Cm(maj7):	C E♭ G B
Ninth	1 3 5 ♭7 9	C9:	C E G B♭ D
Minor Ninth	1 ♭3 5 ♭7 9	Cm9:	C E♭ G B♭ D
Major Ninth	1 3 5 7 9	Cmaj9:	C E G B D
Eleventh	1 3* 5 ♭7 9 11	C11:	C E* G B♭ D F
Minor Eleventh	1 ♭3 5 ♭7 9 11	Cm11:	C E♭ G B♭ D F
Thirteenth	1 3 5 ♭7 9 11* 13	C13:	C E G B♭ D F* A
Minor Thirteenth	1 ♭3 5 ♭7 9 11* 13	Cm13:	C E♭ G B♭ D F* A

*indicates that a note is optional.

A **double flat** ♭♭, lowers the note's pitch by **one tone**.
A **double sharp** ✗, raises the note's pitch by **one tone**.

GLOSSARY OF MUSICAL TERMS

Accidental — a sign used to show a temporary change in the pitch of a note (i.e. sharp ♯, flat ♭, double sharp ✗, double flat ♭♭, or natural ♮). The sharps or flats in a key signature are not regarded as accidentals.

Ad lib — to be played at the performer's discretion.

Allegretto — moderately fast.

Allegro — fast and lively.

Andante — an easy walking pace.

Arpeggio — the playing of a chord in consecutive single notes.

Bar — a section of music occurring between two bar lines (also called a 'measure').

Bar chord — a chord played with one finger lying across all six strings on the guitar.

Bar line — a vertical line drawn across the staff dividing the music into equal sections called bars.

Bass — the lower regions of pitch in general. On guitar, the 4th, 5th and 6th strings.

Chord — a combination of three or more different notes played together.

Chord progression — a series of chords played as a musical unit (e.g. in a song).

Clef — a sign placed at the beginning of each staff of music which fixes the location of a particular note on the staff, and hence the location of all other notes.

Coda — an ending section of music, signified by the sign ⊕.

Common time — an indication of $\frac{4}{4}$ time — four quarter note beats per bar (also indicated by **C**).

D.C. al fine — repeat from the sign (indicated thus 𝄋) to the word 'fine'.

Dynamics — the varying degrees of volume, e.g. softness (indicated by the term 'piano') and loudness (indicated by the term 'forte') in music.

Eighth note — a note with the value of half a beat in $\frac{4}{4}$ time, indicated thus ♪ (also called a quaver).

Eighth rest — indicating half a beat of silence is written: ♪

Enharmonic — describes the difference in notation, but not in pitch, of two notes.

Fermata — a sign, ⌒, used to indicate that a note or chord is held to the player's own discretion (also called a 'pause sign').

Flat — a sign, (♭) used to lower the pitch of a note by one semitone.

Forte — loud, indicated by the sign *f*.

Half note — a note with the value of two beats in $\frac{4}{4}$ time, indicated thus: ♩ (also called a minim).

Half rest, indicating two beats of silence, is written: ▬ on the third staff line.

Harmony — the simultaneous sounding of two or more different notes.

Interval — the distance between any two notes of different pitch.

Key — describes the notes used in a composition in regards to the major or minor scale from which they are taken; e.g. a piece 'in the key of C major' describes the melody, chords, etc., as predominantly consisting of the notes, **C, D, E, F, G, A,** and **B** — i.e. from the **C** scale.

Key signature — a sign, placed at the beginning of each staff of music, directly after the clef, to indicate the key of a piece. The sign consists of a certain number of sharps or flats, which represent the sharps or flats found in the scale of the piece's key.

Leger lines — small horizontal lines upon which notes are written when their pitch is either above or below the range of the staff.

Legato — smoothly, well connected.

Lick — a short musical phrase.

Major scale — a series of eight notes in alphabetical order based on the interval sequence tone - tone - semitone - tone - tone - tone - semitone, giving the familiar sound **do re mi fa so la ti do**.

Melody — a group of notes of varying pitch and duration, and having a recognizable musical shape.

Metronome — a device which indicates the number of beats per minute, and which can be adjusted to any desired tempo.

Moderato — at a walking pace.

Natural — a sign (♮)used to cancel out the effect of a sharp or flat. The word is also used to describe the notes **A, B, C, D, E, F** and **G**; e.g. 'the natural notes'.

Note — a single sound with a given pitch and duration.

Octave — the distance between any given note with a set frequency, and another note with exactly double that frequency. Both notes will have the same letter name.

Open voicing — a chord that has the notes spread out between both hands on the keyboard.

Pitch — the sound produced by a note, determined by the frequency of vibrations. The pitch relates to a note being referred to as 'high' or 'low'.

Plectrum — a small object (often of a triangular shape) made of plastic which is used to pick or strum the strings of a guitar, bass, mandolin or banjo.

Quarter note — a note with the value of one beat in $\frac{4}{4}$ time, indicated thus ♩ (also called a crotchet).

Quarter rest: ⅃ indicating one beat of silence.

Repeat signs — used to indicate a repeat of a section of music, by means of two dots placed before a double bar line.

Rhythm — the aspect of music concerned with duration and accent of notes.

Riff — a repeating pattern which may be altered to fit chord changes.

Semitone — the smallest interval used in conventional music. On guitar, it is a distance of one fret.

Root note — the note after which a chord or scale is named (also called 'key note').

Sharp — a sign (♯) used to raise the pitch of a note by one semitone.

Staccato — to play short and detached, indicated by a dot placed above the note.

Staff — five parallel lines together with four spaces, upon which music is written.

Syncopation — the placing of an accent on a normally unaccented beat.

Tempo — the speed of a piece.

Tie — a curved line joining two or more notes of the same pitch, where the second note(s) is not played, but its time value is added to that of the first note.

Timbre — a quality which distinguishes a note produced on one instrument from the same note produced on any other instrument (also called 'tone colour'). A given note on the guitar will sound different (and therefore distinguishable) from the same note on piano, violin, flute etc. There is usually also a difference in timbre between two instruments of the same type (e.g. two pianos).

Time signature — a sign at the beginning of a piece which indicates, by means of figures, the number of beats per bar (top figure), and the type of note receiving one beat (bottom figure).

Tone — a distance of two semitones.

Transposition — the process of changing a piece of music from one key to another.

Treble — the upper regions of pitch in general.

Treble clef — a sign placed at the beginning of the staff to fix the pitch of the notes placed on it. The treble clef (also called 'G clef') is placed so that the second line indicates as G note.

HOW TO TUNE YOUR GUITAR

TUNING TO ANOTHER INSTRUMENT

If you are playing along with another instrument, it is essential that your guitar be in tune with that instrument. Tune the open strings of your guitar to the corresponding notes of the accompanying instrument. E.g., To tune to a piano, tune the open 6th string to the **E** note on the piano, as shown on the keyboard diagram. Then tune your guitar to itself from this note, using the method outlined below, or tune each string of your guitar to those notes of the piano shown on the keyboard diagram.

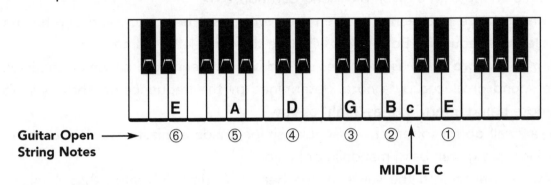

Guitar Open String Notes

MIDDLE C

TUNING THE GUITAR TO ITSELF

If you do not have another instrument to tune to, you can tune the guitar to itself by using the following method. However, this usually requires many months of practice. You will probably need your music teacher or musician friend to help you tune when you are learning.

1. Place a left finger on the **6th** string (thickest string) at the **fifth** fret, and play the string.
2. Play the **open 5th string** (an **A** note). If this note sounds the same as the note you played on the **6th** string at the **fifth** fret, the **A** string is in tune.
3. If the open A string sounds **higher**, it means that it is **sharp**. Turn the tuning key slowly in a clockwise direction. This will lower the pitch of the string. Play the two strings again and compare the notes. Keep doing this until the open A string sounds the same as the E string at the fifth fret.
4. If the open A string sounds **lower**, it means that it is flat. Turn the tuning key slowly in a counter-clockwise direction. This will raise the pitch of the string. Play the two strings again and compare the notes. Keep doing this until the open A string sounds the same as the E string at the fifth fret.
5. Tune the **open 4th string** (a **D** note), to the note on the **fifth** fret of the **5th** string, using the method outlined above.
6. Tune all the other strings in the same way, except for the **open 2nd string** (a **B** note), which is tuned to the note produced on the **fourth** fret of the **3rd** string (see diagram).